Adirondack Community College Library

DISCARDED

P9-APE-344

Richelieu

Richelieu
The Thrust for Power

by PHILIPPE ERLANGER

translated by Patricia Wolf

STEIN AND DAY / *Publishers* / New York

Translation copyright © 1968, Stein and Day, Incorporated
Copyright © 1967, Philippe Erlanger and Librairie Académique Perrin
Library of Congress Catalog Card No. 68-31678
All rights reserved

Published simultaneously in Canada by Saunders of Toronto Ltd.
Designed by Bernard Schleifer
Printed in the United States of America

Stein and Day/*Publishers*/7 East 48 Street, New York, N.Y. 10017

"One must sleep like a lion—with open eyes."

RICHELIEU

"Many men would save their souls in private life who damn themselves as public figures."

RICHELIEU

Contents

Richelieu

I

The Year 1585

1585 WAS a year of decision for Europe and for its civilization. History was repeating one of its recurrent themes, familiar to us in the twentieth century: an ideological conflict raged between two violently opposed forms of imperialism and nationalism. The Protestant revolt unleashed at the beginning of the century had overrun the northern countries, England, the Germanies, half of the Low Countries, and a large section of France, and had sown its seed everywhere else. Its triumph appeared certain until the Counter Reformation, inspired by the Jesuits and supported by a secular arm, the Spanish monarchy, blocked its advance by setting up a frontier zone between the North and the Mediterranean lands. France and the Low Countries were left in the middle: a battleground of two religions and two hegemonies.

Yet the duel was not merely between the Church of Rome and the Reformation. For the cause of militant Catholicism coincided with the interests of the House of Austria, especially of its head, Philip II, ruler of Spain, the two Sicilies, Milan, the Low Countries, Portugal, Mexico, Peru, and the Indies, into whose hands had passed the spiritual sword of the Holy See, too powerless now to wield it. Philip's rigid despotism, fortified by the Inquisition, was relentless in hunting down any trace of independent thinking. His victory would thus mean the triumph of a

9

totalitarian system pledged to maintaining the old order. This had already happened in Italy.

But there was another and quite different stake: the mastery of the sea was essential to the sprawling Spanish Empire, and both the English and the rebellious Dutch were beginning to dispute it.

The leaders of these two blocs, Philip II and Elizabeth of England, had no desire to fight each other. For twenty-five years they had co-existed peacefully, preferring to test each other's strength indirectly and to nurture civil war in France. The French were in a position to tip the scales of power, but Catherine de Medici, determined to keep her country independent, had never wanted to do so, and Henry III, her son, was even less eager. This earned them the hatred of extremists in both camps.

In 1584 the death of the Duke of Anjou, the King's brother, sparked the powder keg, for it left a Protestant heir to the throne: Henry of Bourbon, King of Navarre, whose right of succession was upheld by the last Valois, Henry III.

At this point the Catholic party and its leader, Philip II, took courage and decided to launch a general offensive. A Spanish turncoat informed the French of a plan to assassinate Henry II as well as the King of Navarre, the Queen of England, and the Prince of Orange. A tremendous invasion was to follow this quadruple murder to which the Pope was not opposed. Spanish shipyards were already at work building the Armada that would transport Philip II's troops.

The warning shot was the death of William of Orange, felled by a fanatic's musket. Henry III stood alone against the storm threatening to reduce France to a mere satellite, almost a colony, of Spain. His own mother, Catherine de Medici, a sworn enemy of Navarre, turned for support to the Holy League, instrument of the Counter Reformation, and to Henry, the Duke of Guise, who aspired to the crown. While the King was deliberating an alliance with Navarre and the Protestants, the League acted. On May 21 Guise and the great nobles, his allies, took over most of the cities. Isolated and without support, Henry III was forced to capitulate and to grant the League's demands. On July 18 Parliament sanctioned the reversal of the King's policies by revoking the peace treaties, outlawing heresy, and requiring Protestants to be converted or to leave the country.

What followed was the outbreak of a new civil war, the longest and worst yet, lasting thirteen years. France fell into complete anarchy. Shop-owners and merchants hoarded food and arms; châteaux closed their drawbridges; monks learned to use the arquebus and halberd. Swarming over the land came foreign mercenaries, the scum of Europe, holding the countryside to ransom. The French economy collapsed. Philip could now safely prepare to invade an England gripped by the fear of siege.

Each evening, high in the observatory of her residence at Soissons, Catherine de Medici called on her astrologers to read the future. Not one of them predicted that two months after the breakdown of royal authority, a child would be born destined to bring leadership to France and absolute power to the monarchy.

II

Born into Turmoil

T HE Rochechouart family, one of the oldest among the feudal nobility, considered itself almost the equal of the House of France: the King's mistress, Mme de Montespan (*née* Rochechouart), was to make this quite clear one day to Louis XIV. Thus, the whole of Poitou was astonished at the marriage of Françoise, daughter of Master Antoine, bailiff of Toulouse and gentleman of the Privy Chamber under François I, to Louis de Plessis, "gentleman-landowner, lord of Richelieu and other domains," as stated in the marriage contract.

But the truth was that Françoise de Rochechouart had neither youth, beauty, nor wealth. She was reduced to dancing attendance on her rich cousin, Anne de Polignac, Countess of La Rochefoucauld, who lived in splendor at the Château de Verteuil, where the marriage was celebrated in 1542. In fact it could almost be called a misalliance in reverse since the du Plessis, whose name goes back to the time of Philippe-Auguste, descended from some Clérambaults and Le Roys who had enjoyed rather important positions at Court. The Richelieu property came from the Clérambaults and had brought the younger branch of the du Plessis considerably farther up the social ladder than their elders.

Françoise de Rochechouart was supposed to have a dowry of 12,000 livres, but barely one-third of this was actually paid. During the nine years of their marriage (Louis died in 1551, still a young man), she bore her husband three sons and two daughters. Widowhood left her more bitter than ever at having stooped to marry beneath the level of her great family pride. She was a harsh and forceful woman, imperious, peevish, untouched by the weaknesses of her sex. The graces of the Renaissance had not refined her medieval coarseness. In a number of ways Cardinal Richelieu resembled his fierce grandmother.

François, the second son, was sent to the Court of Charles IX where he became a page. In Louis, the eldest, a lieutenant aide-de-camp with the Duke of Montpensier, his mother instilled the pride, violent temper, and aggressiveness common to gentlemen of those times. Between the du Plessis and their neighboring relatives, the Maussons, a long-standing vendetta smoldered, and following a quarrel over precedence in the church at Braye, the head of the Mausson family ambushed Louis and killed him.

Whereupon Françoise de Rochechouart recalled her son François from the Court. She took charge of his education and raised him with the fixed purpose of avenging his brother's death. Mausson was aware of this and planned accordingly. He had his doorway and the river bank connected by an underground passage so that he could always cross to Champigny in safety. But one day, François, from a hiding place among the trees bordering the river, heaved a cart wheel into the water just as Mausson started across on horseback. The horse reared and threw its rider; Louis's assassin thus perished according to the law of "an eye for an eye"—a law which the Cardinal was later to invoke on numerous occasions, mercilessly and to its limits.

Although under Charles IX a man's life was not worth very much, still this affair looked too much like murder, and Richelieu was condemned to be broken on the wheel. The sentence was carried out only in effigy, however, since the prisoner hastily left France.[1] He traveled extensively, and it is probable, though undocumented, that he accompanied the future Henry III to Poland, arranged his flight, and returned to France with him. In any event, about 1575 he was enjoying royal favor and the valuable protection of Barnabé Brisson, President of Parliament; these connections enabled him to "erase" his crime.

An interesting detail is that President Brisson bought the Mausson château and sold it to Richelieu in exchange for some land in Picardy.

---

[1] At least this is the version of Taschereau whose geneology, published in the *Revue Rétrospective* (1870), is openly hostile to the Cardinal.

Thus the du Plessis gained title to their enemy's property, and the vendetta ended in total victory.

François married very early, about 1566, when he was close to nineteen. What a difference there was between this marriage and that of his parents! The haughty Françoise de Rochechouart's daughter-in-law came from a middle-class family; her father, François de La Porte, was a lawyer in Parliament who had only recently become a landowner. La Porte lived in Paris on the rue Hautefeuille but was a native of Parthenay, and in those days it was rare to marry outside one's province. He was a remarkable man. Dreux de Radier described him thus: "As a lawyer in Paris he was outstanding in all the qualities that make a great man. His unselfishness and generosity as well as his talents were widely admired. If vanity is pardonable, no one was more deserving of pardon than he." La Porte, who, according to Saint-Simon, came by his name because "he was gatekeeper for an adviser to Parliament," had no conception of modesty. His famous grandson took after him in this respect and, fortunately, also inherited the ability to plead a case and to present both sides of an argument with seeming objectivity while managing to win acceptance for his own view.

La Porte was rich, the Richelieus half-ruined, and this is what led the dowager to depart from her principles—on the whole rather fruitlessly, for Suzanne de La Porte inherited only what her mother had left her. So the new Mme. de Richelieu, a bride at sixteen, lost forthwith her chances for happiness. But her sweetness and resignation were well suited to the role of a bourgeoise, who, almost by mistake, had married into an arrogant and ambitious family. She was an excellent mother to her children, modest, virtuous, and level-headed. The Cardinal came to dislike women of any other type.

Perhaps because François traveled so much, he and Suzanne had their children rather long after the marriage. Three sons and two daughters were born between 1578 and 1585 when M. de Richelieu's fortune was already rising. A melancholy and taciturn man (justly nicknamed Tristram the Hermit), he had mastered the courtier's art and would pass this on to his son.

While keeping in the King's good graces, he struck up a friendship with one of the royal favorites, Baron d'Arques, later known as "Archimignon" [2] when he became the Duke of Joyeuse. This friendship yielded

---

[2] The effeminate courtiers in Henri III's entourage were known as "mignons" (darlings). (Trans.)

François the title of Provost of the Household, then Grand Provost of France (Saint-Simon takes issue with the latter title). It was a costly honor, for in those days there was a price on public offices and this one came very high: 36,000 livres. Richelieu had only 4,000 écus! Arques and President Brisson lent him the rest.

The Grand Provost's enduring loyalty to the King was so well known that it inspired one of the Court toadies to compose the following anagram, in the manner of the times: "François du Plessis: Foi aux fleurs de lys" (Faithful to the fleur-de-lis). Henry III had few men he could trust, and he relied on François for a number of difficult missions. There still exist records of receipts for monies paid to "Tristram the Hermit" for affairs "which the King does not wish mentioned." One of these must have been particularly important, for the Grand Provost was rewarded munificently: on January 1, 1585, in return for an undisclosed "service," the sovereign made him a Knight of the Holy Ghost "by absolute authority." The Order's general chapter was not even convened, probably for fear the new member's nobility might be found insufficient. His armorial emblems drew some disparaging comments in regard to the "supporter, crest, wreath, torse, and mantle."

François de Richelieu's role as a secret agent adds piquancy to the family history when one thinks of the highly efficient police organization established during his son's ministry, which succeeded in uncovering numerous intrigues.

Most of the elements of Cardinal Richelieu's personality—including his driving ambition—are thus traceable to his forebears. Yet the major element is missing, something strange and disquieting that is not found in the generations prior to his. It is a certain irrational, peculiar turn of mind which was to degenerate to madness in his brother, his sister, and his niece, and which, along with certain excesses, brought him genius.

*

Was the Grand Provost's third son born at Richelieu or in Paris? The issue has never been settled, and rather than attempt to settle it here, we shall simply support the opinion of the interested party, himself who, in a letter dated 1633, called himself a Parisian.

The event took place on September 9, 1583, probably at an address on the rue du Bouloy. We know for certain that he was baptized the following May 5 in the Church of Saint Eustache. Françoise de Rochechouart was his godmother; Marshal Gontaut-Biron and Marshal d'Aumont served as godfathers. "There was no celebration," a contemporary biographer tells us, "for the danger threatening both mother and child called for mourning rather than rejoicing." [3] It had been a long and difficult birth, and the child would always be frail.

It was natural for the Grand Provost to remain close by his sovereign during this critical period. Henry III saw the situation thus: "They have surrounded me like a wild beast, waiting to trap me in their net." It is to François de Richelieu's honor that despite rampant treason in the Court, he never waivered in serving the hated and misunderstood King who waged a lonely struggle to save France.

May 13, 1588, the Day of the Barricades,[4] seemed to have given a decisive victory to the League and to the Spanish party (the Armada set sail on the 29th). But Henry III evaded the street fighting—which could have toppled the monarchy as it did in 1792 and again in 1830— and made his way across the Tuileries Gardens where a single gate, leading to the countryside and safety, had been left open. At the entrance, later known as the Conference Gate because of this episode, Richelieu stood waiting for a troop of angry League members who had dashed out in pursuit of the King. He parleyed so successfully that Henry had time to get a start on them and escape unharmed.

On December 23, four months after the disaster of the Armada, the murder—or rather execution—of the Duke of Guise took place at Blois; in his pocket a letter to Philip II was found which justified his death: "700,000 livres a month are needed to sustain civil war in France. . . ." Richelieu was put in charge of arresting the principal League delegates to the States-General.

The following spring he tried vainly to prevent Poitiers from joining the rebellion. He was present at the memorable reconciliation of Henry III and Henry of Navarre; in the embrace of these two Princes lay the salvation of France. He was at Saint-Cloud when Jacques Clément's dagger killed Henry III and opened a new era of disaster.

The King had forced the great Catholic nobles to recognize Navarre. But no sooner was the monarch dead than the majority of those proud and greedy feudal lords refused to submit to a shabby princeling, an

---

[3] Abbé Michel de Pure, *Vita Eminentissimi Cardinales Arm. Joan Plessei Richelii.*

[4] An insurrection, instigated by the League and directed against the King, which broke out in Paris. (Trans.)

adventurer. Richelieu knew which card to play: he did not follow Epernon [5] and the others but openly threw in his lot with Henry IV.

He fought at his monarch's side at Arques, Ivry, Vendôme, Le Mans, Falaise, and at the siege of Paris. The King retained him as Grand Provost and appointed him Captain of the Guard. On June 10, 1590, malaria took the life of this valuable and trusted officer.

Armand-Jean du Plessis, the future Cardinal, was less than five years old and in very poor health when this misfortune struck the family. If François de Richelieu had lived, his career would have been a brilliant one, but he died impoverished and debt-ridden, at the lowest ebb of his King's fortune. The gold chain of the Order of the Holy Ghost had to be pledged to pay his funeral expenses.

Still, the family patrimony included numerous landholdings: châteaux at Richelieu, La Vervolière, Mausson, and Châteauneuf; estates at Chillou, Beçay and Le Petit Puy as well as the house and priory at Coussay-les-Bois. But the income from all of these was small while expenses were crushing, and civil war periodically destroyed the villages and crops. Everything was heavily mortgaged apart from the dower of the grandmother, Françoise de Rochechouart, to whom the uncertain assets of these properties now belonged.

In addition, Henry III had awarded the income from the bishopric of Luçon to his Grand Provost around 1584, for the impoverished monarchy had reached the point of using church revenues to remunerate its servants. The bishops of Luçon, first Jacques de Richelieu, François's uncle, then François Yver, who was never consecrated, acted as administrators for the du Plessis family's affairs, which did not please the canons in the least.

In the face of this disastrous situation, the unfortunate Mme de Richelieu was forced to renounce any hopes she might have nurtured and to retire with her brood to the château ruled over by her unbearable mother-in-law, in the heart of Poitou, chosen theater for the civil war which had now reached the apex of its fury.

*

To understand Armand's first impressions of the outside world, we must recall what conditions were like in the country, in his province, and

---

[5] The Duke of Epernon was Admiral of France and one of Henri III's favorites. (Trans.)

in his family during his childhood. What remained of that kingdom of lilies, which Emperor Maximilian said that God would have given to His youngest son if He had had one? We find a heretic King, excommunicated and reduced to the role of a gang leader; a family of foreigners, the Guises, camped on the steps of the throne but unable to ascend it; the Catholic party, swept along by its leading wing, the League, outwardly strong but so weak in reality that it relied on an hereditary enemy, the King of Spain; a Protestant republic in the South; a revolutionary government in Paris; a return to feudal conditions whereby the great nobles were absolute masters of their cities, their châteaux, and their regiments; nomad armies who were kinder to the enemy than to the towns and countryside they systematically ravaged; an incredible chaos in the economy; the failure of justice, police protection, trade, finance, or laws—except the laws of warfare.

This was a war opposing Catholics and Protestants, royalists and members of the Holy League, Spaniards, who were allies of the League, and Englishmen, supporters of the Huguenots; a war to which bandits the world over happily flocked. France was prey for the hunters, a wasteland delivered up to flames, plunder, famine, pestilence, and foreign occupation. "My city" is how Philip II referred to Paris, where he kept a garrison.

The idea of nationhood, the principle of unity, seemed to have met defeat; only the international religious orders counted. League members acted as soldiers of the Pope as well as of the King of Spain, while Calvinists favored Geneva and England over French Catholics. Unconcerned for their country, citizens made private alliances that reached beyond the borders. Echoes of this confusion came to the child Armand and left him with a permanent hatred of disorder.

Crushed and torn apart, Poitou was among the provinces that suffered most. It was preponderantly Catholic and was almost hemmed in by three powerful Reform fortresses, La Rochelle, Saumur, and Chatellerault, in addition to several smaller Protestant strongholds. Countless battles, both major and minor, were fought there, all the way from Jarnac and Moncontour, not to mention ambushes, massacres, pillage, and burning of towns.

Poitiers was besieged for the third time in 1591 by Henry IV. The luckless inhabitants could only moan: "Between friend and foe there is no difference, for they act the same!" A city fallen into the hands of its assailants would suffer the tortures of martyrdom for three days on end; such was the fate in 1593 of Fay-la-Vineuse. Henry IV was the first to limit the pillage to twenty-four hours; the Duke of Mercoeur, Governor of Brittany and western commander of the League, was not so considerate. Besides this, ransom had to be paid to bands of irregulars wandering about in search of loot: cavalrymen from Albania, German mercenary cavalrymen, armed attendants from Italy, Spanish or Swiss adventurers.

Richelieu's family was in a particularly dangerous situation for, being Catholic Royalists, they were exposed to reprisal from both the League and the Huguenots. Between the ages of six and ten, Armand grew up in an atmosphere of terror. He and the family lived in near seclusion in the château at Richelieu, where his mother had to put up with old Françoise's tyranny, take care of her "poor sickly boy," as she called this son who was always running a fever, and reorganize her late husband's affairs.

Fortunately, Suzanne inherited a practical head from her lawyer father. When La Porte died, he left her in the guardianship of his chief clerk, Bouthillier, who honored the trust without suspecting what an extraordinary opportunity had presented itself for his own family. Under his guidance, Mme de Richelieu went to court, argued, paid, came to terms, and retrieved her losses. Her good sense and fierce persistence succeeded in rehabilitating the family heritage.

And all the while she prayed each evening that their châteaux would not be burnt to the ground, or their estates pillaged, or the entire household butchered after first being put to unspeakable torture at the whim of some captain in need of money and distraction. The slightest alert set the bell ringing; the drawbridge was hoisted and Heaven's protection implored. Sometimes they spent the entire night waiting for an assault. It was fortunate that the château had been built during the Hundred Years' War, a period of equal turbulence, for the house, of hewn stone and slate roofs, surrounded by beautiful gardens, a vast park, and woods, was blessed with thick walls. The Cardinal would always cherish this place, but we may well believe that if it recalled happy memories, it also left an indelible reminder of menace and alarm. Louis XIII's future minister was personally affected by the backlash of misfortunes brought on by the country's disintegration.

As to his class background, it provided him with valuable experience, since, owing to a combination of circumstances, his relatives represented three different social categories: the old feudal caste, the gentry, and the bourgeoisie. His grandmother, who was to live on past the year 1595, had the pride, cruelty, and fighting spirit of the old regional dynasties. All the impatience of grasping and needy country squires seethed in the Richelieu blood. Suzanne's capable management of the household, her diligence, and her skillful handling of money were those qualities which, for a century, had enabled the middle class to successfully attack the positions of nobility.

The education of gentlemen was deliberately scorned, and François de Richelieu had acquired only the most rudimentary learning. His widow, however, steeped in another tradition, had no intention of limiting her son's instruction to religion and physical exercise. At an early age Armand had a tutor, whose identity is somewhat uncertain—Hardy Guillot, according to some; others say Charles Cerveau—who later became Prior of Saint-Florent de Saumur.[6] We do not know just how much this early training benefited the boy.

In 1593 France at last emerged from the shadows, first through the failure of Philip II, who had counted on putting his daughter, the Infanta Isabella Clara Eugenia, on the French throne, then with the conversion of Henry IV. In the following year the King returned to Paris, having ransomed most of the principal cities from rebellious lords. There was still some fighting, but the Horsemen of the Apocalypse were vanishing in the distance, and life was returning to normal.

Mme de Richelieu had a brother, Amador de La Porte, who was a Commander of the Order of Malta, and family solidarity came into play. This worthy man offered to look after young Armand and took him to Paris, where he was enrolled in the famous College of Navarre, the same institution where the King had studied, but which, like the entire country, bore the disastrous stamp of civil war.

---

[6] Both of these men held the position mentioned; hence the existence of conflicting versions.

III

"Who Shall Be Like unto Me?

THE Paris that Armand du Plessis encountered at the age of nine was just recovering from terror and occupation, still layered with the filth of the Middle Ages, protected by walls and towers bearing reminders of the recent fighting; a Paris of dark, twisting, narrow streets, bridges weakened by time and overuse, a multitude of convents, churches, palaces, crumbling hovels, and murderous alleys swarming with crowds as motley as those in an Oriental marketplace; a city where mud from constant flooding left its sickening stench and permanent record.

The plumed hats, cassocks, and austere doublets of the bourgeoisie mingled with dresses of satin and fustian, liveries, and tatters in a seemingly endless tumult. The great scarcity of carriages did not prevent traffic jams. Every street was alive with the most alarming species: beggars, cripples, ruffians, thieves, prostitutes badgering the passers-by and always on the lookout for interesting opportunities. Lackeys, schoolboys, and hooligans competed in mischief-making. The famous Cour des Miracles [1] served as a den for six or seven thousand thieves who, at night-fall, would melt into the countryside.

Released at last from an ordeal that had dragged on for thirty-five

---

[1] An old section of Paris between the rue Réaumur and the rue du Caire. (Trans.)

years, the capital seemed to sigh with relief and hope. Gilded gentry and starving workmen alike longed to enjoy life, and rounds of pleasure-seeking began in earnest with the revival of drinking parties, masquerade balls, and feasts. Still suffering the effects of war, filth, and misery, Paris was on its way to becoming once again what Montaigne called "the glory of France and one of the world's most beautiful ornaments."

Nor had the famous University of Paris escaped the marks of war. Certain of its colleges were still being used as stables; the College of Navarre had just got rid of the collection of soldiers, peasants, and vagabonds that had been camping there and had managed somehow to restore order and re-establish its former dignity by the time young du Plessis arrived in his small boots of soft, elegant leather, lace collar, and plumed hat, escorted by his tutor, Abbé Mulot, and Desbournais, his valet. For this is the way students from good families went to school, and Uncle Amador had seen to everything.

Amador must have gone to considerable trouble to have his nephew admitted, for it was not easy to enter the temple of learning. Famous men such as Ramus [2] and Guillaume Postel [3] had succeeded only by becoming the servants of rich students—which, in itself, bespoke their passion for learning, since the college resembled a penal colony. Students rose at four in the morning and studied until eight at night with only three breaks: two for recreation and one for Mass. Holidays were spent at prayer. There was little heat; food was scarce and abominable. A typical meal for the youngest boys was half a herring and an egg, while the older students received about ten ounces of wine, a half-ounce of butter, a plate of vegetables without meat, a herring, and a piece of cheese.

Added to hunger and cold was a savage system of discipline, which Montaigne described: "All one hears are the cries of suffering children and of drunken, angry masters with bloated faces and whips in hand."

Although the harsh regime was somewhat eased for children of the wellborn, it left its impression nonetheless on Richelieu. Many years later, when his former Rector, M. Yon, paid him a visit, Richelieu, who was then the great Cardinal and the terror of Europe, received him with

---

[2] Pierre Ramus (1515–1572), a philosopher who rejected Aristotelian doctrines, was converted to Protestantism and died in the Massacre of St. Bartholomew. (Trans.)

[3] Guillaume Postel (1510–1581) was a linguist and celebrated Orientalist who traveled widely in the East. (Trans.)

respect that still carried a hint of fear. The memories of his school years had stayed with him, for his old tutor, Abbé Mulot, had become his confessor, Desbournais remained his valet, and his former lackey, Le Masle, was then his secretary.

The cruelty of the academic system brought out certain aspects of the boy's character which otherwise, because of his frail constitution, might have developed into timidity or submissiveness. Armand had neither of these; he showed great courage, a rebellious spirit, and a surprising appetite for praise. Neither punishment nor threats could budge him, whereas promises and compliments made him quite pliable. Abbé Michel de Pure, his biographer, tends to panegyrize, yet the portrait he left us of Armand during this period of his life is not so exaggerated: "His thirst for praise and fear of blame kept him on the right path. He was able to swallow the whole system of grammar in a single gulp, so to speak. Soon his stunning brilliance became apparent. What other children do as children he did with full consciousness: *he was aware of everything he said and did.* When called on to recite, he knew how to forestall the next question by interjecting an embarrassing one. In short, one cannot describe this superb mind's admirable gifts, which, like a shower of sparks, were constantly bursting forth."

Courses of study were divided into three parts: grammar, the arts, and philosophy. The *chria* or *sententia*, literary training, formed the basis of the system. Students had to prove, for example, in three steps that "if the roots of knowledge are bitter, the fruits are sweet," or they might have to declaim against tyranny. Unfortunately, no written theme on this subject has come down to us from the budding despot. The study of philosophy covered two years, the first of which was entirely devoted to Aristotle, the second to physics and metaphysics.

As a rule, a young gentleman was in a hurry to finish school and would limit himself to grammar and art, which was a good deal considering that many a nobleman of the previous generation could not even read. Armand first took up Latin and a little Greek (a grammar course), then philosophy, which familiarized him with Euclid and the art of disputation "under any and all conditions," preparing him to become an excellent dialectician.

A remarkable intelligence enabled him to finish his studies in record time. It is worth noting that he was at school during a transition period in the universities when the anachronism of the educational system was altogether apparent but had not yet been modified, and so he could not benefit from the important reforms of Henry IV and the teaching of the Jesuits, which would sweep away antiquated texts and methods. Armand du Plessis did not have the broad culture that a person such as the Grand Condé would later be able to absorb, and his enemies sometimes amused themselves by uncovering certain gaps in his learning.

Despite recurring illness, the boy's pugnacity, boldness, and quick temper drew him toward a military career. The choice was a good one, for his eldest brother, Henry de Richelieu, who would inherit most of the family fortune, was already in the limelight at Court; and Henry IV, in a rare showing of gratitude, had granted him a pension. There he was one of the arbiters of fashion—which did not prevent him on occasion from hatching a plot or two. Devoted to the new Queen, Marie de Medici, he was privileged to enter her private apartments in the Louvre, where her favored Italian courtiers gathered to weave their intrigues in a setting that resembled a miniature Florence.

Henry de Richelieu was to follow in his father's footsteps and make his fortune in the service of Their Majesties. Alphonse, the second son, would be awarded the Bishopric of Luçon, Henry IV, in a most paternal manner, having refrained from installing a bona fide bishop there. Armand's destiny was that of youngest sons: since there was no inheritance for him, he would have to attach himself to some prince or important person and be a soldier.

On leaving college, he was presented with a sword and the title of Marquis of Chillou, then handed over to M. de Pluvinel, Director of the Academy, to be trained as a gentleman.

M. de Pluvinel had traveled widely and was an admirer and imitator of Italian manners, as indeed was the entire European nobility. He opened a riding school on the rue Saint-Honoré near the rue Dauphin, in what was once the Hôtel de la Corne de Cerf; the school was an immediate success and received royal recognition. In 1598 the Venetian ambassador spoke of it in an official letter to his government: "To train the nobility in the paths of virtue, His Majesty has founded an Academy in Paris where the daily lessons are conducted by the King's Master of the Horse. This Master provides the young men with mounts from the royal stables, teaches them to ride, and gives them thorough training in all aspects of horsemanship. There are instructors of fencing, table manners, music, and mathematics, and one or two valets are assigned to each student depending on his means: all of this for the price of 1,000 écus a year. Other academies based on this model have been established in different cities, such as Rouen and Toulouse, and if they spread any farther, I predict that far fewer young Frenchmen will be coming to Italy, and, furthermore, the city of Padua will suffer from it."

The Academy molded what was to be "the well-bred man" until the end of the seventeenth century: a man whose cardinal virtues would be bravery and the religion of honor; a man constantly concerned with his appearance, with a keen mind and agile body; a seasoned soldier and a rounded athlete. The two pillars of this education were horsemanship and fencing, but the young gentleman learned many other skills, including tilting at the ring and at the quintain as well as court etiquette.

M. de Pluvinel had the last word as to proper behavior and language, the correct curl of a plume and height of a hat; he set his stamp on a generation of men. Richelieu bore that stamp the rest of his life, as did one of many foreigners who came to acquire the "fine airs" of Parisians: George Villiers, future Duke of Buckingham.

At seventeen the Marquis of Chillou was a proud young man, extremely concerned with his elegant appearance and manners, hotheaded and full of enthusiasm; it was quite evident that his special gifts would carry him far. People considered him a handsome man; he was tall and overly slender, with an angular profile and sparkling eyes set in a pointed face: a young eagle who, either in the army or at Court, would surely make a dazzling impression.

Destiny had other plans, however. Alphonse de Richelieu, who had held the title of Bishop of Luçon since the age of twelve and who was mentally disturbed, suddenly developed a mystical fervor. To everyone's astonishment, he vehemently refused to accept the bishopric and, instead, became a Carthusian monk.

Mme de Richelieu was in despair. This headstrong act threatened to undo all the work she had so painfully put into rehabilitating the family fortune. And people of modest means simply did not pass up the income from a bishopric.

It is enlightening to relate this last idea not only to the thinking of the bourgeoisie, for whom money continued to be the guiding principle over a long period of time, but also to the religious zeal that permeated and colored each moment of existence. The ardor of men enraptured with God could lead them to withstand incredible suffering and to

25

commit the foulest atrocities; but it raised no questions as to the ethics of traffic in holy matters or of exploitation of a church office in the same way farmers work the land for everything it will yield.

In fact there was complete dichotomy between faith and morality, and one can never hope to understand the history of the seventeenth century without an awareness of this phenomenon, which perhaps had vexed the half-mad Alphonse de Richelieu.

Armand was incapable of such a relation. He had strong family spirit and adored his mother. To give up the prospects of a life of fighting and adventure was an enormous sacrifice, even though a bishop was not required to have an angelic temperament, but the young man resigned himself and bravely returned to school to study theology.

The theologians, as Luther had put it, still "had to themselves the most agreeable place in the city, a private street, closed off by gates at each end, which was called the Sorbonne." The buildings dated back to the time of Saint Louis.

The man destined to destroy these buildings set himself up there with an extensive household staff including a doctor, a secretary, and servants. He plunged eagerly into his new studies, determined to be as brilliant a churchman as he would have been a soldier. Time was running short; there was much ground to be covered before this bishopric could be his, and the canons were angry that the post remained vacant. They had already brought suit against the Richelieus to force them to pay for the cathedral's restoration out of church revenues. While legal action was taking its course, Armand went back to his philosophy, already a little hazy in his memory, and buried himself in theological subtleties. His impatience was motivated not so much by a desire to protect his church interests as by the need to assert himself, to dominate his peers once he came to power.

It did not take him long to discover that traditional scholarship did not suit this objective. He would not accept rules unless they were to his liking or, better still, in his own interest. So this boy of seventeen became his own master and called in a scholar from Louvain named Cospéau and an English expert in debate, Richard Smith. Armand himself determined the plan of work; his aim was to become proficient in disputation, which is an excellent method of stimulating the memory and intelligence. For eight hours a day he stimulated those faculties to the point of impairing his health. This was another mental exercise derived from the neo-Stoicism which, from Montaigne to Pascal, characterized one of the stages of French thought.

The *Manual* of Epictitus was "one of the Bibles of the period" and became the source of a system of knowledge which was developed and has come down to us in the writings of Guillaume du Vair. "This neo-Stoicism with its attractively presented morality, which enabled Balzac to die like a Christian Socrates and inspired Descartes's 'generous man' as well as the Cornelian hero, was wedded to devout Catholicism, but perhaps, fundamentally, the two were opposed. . . . It lacks humility. All Stoicism sins through pride." [4] Richelieu would often display the marks of Stoic influence, particularly in his self-absorption.

Undoubtedly, it was to display his new talents that he invited the gentlemen from the Sorbonne to take part there publicly in a philosophic debate. Frightened and shocked, these worthy gentlemen refused. After all, such a thing had never been done. The persistent young man had better success with the deans of the College of Navarre, but for arbiter of this oratorical joust, he had to be satisfied with one M. Itain, who did not even have his degree!

In 1606 the canons of Luçon won their case, and M. Yver gave in. Henceforth official documents relating to the diocese were executed by a bishop whose name was left blank. The affair verged on scandal. At Mme de Richelieu's entreaties, the King consented to confer the title on a boy who was five years short of canonical age. But had he not already appointed one of the royal bastards to the bishopric of Metz at the age of six?

The only thing needed was the Pope's authorization, and for this Henry IV sent off his ambassador, Halincourt, to Rome bearing a royal letter, the tone of which was urgent: "I am assured that his [Richelieu's] merit and competence can easily make up for this one shortcoming [the candidate's youth]. . . . He is capable in every way of serving in the Church of God, and I know that he shows great promise of proving his value."

No one in Rome had any reason to be in such a hurry. Meanwhile, Armand worked furiously, obtained his first diploma during the summer, and, through special permission, was able to complete the first course of

[4] Jacques Chevalier, *Les maîtres de la penser.*

27

study in record time. But his eagerness did nothing to change the slow habits of the churchmen in Rome. Realizing this, he decided to take his cause personally before the Papal Court.

To discover Rome is always an event for a young man; in this case the event was to have far-reaching effects.

Rome at the beginning of the seventeenth century, still in her primacy and glory, was enjoying a veritable springtime now that the ambitious Italian princes no longer threatened the peace. With the end of the Italian wars, the city regained its tranquility, undisturbed but for the excesses of its own citizens. Rome's prodigious wealth seemed paradoxical, since it was not a maritime city, carried on very little trade, and professed to despise worldly goods. The explanation lay in the flood of American gold which the masters of the West Indies, almost all of them Catholics, poured into the Holy See in exchange for favors. Collected in lowly parish churches, scooped out of kings' privy purses, the precious metal flowed toward the Eternal City, transforming it within two generations. As Stendhal pointed out: "The countries where authority is secure are those which accomplish the greatest works." Rome had become a vast construction site. While Saint Peter's was nearing completion and the Church of the Gesù going up, all the religious orders competed not only to beautify the city but to propagate the new forms of architecture, a rare illustration of the growing revival of mysticism.

This "revolution from above" brought with it a civilization geared for war. Art was not an end in itself but a weapon of propaganda to combat the austerity of the Reformation: the repeated impact of pictures, as we know from modern advertising methods, served to affirm Church dogma and, to some degree, helped to check the spread of Protestant rigorism throughout the world.

Rome's administrative structure took shape as her architectural decoration progressed. Since the time of Pope Sixtus V, the Congregations had held a large share of papal power, and as the number of Cardinals, administrative departments, secretaries, and employees increased, the old feudal framework crumbled.

A keen-eyed observer in Rome would also have noted that wealth was much less likely to be the reward of labor than in other cities. Luxury displayed itself in the most enticing wrappings, purified by the holy occupations of those who enjoyed it, while dissipation was its shameless companion. Despite the growing number of places of worship as well as the influx of pilgrims and churchmen, prostitution flourished on an enormous scale. Every traveler remembered the courtesans of Rome, their palaces, and their jewels.

But alongside abundance there was great poverty; with increased prosperity came also the proliferation of beggars, cripples, robbers, and ruffians. Rome was the capital of opulence and want, true believers and bandits, asceticism and debauchery. Hardly seven years had passed since the tragedy of the Cenci family, but apparently the unruly nobility had not learned from it the need for controlling its passions.

The Borghese Pope Paul V tried to ease the cruel misery of the Roman campagna, took an interest in the peasants, and fought against crime by attempting to limit the trains of dependents which the great families supported. On the other hand, this stern judge of morals had managed to make an institution of nepotism. It was common knowledge that the Pope's family governed the Church and thereby netted an immense fortune. Each pontificate thus introduced a powerful tribal organization, and the strength of the whole depended on the outcome of struggles or alliances between the members.

During the six months he stayed in Rome, Armand discerned these phenomena and learned some valuable lessons. His intelligence was appreciated by the haughty Cardinal de Joyeuse, brother of Henry III's "Archimignon," and by Cardinal de Givry, as well as the Cardinal who was the Pope's nephew and prime minister. They took him behind the scenes where papal schemes and diplomacy were elaborated. "He was struck by the behavior of this Roman Court where deep-seated ambitions masked themselves for years under a cloak of humility and disinterestedness. Thenceforth he was determined to restrain his natural impetuosity and to discipline his conduct in accordance with his ambitions." [5] In other words, he learned the courtier's art and made dissimulation a strict rule.

The young priest was always on the watch for an opportunity to draw attention, and nothing served him better than the remarkable memory he possessed. One day, after a very long sermon had been delivered in church, Armand, at the close of the service and before a stupefied audience, repeated it word for word. Hearing of this exploit, the Pope asked that he come before him and repeat it. Richelieu not only accomplished this in admirable fashion but composed another sermon on the same

[5] Gabriel Hanotaux, *Histoire du Cardinal de Richelieu*

theme "with such an abundance of ideas and quotations, such noble spirit and choice of feelings and words, that the cry went up of a miracle." The cry was all the louder since it was obvious that the Holy Father had fallen under the spell and magnetism of the young prodigy.

Luçon's future bishop obtained other audiences with Paul V. The Pope was an extremely suspicious man, equal in that respect to what Louis XIII must have been. Richelieu thus had occasion to test his system for winning over princes who were least inclined toward candor and was so successful that His Holiness spoke to him on a number of delicate subjects—principally, Henry IV.

The "red dog of the Apocalypse," [6] now returned to the Church, was a constant source of concern to the Holy See. There was always the fear that he might lead a Protestant crusade; nevertheless, the Pope was not displeased that he provided a sort of buffer against Spanish tyranny.

The Holy Father did not divulge all these thoughts to Richelieu. He merely expressed regret at the French monarch's disturbing behavior and cautioned that this type of conduct could return the King to "his former errors." In fact what he really wanted to find out was whether he could safely risk giving secret support to His Most Christian Majesty against the Catholic King. Richelieu's defense of his sovereign gratified the Holy Father's hopes, and the latter voiced his satisfaction in a pun: "*Henricus Magnus armandus Armando*" (Henry the Great armed by Armand).

Supporters and detractors of Richelieu disagree violently as to how he obtained his dispensation; there is truth on both sides.[7] At the Consistory of September 17, 1606, Cardinal de Givry proposed the young priest for nomination. On December 9, the Pope granted the dispensation, explaining that it was done "not on the King of France's recommendation but because of your personal merit and despite the fact we have been told that you are only *twenty-three years old*." Paul V might have added that it is proper for a man who is wise far beyond his years to be ordained before his time.

All this would be highly edifying were it not that Armand had just reached *twenty-two* and not twenty-three: he had submitted a falsified birth certificate. Once he was duly consecrated by Cardinal de Givry on

---

[6] The League's preachers had branded the heretic Bourbon King with this epithet.

[7] Cf. Abbé de Pure, *op. cit.*; Mathieu de Morgues, Dom Meurisse, *Histoire des évêques de Metz*; Abbé Lacroix, *Richelieu à Luçon*.

April 17, 1607, he wanted to avoid any future consequences of this fraud and, with supreme cleverness, made a personal confession to the Pope. Paul V had been around in his time; the enchantment was not broken. Better still, privately, as a connoisseur, this shrewd politician must have appreciated the young man's finesse. Whatever the reasons were, he granted his pardon, adding a prediction which, for those times, was tantamount to a tribute: "This boy will turn out to be a first-class scoundrel!"

Armand left Rome shortly afterward and never returned. Once he was back in Paris, he did not hesitate to resume his studies and provided the uncommon spectacle of a bishop in the schoolroom. Humility was not the motive, for as soon as he had passed his examinations, he applied for permission to teach, and a dispensation no less exorbitant than the others offered him the "hospitality" of the Sorbonne. From then onward, his courage, his capacity for work, and his ambition became known. Furthermore, M. de Luçon had made it a point to enlighten anyone who did *not* know, for at the head of each of his three doctoral theses appeared a motto taken from the Scriptures, and in seeming glorification of the Church: *Quis erit similis mihi?* (Who shall be like unto me?)

IV

The Courtier-Bishop

ROME'S climate in this period was murderous. It had aggravated the fevers from which Richelieu had suffered since childhood and caused them to set in more or less permanently. The young prelate's furious working pace, his consuming activity, and restless ambition acted to fan the glowing fever. France's future master was never to know the delights of untroubled sleep, a normal pulse and temperature, or a clear head not pommeled by throbbing temples. Faced with these odds, how many others would have lost heart and given up the rough climb to the heights of fortune and power?

Armed with the endurance and will power of a Stoic, Richelieu absolutely refused to regard his health as an obstacle. Many others would come to know the inflexibility which he first exercised on his own body. Never would he allow sickness or suffering to slacken his drive. His innate hardheartedness, common to men of his class, increased with poor health; for short of being a saint, the man who must struggle daily with physical pain will never be merciful—and can easily become inhuman. It is probably because of his prodigious self-discipline that the Cardinal never gave in to weaknesses which might have made him less odious to his contemporaries and caused no harm to his memory.

For the moment, his aim was not to dominate but to please, and he was fortunate in having the ability to do both equally well. So he went to the Court, which, now that the disorders were ended, had become "that great sun which gives life, light, and strength." There, a man could obtain favors, offices, and pensions, and a royal smile could change his destiny. To be near the King was the highest blessing, a veritable ideal. Thus did many bishops live in the shadow of the Prince, leaving their dioceses in the care of canons. They cut a fine figure.

The clergy had emerged victorious from one of the bitterest struggles in its history, both because the leader of the Protestants had been obliged to rejoin the Catholic Church and, more important, because he had dealt with the episcopate rather than the Holy See. From this union of Church and State issued a highly unstable type of national religion: since the King was the object of worship in France, there was a cult of the King.

Richelieu adopted this doctrine of Gallicanism unconditionally, despite his recent visit to the Pope. He reasoned that if it enabled the King to maintain the loyalty of his subjects and to reject the claims of foreign powers, it meant in return a privileged position for church dignitaries. Since the signing of the Concordat of 1515, many cardinals and bishops had been given high posts and seats in the Council. The prelates, their chimers adding a touch of scarlet and purple to the carnival scene endlessly unfolding around the monarch, were more interested in these worldly splendors than in the well-being of their flocks. It was said they considered themselves "exempt from virtue."

Richelieu appeared shocked at all this and wrote one day: "Only scandal and poor examples were to be found among those who ought to have provided moral instruction." Was this a desire to flatter Henry IV, who was trying to reform the clergy, or the genuine indignation of a pious soul?

During this period religion permeated every gesture and thought of Christians; for most Frenchmen, it superseded the concept of patriotism. Social and private life were extensions of it, just as were international politics where the Protestant and Catholic blocs continued to confront each other.

Sceptics and freethinkers, the spiritual heirs of Montaigne, made up a tiny minority and risked great danger. Chief among them was the King, who publicly prostrated himself in the mud before the Holy

Sacrament, hoping to be pardoned for the toleration, branded treasonable and blasphemous, that he had practiced in a moment of madness: "I share the religion of all those who are good and honest men."

During the civil wars of the sixteenth century, all the atrocities had been committed for the glory of God; religious spirit had been vilely degraded. It began to revive with the help of such people as François de Sales, on whom Henry IV would have liked to bestow the miter; Vincent de Paul, Queen Margot's [1] chaplain, whose circuit stretched from the royal palaces to the Paris sewers; the first French Carmelites; a young revolutionary abbess named Angélique Arnaud, as well as Jeanne de Chantal, Bérulle, Mme Acarie with her vast "clientele of souls," a handful of well-born young men turned reformists of the monasteries (Beauvilliers, Champigny, Archange de Pembrock), and the "apostle of the illiterate," César de Bus.

It is not known that the Bishop of Luçon participated in this vast movement of spiritual renewal. A complete stranger to mysticism, he was basically closer to the worldly prelates of Valois times than to people like Donnadieu, Fremyot, or Du Laurenc, new bishops cut in the fashion of Henry IV, who had entirely different principles. However, since the King desired the abuses to end, Richelieu attacked them with all his ardor.

There was no question of hypocrisy here, for the young Sorbonne scholar had no way as yet of measuring the strength of his own ambition, nor could he know that instinct drove him to identify with the *status quo* in order to best serve his aspirations. The path to follow was clearly marked: a great career demanded that a man be a declared believer and Gallican, that he distinguish himself, with voice and pen, as a defender of the Church, just as a soldier must make his reputation in battle.

There was a popular saying that "guns aim at small targets, while books reach out to the world." Catholics and Protestants continued to sling claims and counterclaims at each other. No festivities charmed the public quite as much as theological controversies. The debates between Cardinal Du Perron and Duplessis-Mornay drew vast audiences, and at the time of her marriage to the Duke of Bar, Catherine of Bourbon, the King's sister, presented entertainments in the form of confrontations between theologians. In addition to attacks on Protestantism, there were a number of equally passionate subjects of debate: Gallicanism, ultra-

---

[1] Marguerite of France, Henry IV's first wife. (Trans.)

montanism, grace, penitence, Molinism, and Thomism (Jansenism had not yet made its appearance).

Richelieu was determined to be a brilliant orator and had no trouble succeeding; it was the same for every undertaking to which he pledged himself. Soon he preached at the Court and drew great praise.

By 1608 his reputation for oratory was established, which is proof mainly of his cleverness in adapting to changing taste, for the taste of that day was entirely worthless. Pedantry was in vogue, along with bombast, euphuistic conceits, preciosity, and ridiculous mixtures of sacred and profane expression: an orator who evoked Jupiter and St. Augustine in the same breath, or the Apocalypse and Hippocrates, was roundly applauded.

One of the first to laud the exemplary talents of M. de Luçon was Cardinal Du Perron, the King's Chaplain, whose fame rested upon his having persuaded Henry IV to recant heresy. Richelieu had taken a wise step in winning the confidence of this remarkable man, whose rise to power provided the young bishop with a model. Son of a Protestant minister, Du Perron's conversion had caused quite a stir. He became Reader to Henry III and was considered an infant prodigy of humanism; a friend of the Pléiade circle of poets, he himself composed a good deal of verse, often quite audacious. In 1587 a moment of absent-mindedness almost ruined him. Since he nourished his Muse at a number of different tables, he flattered all his hosts and all the parties. Thus when the Duke of Joyeuse was killed in the battle of Coutras, he composed a panegyric in his honor—then turned around and produced a satire on the same subject. At the time of the state funeral, intending to hand Henry III the funeral oration, he was upset over something and made the mistake of giving him instead a dialogue composed of five hundred waggish verses poking fun at the homosexual affairs of "Daphnis and Aristaeus."

Apparently the King did not hold it against him; four years later this literary chameleon joined the priesthood and became a theologian renowned for his bitter attacks on his former faith. This is why he was called to preach for Henry IV and then made Royal Chaplain. But despite its virtuous trappings, the close relationship between the King and his confessor may have grown out of the fundamental scepticism they shared. In any event, within a few years Du Perron became Bishop of Evreux, then a Cardinal, and finally Archbishop of Sens—hardly having set foot outside the Court.

RICHELIEU

Richelieu must have evoked in Du Perron the tenderness of an old man watching an apprentice who reminds him of what he was like as a youth.

But Armand had other patrons to help him charm the King, who was already favorably inclined. And, indeed, the monarch, nearing the end of his days, was genuinely fond of this young eagle, so impatient to test its wings. "You, my bishop. . . ," he would say, as if to a disciple.

While Richelieu's intelligence could be astounding, his serious, gruff, inflexible manner, his determination to succeed, even his Stoicism seemed out of tune with the supreme versatility, the humor, and the indulgence of this great pleasure-seeking sovereign. Yet he was either prescient or, now that he had become a seasoned courtier, knew exactly how to touch the King's emotions. A piquant detail: during his first stay at Court, M. de Luçon seemed to take no notice whatever of the Queen, Marie de Medici. It was another proof of his cleverness, for at that time Henry IV was in the midst of a quarrel with his wife. On the other hand, Henry de Richelieu continued to protect the family interests through Her Majesty.

"You, my bishop. . . ."

The words were full of promise. But where those close to him were concerned, this shrewd King was sparing of everything except promises. Richelieu came to understand that he would have a long wait before gaining importance. Much has been said about his motives for choosing the poorest bishopric in France over the delights and intrigue of Court life. The principal reason, in our view, was his need to act, to command, to govern. Such a young man (he was twenty-three) was better off managing the affairs of a miserable diocese than lending his sparkle to the halls of the Louvre. And anyway, he left himself free to appear now and then at the palace and to speak from the pulpit, confident in the reputation he was sure to gain by attending to his official duties.

He took respectful leave of everyone, from the King down to the lowest clerk, then borrowed a carriage from a friend, M. de Moussy. He left Paris at the beginning of December, 1608, burning with an attack of fever—as if to defy nature and the season as well as the astonished Court.

V

The Slough at Luçon

IT was no trip to make in the dead of winter, across countryside generally under water, blanketed with forests and disease-bearing marshes, infested with robbers and wild animals. Toward the middle of December Richelieu reached his native province, where Protestant influence was still as strong as ever since Duplessis-Mornay himself, called the Pope of the Huguenots, was Governor. This "silent, dull, monotonous, gently languid" region, wrapped in wintry mists, was the precise antithesis of Richelieu's temperament. Perhaps in private he longed for the excitement of Court life, especially the adventures that not long ago seemed certain to lie ahead.

He stopped at Fontenay-le-Comte, where the townspeople, boasting a few good heads in their midst, came out to welcome him; their delegation was followed by the canons of the Luçon chapter. The young Bishop greeted them with perfect ease and tact. After paying his respects to the people of Fontenay, he turned a cordial face to the canons, those old enemies of the Richelieu family. Only in Luçon did he put them in their place by disdainfully granting them "the amnesty of forgetfulness" for having been "so extremely disagreeable" toward him whom "God had made their leader." Next, he harangued the populace in effective fashion:

"Gentlemen: I have come to live with you and make my home in this place, and I am gratified by the welcome I see in your faces and hear in your words. Thank you for this evidence of your good wishes, which I shall try to merit in carrying out my duties. . . . I know that among us there are some who do not share our beliefs [an allusion to the Protestants], but I hope that affection will bring us together. I shall urge you in every possible way to embrace this purpose which will benefit them as well as ourselves and will gratify the King whose pleasure is our duty."

Henry IV would have applauded.

On the feast day of St. James (December 21, 1608), M. de Luçon celebrated his first solemn pontifical mass. When the last of the incense had cleared, he was left to face the wretched life awaiting him.

Everything was depressing—starting with the landscape, the little brook and vast marshes encircling the city, the ill-defined roads wandering between rows of ditches, the mazes of mud, the peasants' huts which a contemporary traveler, Jouvin,[1] called the most wretched in France, the canals and flooded pasture land, the cakes of cow dung left to dry in the sun as fuel for the peasants, who might otherwise perish from the cold, for wood became rotted from the dampness.

The bishop's residence was a ramshackle affair resembling a little island lost in a sea of mud. There was no garden. It was impossible to take a walk or even set foot outside the door in winter for fear of sinking into a bog. Inside, it was bitterly cold, and lighting a fire only loosed clouds of smoke. Spring brought with it heavy, incessant rains; summer meant unbearable heat; and autumn reopened the sluice gates. The perpetual dampness "laid a crushing weight of grievous apathy on body and spirit." The gray swamp waters mirrored clouds in the gray sky, while the land seemed to stretch out to the horizon in a hopeless flat line.

"My house is my prison," wrote Richelieu to Mme de Bourges, the wife of a Paris physician, in all probability, of whom we know nothing beyond some valuable correspondence which gives us a glimpse of the proud young bishop at grips with an unbearable situation. "I am penniless," he went on to say, but by making sacrifices he was able to hire servants and acquire furniture as well as a silver service: "It will enhance my nobility."

And soon, indeed, he was assuming the air "of a great gentleman," a matter of prime importance to him, and rightly so. For he was obliged to confront the canons, angered at having lost their power owing

[1] A. Jouvin, *Le Voyage de France,* 1672.

to the whim of this boy. His natural authority won him an initial victory, for as La Fontenelle de Vaudoré tells us, "a bishop only twenty-four years old laid down the law to his chapter and offered proof in every respect of his superior mind." So the repair of the cathedral and the bishop's residence were carried out without incident.

Richelieu was a fighter. He enjoyed having to struggle in defense of his wretched flock, as well as against the Protestants, on whose frontier he occupied something like an outpost. His ancient support of the peasants would end when he became Louis XIII's minister. Whether it was Christian charity or simply a tactical maneuver, Armand used his connections to obtain relief for the poor and tax abatements. He even wrote to Sully, the formidable Financial Secretary, in an incredibly obsequious tone, proving how completely he could stifle his pride when dealing with Important People. We do not know what he obtained from Sully, but he managed to make himself popular in his diocese.

As soon as road conditions would permit it, he set out to make direct contacts, hurrying from one village to the next, asking questions, looking around him, drawing conclusions. This episode is extremely important in formulating an objective judgment of Richelieu.

Thanks to Henry IV, the peasants were enjoying a golden age that would not return until the Revolution. But they were victims nonetheless of implacable tax collectors, extortionary public officials, greedy usurers, and abusive Church practices. As a matter of fact, in that very year the English Ambassador, Lord Carew, remarked in a letter: "In France there is an unwritten rule that the common people must be battered and demoralized by extortion and oppression, for otherwise they would be on the verge of revolt. As a result, they are at this moment so overburdened by the load they carry that it is impossible for them to walk or move, much less kick out or run."

Richelieu saw this with his own eyes. He was not one of those court dandies who, without ever having come near them, mocked the "uncivilized tribes" [2] whose labor made possible their lavish existence. When forced to make a decisive choice between the grandeur of France and the welfare of her people, he did it with full knowledge of the issues involved.

In 1609 we find him in the role of the "good shepherd," voicing indignation at the priesthood's incompetent teaching. The village priests,

---

[2] The expression comes from St. Vincent de Paul.

whether they shared the common folk's misery or played a lordly role, were all-powerful in their parishes but appallingly ignorant. When the decisions of the Council of Trent [3] went into effect, the majority of priests could not understand a word of them.

A few pious souls were troubled by this decadence. The idea of seminaries was conceived by Bérulle and, more notably, by a former cattle drover, a rough, clumsy wag of a fellow, M. Bourdoise. For Richelieu's part, he set about introducing drastic reforms aimed at promoting the education of the ignorant masses and the struggle against heresy. Taking as his model St. Charles Borromeus,[4] he decided to recruit priests competitively, frowning upon letters of recommendation which, up to that point, had played a decisive role in determining appointments. He wanted to mold these priests into instruments of his own design and, like an army commander, to give orders that his lieutenants would execute. His method would be the same when he took power.

Under his direction, Flavigny, his Vicar-General, drew up a 78-page manual (*Briefves Instructions*) which was modeled on Richelieu's own "Regulations for the Synod" (*Ordonnances synodales*). This work contained none of the casuistry or rarefied arguments so highly prized at the time. Richelieu was a precursor of Descartes and also an opportunist; the two tendencies were manifest in his outline of the duties of the faithful to God, the Church, and the King, as well as in his definition of the proper attitude towards Protestantism. He could not abide heresy or the intolerable disorder it brought, but, knowing its strength, he advised a flexible approach—which, later on, would have made a Jansenist's blood boil.

His writing as a whole demonstrates "that his Catholicism was based as firmly on a political ideal as on a religious one, and that to him it represented the supreme form of government as well as a guide for the inner life." [5] This is also apparent in his "Education of a Christian" (*Instruction du Chrétien*), a catechism whose simplicity has earned it much praise. Completed by 1609, although not published until 1618, this manual is scarcely doctrinal and aims at reaching the minds of the uneducated. In it the King is not compared to God, and God is compared

[3] The Council of Trent, convened several times between 1545 and 1563, was the Roman Catholic response to the criticisms of the Protestant Reformation and set the pattern for modern Catholicism. (Ed.)

[4] Archbishop of Milan (1538–1584) and Catholic reformer. (Trans.)

[5] Auguste Bailly, *Richelieu*

to the King! "A King, sovereign in France, is evidence of there being no other equal to himself and that everyone else is his inferior: so God, sovereign of the world, has no equal and is unique." Here in a nutshell is the theory of divine sovereignty to which Henry IV ventures only discreet allusions and which will serve as the foundation of his successor's rule.

The *Instruction du Chrétien* has another interesting aspect. It destroys the concept of Richelieu as a man governed strictly by cold logic. The future Cardinal came of an epoch when men were as familiar with wonders as an African tribe is today. Messages from the great beyond came pouring in, and nothing was quite as normal as the supernatural. Never was the power of the Devil or his sorcerer-henchmen more widely recognized, feared, or craved or more closely bound in some way to daily life.

The Bishop of Luçon was no more free of these dreadful superstitions than was the minister who sent Urbain Grandier [6] to the stake. His catechism vigorously denounced "those who, by means of magicians and sorcerers, invoke demons in whatever way and for whatever purpose, who use such monsters or their own powers to reveal hidden things . . . those who, by means of sorcery, prevent the consummation of a marriage, or, having prevented it, undo the spell or cause it to be undone by use of the same sorcery instead of seeking the Church's help."

Another passage, entirely farfetched to the twentieth-century mind, proves how class-conscious Richelieu was and how deeply he espoused the ideas of the still-feudal nobility whose worst enemy he was to become: "He who marries a woman not of his class against the wishes of his father commits a mortal sin; if she is of the same class, the sin is only venal." From a social point of view, Richelieu could never be a revolutionary.

In his dismal palace, where social life was practically nonexistent— and he would not have had the means anyway to entertain guests of rank—M. de Luçon did an enormous amount of reading. Often he would set off for Poitiers to visit La Rocheposay, a friend since childhood, who should have worn a suit of armor rather than a miter. Poitiers prided itself on its educated bourgeoisie and on its university, which attracted a good

---

[6] Urbain Grandier (1590–1634) was a priest in Loudun who was accused of committing the nuns of Loudun to the Devil's power. Jean Martin de Laubardemont was the state official whom Richelieu appointed to judge the case and who sent Grandier to the stake. (Trans.)

many foreign students as well as a number of eminent jurists. The traditions and influence of the sixteenth century were firmly established there; Richelieu steeped himself in them, which undoubtedly explains why, in the domain of thought, he was the last son of the glittering and ruthless Valois era rather than the harbinger of a new age.

He continued to sharpen his mind by practicing disputation and composed lengthy theological treatises. His debates with Protestant ministers did much to build his fame.

*

So here we have a bishop entirely devoted to his mission, completely absorbed, so it seems, in comforting and educating the common people, reforming his clergy, preaching, writing devotional books, studying the Scriptures, debating the Protestants, making official tours, and administering his diocese. But there are moments of leisure when his thoughts turn to his real desires. To regain his strength and courage, he forgets the tedious task of enlightenment to which he is committed; he dreams, and the dream brings disappointment, for never will imaginary creations satisfy this demon for action. He needs much more: in place of the reality, its nearest concrete image.

So M. de Luçon wrote another sort of catechism for his own use—not that he needed a reminder of the precepts that had become his bedfellows since the trip to Rome, but by writing them down he felt in a position to apply them. This defender of the Church thus became the author *Instructions que je me suis données pour paraître à la cour* ("Instructions to myself on how to appear at Court").[7]

He imagined himself already back in Paris and choosing (this is the most important element) a lodging which "will not place him far from either God or the King."

He analyzed the personality of Henry IV and how to approach him: "The King likes witty conceits and surprise retorts. He cannot *stand* anyone who does not speak out boldly, but he demands respect at the same time. The important thing is to figure out what mood he is in. . . ."

---

[7] This manuscript was found and published in 1880 by Armand Baschet. Despite Lair's opinion to the contrary in his *Notice sur les Mémoires de Richelieu* (1905), there appears to be no doubt that it is the work of Richelieu.

No detail should be neglected: "Be careful to stop talking when the King is drinking."

At Court it was a fatal blunder to appear arrogant or importunate, and there was a whole list of other maxims to guide the ambitious man. "Do not seem distracted, or let your eyes wander, or look sad and melancholy when someone is speaking; give lively attention and ready grace to what is said, but more so by observation and silence than by words or applause."

Richelieu knew how a haughty or impulsive remark—and he had a penchant for both—could ruin the day: "When dealing with or speaking to gentlemen of rank, I had trouble controlling and restraining myself. There, the more honored and respected you are, the more humble and respectful you must appear."

Keep constant control over yourself; never give in to a spontaneous urge; watch carefully what you write, for it is lasting. The problem of writing is difficult, since correspondence has to be answered, yet you must make the least possible use of your pen. Naturally, you should keep a copy of every personal letter you send, and compromising letters should be burned immediately: "Let the fire keep those which are a risk to keep in your strong box."

Next came a veritable treatise on dissimulation wherein the virtues of silence were extolled: silence favors the most effective pretense, and notably that which consists of "swallowing offenses which will be avenged on the morrow."

And if by chance it is impossible either to remain silent or to reply with impunity? Well, in that case you must "answer like an army in retreat: not fleeing, not fighting, and without disorder, it aims to salvage men and equipment." Which goes to say that the pious bishop would not hesitate to lie.

It is rare to find a personality so clearly shaped at an early age; it will not change except as the traits become accented. Of course Richelieu was not the type of courtier who would stoop to the lowest acts; he was destined, as Cardinal de Retz later wrote, to "hurl thunderbolts at the human race." But throughout his life, in order to acquire or retain the means of doing it, he excelled at acting out the play whose plot he formulated while the world looked on in wonder at his abnegation.

On Christmas Day, 1609, he preached an important sermon and, in response to an inner urge, the style shifted from popular theological jargon to firm and clear expression. He was discussing politics, or at least political philosophy. "Peace is preserved throughout the land by the obedience of subjects to their Prince and the fulfillment of his commands regarding the welfare of the State. Peace is maintained in the cities when citizens show due respect for the law and for regulations established by those in authority. Peace is in the home when those who dwell there can live together without envy, bickering, or enmity. Peace is in our hearts when reason rules us as queen and mistress; let our inferior parts, wherein the seditious seeds of our appetites reside, obey her; let mind and body be governed by eternal reason, from which our own borrows its small share of light."

We must remember that for Richelieu and the leading intellects of his time, this doctrine was anchored to the memory of a half century of anarchy; it also satisfied the needs of a temperament both despotic and profoundly realistic.

Soon, however, unbridled ambition would sidetrack his sense of reality. The General Assembly of Clergy was due to meet in Paris, and Luçon's young bishop aspired to attend as representative of the province of Bordeaux, to which his diocese belonged. What an occasion to take the limelight before important men and the eyes of the Court! Bouthillier, Richelieu's most faithful friend, who was Abbot of La Cochère and Dean of Luçon's faculty, went off to Bordeaux to plead his friend's cause before the Archbishop, Msgr. de Sourdis.

This Bouthillier, whose father had been left in charge of the Richelieu children's affairs, kept watch over Armand's career, lavishing devotion and affection on him. He was the perfect aide for a man eager to press forward and in need of someone to clear the way for him. Bouthillier had no acting talent, but as a producer and a foil for the star player, he was ideal. He set the stage, did all the running around, arranged meetings, acted as go-between and stirred up rumors calculated to enhance the prestige of his idol.

Appearing before the Archbishop, he presented his request, commenting that M. de Luçon would never have dreamed of applying for this honor had he not been urged to do so by other bishops in the province. Next, Bouthillier solicited the support of important churchmen in the Bordeaux region, spreading enthusiastic praise.

All of this was hopelessly maladroit. Archbishop Sourdis was shocked at the pretensions of a twenty-four-year-old bishop who pushed himself ahead by influence as much as by his own ability; the others were upset at discovering a rival with sharp teeth.

In February, 1610, the provincial assembly elected Sourdis himself and named Bishop d'Aure as executive delegate. Fearing the reaction he would meet back in Luçon, Bouthillier obtained a copy of the minutes of the meeting and, armed with this excuse, returned home.

Richelieu was profoundly disappointed. For the first time his weakness appeared, the flaw which could have been his downfall later on had he not been serving a somewhat dull-witted monarch. His nerves and his sick body did not measure up to his genius. What followed was to recur in other grave situations: he went into what we would call a depression.

All courage gone out of him, he sank into deep melancholy. His whole career seemed threatened, lost, despite the letters full of esteem and even deference which came to him from such eminent persons as the Bishop of Orléans and Father Coton, the King's confessor. Armand rejected all consolation. He left the diocese, turning his back on the ill-concealed rejoicing of his chapter, and went to shut himself up in Coussay, where, fever-ridden, he sought to bury his sorrow in the dense thickets of theology.

VI

Friendly Encounters

RICHELIEU might well have taken heart and hope from the number of friends who were his devoted admirers. Henry de Richelieu had sparked considerable interest in his brother on the part of a woman whose reputation for virtue, in that appallingly dissolute society, was astonishing: Mme de Guercheville, lady-in-waiting to the Queen.

Outside the Court, Richelieu's friends were of more modest background, but people of some influence nevertheless. During his visits to Poitiers he had come to know an exceptional man, the Vicar-General of La Rocheposay, and a close friend of Bouthillier, Duvergier de Hauranne, as ambitious a soul as the bishop himself. "I have no less a gift for leadership than the greatest rulers in the world," he would boast, this overbearing, ruthless, and tormented priest who was shortly to become Abbot of Saint-Cyran.

La Rocheposay, Duvergier de Hauranne, Richelieu—a formidable trio that used to meet "for amusement's sake" at theological disputes in the Poitiers diocese. Between 1605 and 1610 M. de Saint-Cyran had seen a good deal of the Flemish scholar Jansen, and the two had had long discussions on St. Augustine and on the means of reforming the Church and men's souls. When tired from their work, the two apostles would seek their favorite relaxation, a game of racquets in the great hall of the

Château de Hauranne. At the time of his debates with Richelieu, Saint-Cyran was not yet the founder of French Jansenism. It is a pity we know nothing about the conversations of these two men whose ideals were to become diametrically opposed.

The Christians who were persuaded by M. de Saint-Cyran and his disciples to accept a life of sacrifice and await uncertain salvation would be lost to the task that the Cardinal was later to set for France. As early as 1610 Richelieu may have considered the necessity of gathering all the country's resources under one standard and may have recognized the danger of religious fatalism. It is probable that he did, for his meditations, despite their appearance, were concerned with problems of government and not eternal life. It would be interesting to find some trace of the debates between these imperious friends, so certain of their extraordinary abilities and absolutely at cross purposes, though perhaps they did not know it yet.

Richelieu, if he was not the dupe of his own play, acted his role flawlessly, creating a perfect illusion. He attracted the mystics, the most fiery and aggressive of whom was a Capuchin missionary who had been appointed in 1605 to preach the Word in Huguenot territory. François Le Clerc du Tremblay, known as Baron de Maffliers and later famous under the name of Father Joseph, had given up soldiering to join the most austere religious order but had lost none of his ardor or organizing ability. Unlike most monks during this period, the Capuchins were uncompromising, and their severity and Gospel-inspired poverty attracted many young gentlemen hungering, as youth often does, for a way of life exactly opposite to the one they knew. Some of these elements were behind the calling of François du Tremblay, in addition to pride mingled with love of God, and a taste for heroism. "I lead a soldier's life," he wrote to his mother, "with the difference that soldiers die in the service of men, while we hope to receive life in the service of God."

Here was a soldier armed with eloquence, burning conviction, a variety of talents, a propensity for ecstasy, and the spirit of adventure. Soon he was dispatched to combat Protestant influence in the provinces of his choice, Touraine, Anjou, and Poitiers, where he wrought miracles, "with one hand making the citadels of heresy tremble, with the other, restoring the ramparts of the true Church." His principal achievement, despite the opposition of Duplessis-Mornay, was the founding of a Capuchin monastery in Saumur. During the same year (1609), Richelieu invited the Capuchins to lead Lenten prayers in his diocese, and thus began his relations with Father Joseph, eight years his senior.

Father Joseph was a good judge of people and was impressed by Richelieu, although he did not recognize the same pious anger in the bishop that smoldered within himself. Each of these men had extraordinary abilities as well as strength of character and courage; it was these qualities that drew them together.

An incident that aroused the entire kingdom brought the two men into collaboration. The powerful Abbess of Fontevrault, Eléonore of Bourbon, who was also the King's aunt, had worked hard for the Capuchin triumph over Duplessis-Mornay. Her reward was meager, however, since Father Joseph, who was the confessor of her coadjutrix, Antoinette d'Orléans, incited this princess to reform the famous convent. Antoinette d'Orléans had been forced by royal command to leave the Feuillantines [1] of Toulouse and go to Fontevrault to quash the scandals resulting from an excessively permissive rule there. She, too, was an exalted militant. She tried to reinstitute fasting as well as the rule of silence, manual work, wearing of rough homespun habits, and denial of visitors to the nuns. The latter rebelled with the tacit support of the good Abbess, but Father Joseph would not allow Antoinette d'Orléans to yield, carried on the struggle through her, and was personally involved in a good many intrigues. He asked for support from the Bishop of Luçon and received it forthwith. This brought them together—without, however, solving the problem.

A deep affection grew between them, as their correspondence shows, one of the rare affections which was to last throughout the Cardinal's life. And the reason was that politics managed to unite rather than to separate them.

In fact, nothing counted for Richelieu save his ambition to dominate. He made friends easily but was scarcely touched by feelings of friendship. His coldness might have alienated a good many useful people had he not taken care to mask it. He had developed an attitude of overflowing, even tearful, compassion which was all the more persuasive considering the rarity of such a quality among men of science and reason. But beneath this "tenderness," which was destined to become singularly

[1] Strict followers of St. Bernard. (Trans.)

48

useful, there lay a barren heart where few feelings were encouraged to grow.

Did Richelieu have any feelings toward women? The question would be strange if churchmen of that period had not been extremely free with their vows. Fined down even more by fever, Armand was a handsome and imposing man in his purple robe. The eyes of many a Poitiers lady must have fluttered under the warmth of his glance, which could be caressing when it sought to persuade. But any caressing glances seem to have led to nothing. Richelieu wanted to represent a new type of Bishop, one who, in fulfillment of Henry IV's wishes, would restore the forgotten principles of the faith. His growth in other directions was choked by swollen ambition.

After all, he was a misogynist and had written: "As men employ their abilities for good, so women use them for evil. . . . These animals are strange. Sometimes they seem incapable of doing harm because they cannot do any good, but I maintain in all good faith that there is nothing more capable of ruining a kingdom."

Yet, what would have become of him without two of these "animals?"

VII

The Approach

IN May, 1610, Bouthillier was in Paris. It was one of his letters that brought Richelieu the disastrous news: Henry IV had just been assassinated and Marie de Medici proclaimed Regent for Louis XIII, then eight-and-a-half years old.

Richelieu was too intelligent not to have admired the extraordinary qualities of a king to whom he owed much gratitude. He must have pitied the monarch's fate and pitied France, now facing the threat of recurring anarchy. But very quickly his thoughts returned to himself, and, like a war-horse, he trembled at the sound of the trumpet.

Under the firm rule of the first Bourbon, an ambitious youth found few opportunities open to him, through either chance, luck, or his own daring. This would change completely when the country fell into patterns of least resistance, a situation brought on periodically by the existence of a child sovereign. It was easy to foresee the rivalry and conflict, the intrigues and drama, that lay ahead.

Through his brother, Richelieu was familiar with the personality of the Medici Queen: her combined passivity and violence, her dependence on the Concinis, who were favored courtiers and a family to be reckoned with, her extravagant piety, and the influence exerted on her by the Church faction.

Looking over the situation and finding it most favorable, Richelieu wanted to rush headlong toward power. Impatience blinded him completely and gave him the notion that by gaining the Queen's attention, he would be called unfailingly to serve her; inexperienced as she was, he reasoned, still uncertain of her power and surrounded by snares, she would be overjoyed to have such a valuable adviser! This stroke of naïve fatuity is almost unique in the Cardinal's story.

His rash action took the form of an incredible letter addressed to Marie de Medici. After declaring his loyalty to Louis XIII (as if Luçon were a powerful fortress in a country menaced by civil war!), he poured out a stream of hyperboles to the Regent: "We declare that although our joy might seem to be ended after the baleful misfortune which an assassin's hand has spread among us, we do all the same feel unspeakable contentment that it has pleased God, in giving us the Queen as Regent of this State, to dispense to us next, in our woeful condition, the most desirable and necessary good we could have hoped for in our misery, trusting that the wisdom of such a virtuous princess shall maintain all things just as they were established by the valor and wisdom of the greatest king on earth. We swear upon our promised share of the celestial heritage to bear allegiance to her." And there was just as much more in the same confused style that reflected his high excitement.

Fortunately, a glimmer of good sense crept in, and instead of sending this impressive document directly to the Queen, Richelieu asked his brother to deliver it. Henry de Richelieu did no such thing. Bouthillier, who had been told to follow up the matter, sent the Bishop this cautiously worded message: "I believe M. de Richelieu must have advised you that he did not deliver the oath of allegiance you sent, knowing that such a thing was not done by anyone else, just as I, for my part, had ascertained."

Richelieu had hardly digested this note when he made the decision to appear at Court. This time his preparations for the trip were rather clever as he sent off a stream of letters to Sourdis, the Bishop of Maillezais, Father Coton, and countless noblemen. Bouthillier, the eternal go-between, had the pleasure of transmitting some good news: the young prelate was highly esteemed at Court; Father Coton wished him well; M. de Souvré, the King's tutor, was "entirely at his service"; there had even been talk of having him deliver the funeral oration for Henry IV. In short, the climate was favorable, and the footing seemed as sure as it could ever be in the trap-infested Louvre.

RICHELIEU

Richelieu asked Mme de Bourges to find him a house and furnishings, for the time seemed ripe to take that lodging in Paris which was as near to God as to the King. His main concern was "to make a good appearance" when the means were not in his purse. A man might as well forget his dreams if he looked like a beggar: "The greatest pity is the impoverished nobility." Besides, he did not hide the fact from good Mme de Bourges that he was "rather proud." Alongside his impatience and eagerness, there was also the fear of not creating a great enough impression on his return to Court. But hope soon melted the fear.

Richelieu, like many men of genius, had a vision of the future, but of a future still far away and slow to approach. Things would occur as he forecast, but not just yet.

The fierce and proud Sully made a humble plea for an "alliance and friendship" with the Concinis, those fortune-hunters he had wanted to drive out of the country not long ago. The Queen's favorite merely sneered, while his wife, Leonoro Galigaï, provided the reply: "We need no one's help or favor to obtain wealth and honor, for Her Majesty is fond of us for our having served her well. If M. de Sully wishes something, he is more likely to need us than we to need him. . . . Those on whom we once depended shall henceforth depend on us. "

Surrounded by a collection of financiers, sharpers, Court priests, necromancers, astrologers, and cabalists, Leonora, the Queen's childhood friend and indispensable aide, ran a busy and powerful establishment which shortly would include additional services: dispensing jobs, official positions, and pensions. As for her husband, he was a lazy wastrel who openly paraded his arrogance, a fop who played the role of royal lover so ostentatiously that he would often come from the Queen's bedchamber in the act of buttoning up his doublet, leaving the courtiers aghast. After Concini had acquired the title Marquis d'Ancre, one morning, at Her Majesty's levee, the Queen asked for a veil ("voile") and Count de Lude could not resist punning: "A ship at anchor [*Ancre*] needs no sail [*voile*]!"

But the Florentine element did not dare mix in government affairs for the moment. Domestic peace seemed precarious, and the Regent observed extreme caution—except in foreign policy, where she employed exactly the opposite principles of her husband, to the point of seating the Papal Nuncio and the Spanish ambassador in the Council!

Apart from that, there were few changes. Henry IV's old ministers, even Sully, remained in power; their maxim was: "Gain time in order to stay in office, and stay in office in order to gain time." In essence, it was a practical program in view of the current unstable and dangerous situation; and it was workable, owing to the funds that Sully had piled up in the Bastille for use in the event of war. Between May and July, 1610, the colossal sum of seven million livres passed out of the fortress into waiting, often undeserving, hands. Even the Queen came in for her share of the bribes that found their way to Leonora.

Marie de Medici was the image of a shameless, unnatural mother bent on dissipating her son's inheritance. She was indolent and luxury loving, with almost no conception of the public welfare. She hungered for power, meaning the material rewards and satisfactions it brings, and her method of operation consisted in buying her way to a trouble-free life of pleasure.

And thus far, admittedly, none of the catastrophes had occurred which a chorus of oracles had predicted. Almost twelve years had passed between the coming of peace and the passing of the peacemaker. The League's influence was still strong among many Catholics, and the Protestants, by virtue of the Edict of Nantes, made up a little republic, with its own troops and fortifications, its treaties of alliance, and its attitude of bellicose distrust which served the ambitions of its leaders. Their first manifesto, in which Sully had collaborated, smacked of war threats.

No conflict broke out, however. Condé, the eldest prince of the blood, was respected, although he was a dangerous muddle-head who talked of wearing the crown once the divorce [1] and remarriage of Henry IV were annulled. The greedy pack of feudal nobles was kept at bay by the offices and pensions tossed out to it.

But the Bishop of Luçon was not one of the potential troublemakers for the Regent; nor did he belong to the tribe of favorites. So the ministers had no reason to provide for him, much less to find him an office.

Champing at the bit, Richelieu had to content himself with the role of observer at the Louvre. The palace was now quite different from the days of Henry IV. Everyone but the King was armed, and the galleries swarmed with arrogant and avaricious nobles whose perpetual favor-seeking had an air of menace. Like Richelieu, they, too, were in a hurry, for it was in the character of the times. They enjoyed making a perpetual

[1] From Marguerite de France (Queen Margot). (Trans.)

stageplay of their lives, for, after all, who could tell in the morning whether he would be alive that night? The English ambassador admitted: "I can hardly think of one Frenchman who has not killed his man in a duel." The slightest pretext was enough to warrant a challenge, or even "nothing at all, for sheer pleasure." In the year 1606 alone, two thousand sword-rattlers met their end.

Within the select group of individuals from which would come the country's future leaders, there was chaos and a mild form of madness. The daily routine was to go off hunting for a position or for a prebend. Some incident or piece of luck could decide a man's future. "Heredity and patronage were constantly interfering in the ranks of age, merit, and experience." [2] Of course, swords and poison also helped.

In the halls of the palace, Richelieu mingled with the bright-plumaged birds of prey and felt he was not on equal ground. He would have to find another approach.

The hallowed place of power lay beyond the galleries. There, amid the murmur of foreign accents, was the robed Regent surrounded by a sea of other robes: of priests, women, and decrepit counselors, while over them all Concini cast an aura of dusty splendor.

In the pavilion occupied by the King, a child was wilting away, his moral decline eliciting the satisfaction which parents usually reserve for the accomplishments of their offspring. As his silences became habitual, so did his timidity and stammer, his absorption in miniature cannons, handcrafts, and his menagerie, all of which earned the enthusiastic approval of his elders. For what a godsend it was to have an imbecile and hypochondriac on the throne who would spend his days out hunting and let the Court clique do the ruling!

As for this clique, how could one penetrate it? Richelieu did not find the answer. He obtained an audience with the Queen but made no impression on her, which often happens when two people whose lives are destined to interact meet for the first time.

Greatly disappointed and discouraged, the bishop's eager yearning for success gave way to deep gloom. The real fever returned, and he fled Paris.

Back in his diocese, fury and bitterness found expression first in his refusal to live in Luçon because of the climate—which was unquestion-

[2] Gabriel Hanotaux, *op. cit.*

ably bad for his health—and then in attacks on his vicar-general, with whom he had already had some difficulties. His letter had no trace of ecclesiastic unction, and the explosive tone of it forecast what lay in store for those who were to serve him, as well as the High and the Mighty and even foreign rulers: "If an insect has bitten you, you must kill it and not let others feel its sting. . . . I know how to conduct myself, thank God, and know even better how those in my service should conduct themselves. . . . You say that you would willingly renounce the office I have bestowed on you. . . . I do not oblige anyone to accept anything from me. . . . To others you preach free will: you are quite free to apply it yourself."

After this outburst that involved all his own resentment, Richelieu left for Coussay to regain his health. This was to be his sole residence thereafter, except for the Priory of Roches, where the affairs of Fontevrault sometimes took him. Coussay's château was protected by four conical watchtowers and a strong keep and was ringed with ditches and moats. All around it stretched a landscape that was "vast, solitary, restful." There the bishop could take long, meditative walks, then return to his "hermitage," his study in the central tower where piles of books and papers were carefully screened from prying eyes. Still depressed, he led what he called "the existence of a poor monk reduced to selling his books, and to a boorish life." In a letter to his brother, he remarked: "He who counts on going through life without a setback is making a sad miscalculation. No matter how careful a man is, let him remember that mistakes crop up most often where they are least expected." His worries about money had reached the galling stage.

Eléanore of Bourbon died at this time, and Father Joseph sought to replace her with Antoinette d'Orléans. But she, "great servant of God," had obtained papal consent to leave Fontevrault and retire wherever she wished. Seething with anger at this, the priest urged Richelieu to seek an audience with the Queen and ask for her instructions in the matter. The Bishop forgot his hypochondria and let himself be persuaded to return to the Court. He saw Marie de Medici again, this time at Fontainebleau, and, in the most direct manner, renewed his offer of service. For, he reasoned, with Sully in disgrace, there were likely to be other changes at the top.

The Queen did not seem to get the point and simply instructed the petitioner to "keep her advised of developments over there," that is, in the Protestant stronghold of Poitou. As for Fontevrault, Antoinette d'Orléans won out: she went to Poitiers and founded an order of medieval austerity, the *Filles du Calvaire* (Daughters of Calvary).

Although he had failed again, Richelieu was less despondent when he returned to his diocese to supervise the election of a new Abbess, Mme de Bourbon-Lavedan. For he had struck up a friendship with someone very much in favor with the Queen: Bérulle, a saintly man despite his guile and sophistication. At the age of seven, Bérulle had taken the vow of chastity; he claimed to serve God as an "independent." He was friendly to the Jesuits but had profited by their exile in 1595 to build a rival group, the Society of the Oratory. This Society, founded by St. Philip Neri, was used by Bérulle, in accordance with the King's wish, as a training school for a new generation of priests more obedient to their own bishops than to Rome, more divorced from the activities of secular life. Bérulle, too, was responsible for bringing with him from Spain the first five Carmelite nuns to settle in Paris.

For a long time Richelieu had been thinking of founding a seminary in his diocese. However, he wanted nothing to do with the Jesuits. Undoubtedly, Bérulle's prestige was involved in the invitation that the bishop extended, and the Oratorians came into possession of "their second home in the kingdom" in Richelieu's diocese. Bérulle was grateful; he had fallen under the spell, and thereafter the bishop had a distinguished champion close to the Queen.

Toward the end of the year, some serious difficulties between the State and the Protestants gave Richelieu a chance to dabble in politics. Needless to say, he did not let it pass. As a result of offering to help M. de Vic, who had been sent to Poitiers to calm things down, he met Pontchartrain, Secretary of State for Religious Affairs, and he provided both these men with information. He even volunteered to go to La Rochelle to "harangue" the Huguenots.

Troops had been called out to intimidate the heretic province, and Richelieu advised the Queen to take personal command of them. All this without losing sight of his objective, for he wrote to Pontchartrain: "If you think it appropriate to slip a word in the Queen's ear about what I am asking . . . you shall handle it as you see fit." We do not know how Pontchartrain handled it, but nothing resulted—nothing concrete, that is, though to all intents and purposes Richelieu was winning points.

His reputation was growing, there was much talk about him, and his circle of relations was widening.

Feeling more secure, the bishop launched an actual campaign to influence opinion and had Bouthillier observe the results of it in Paris. The Queen was a bigot, a Vaticanist, and totally dedicated to the Spanish cause. So Richelieu paraded and ballooned the same sentiments. Let no one ever mention the Gallican Church to him again! He sent a messenger to Rome to rekindle the Pope's good feelings toward him.

The ultra-Catholic party paid close attention to all this and was delighted to find such an expert at hand. Its pious members extolled this twenty-six-year-old bishop whose youthful ardor seemed to have run its course and who at last was winning the hearts of his flock by good works, kindness, and constant concern for souls in torment.

His religious duties left Richelieu enough time to keep up an abundant correspondence. And what letters they were! What expressions of respect overflowing with humility! M. de Luçon lavished his compliments on Important People "like sacrifices to the gods," as he put it, "even the uncooperative ones." His messages of condolence to the Countess of Soissons on the death of her husband and to Villeroy, the minister, when he lost his daughter, drained the lakes of labored lyricism. He dosed his mortal enemies, Epernon and Sully, with compliments and heaped them upon Cardinal de La Rochefoucauld as well as most of the archbishops and influential churchmen. As for the gentlemen of Poitiers, who were less important but potentially useful, to them he offered his good services and kind words.

All these efforts were not in vain. M. de Luçon was "well reported on" at the Louvre, although no material benefit was forthcoming. He could only pin his hopes on the future when the climate of calm, so painfully maintained by the old ministers headed by Villeroy, would be whipped into a storm by the restless princes.

In February, 1612, Marie de Medici attained the height of her desires and, so she thought, her glory. She could think of no more fitting consecration of the modest House whose name she bore than to unite it to the Catholic monarchy through the marriage of her son and her eldest daughter, Elizabeth, to Spain's royal children. The two engagements—Spain's posthumous revenge on Henry IV—were formally announced and celebrated with memorable festivities in the Place Royale before 200,000 spectators. There were pageants, races for the ring, and fireworks, and on the final night the whole city was lit up by artillery fire. But Condé, the Huguenots' patron, protested that his sect was being menaced and was in a fighting mood.

Strangely enough—although it did not surprise anyone in this anarchistic Court—Concini supported him, despite the fact that a royal favorite had never been so bountifully rewarded: titles and honors, lands and pensions had been heaped upon him. A former conspirator, Baron de Luz, in an effort to win the Italian's favor, advised him to take over the government of Burgundy from the Duke of Bellegambe, an ally of the Duke of Epernon and the Guise faction. Whereupon M. de Luz was murdered by the Chevalier de Guise at the entrance to the Louvre. Concini, acting on behalf of Condé, whose support was essential to him, called for blood revenge and control of the Bordeaux stronghold, Château-Trompette.

The ministers trembled and passed on their fright to the Queen. As it happened, she was quite fed up with Concini's tyranny, which was now well out of bounds: he bullied his wife and, on a number of occasions, upset the Regent so much that she rushed off to find seclusion, dabbing her eyes. Condé did not get Château-Trompette; 100,000 écus went to the Guises; the assassin was made Lieutenant of Provence, and the Duke of Bellegarde was assigned the dead man's estate.

Condé and Concini left the Court in a great huff, followed by the Dukes of Mayenne, Nevers, and Bouillon. It looked like the beginning of another civil war pitting rival families against each other.

The princes hesitated to make the plunge, and Mme Concini managed to reconcile her husband and the Queen. Neither of these women could get along without the braggart, who, when he deigned to return to the fold, was promptly rewarded with a marshal's baton! Now, the enraged Condé decided to take the final step.

Richelieu followed these events very closely, aware that in the impending conflict he would have to make a clear choice between the two parties if he were to break out of his stifling anonymity. And the two parties meant two men, both of whom were outside the government. But what had become of the government? Richelieu saw it thus: "Things were so unstable that the ministers spent more time bolstering their own positions than building security for the country."

All of France watched Condé and Concini. It seemed incredible that in the three years since Henry IV's death, the kingdom had plunged so low that it now had to look to such men for leadership.

At the age of twenty-five, the Prince of Condé was not very bright or courageous or loyal, but his presumption was immeasurable. His appearance and morals were offensive, he was cruel, grasping, and a niggard to the core. While acting as standard-bearer for the Protestants and using every opportunity to arouse their distrust of the Catholics, he was also dealing secretly with Spain. First among the Important Persons, he coaxed and cajoled Parliament, behaving like a full-fledged demagogue.

Opposing him and counseled by his wife, Leonora, a gloomy, owl-like creature who fled the daylight, stood Concini, who, at various moments in his checkered past, had been a croupier in Borgo, a transvestite, and an agent of Spain who had helped plot the murder of Henri IV [3] and who aspired to marry his son off to one of the dead King's legitimized daughters. On leaving Florence in the entourage of Marie de Medici, he had announced to his fellow profligates that he was off to France to make his fortune or die.

Now he crowed: "We'll see how high fortune will raise a man!" With overweening vanity, he called off the list of his booty to a wide-eyed Bassompierre: [4] two townhouses in Paris, magnificent estates at Ancre and Lésigny, the office of Steward of the Queen's Household, 500,000 écus put away in Italy and 600,000 well invested elsewhere, a million in cash. Briefly, his assets would have bought the principality of Ferrara. And as Marshal d'Ancre, he had his Swiss Guard and a following resembling a Court. He wanted even more: control over key territory that would make him semi-independent and, to buttress the edifice of his power, he coveted a dominant position in the government. Now that he had risen so high and was the object of general hatred, he had no choice but to rule the State or fall.

Sometimes, when the rumbling of that hate grew too loud, either he or Leonora would talk about the sensible course of action: close up shop, leave town, and enjoy their fabulous loot in some other place. But, unfortunately, both of them never wanted this at the same time. So they stayed on and, since it was too late to retreat, they kept moving ahead.

[3] Cf. Philippe Erlanger, *L'étrange mort de Henri IV*.

[4] François de Bassompierre (1579–1646), Marshal of France and a diplomat. Later Richelieu had him imprisoned in the Bastille for twelve years for conspiring against him. (Trans.)

RICHELIEU

M. de Luçon appraised the situation objectively. He believed in the Crown, and, through the strange behavior of destiny, it was not the royal blood of France but a Florentine—recently in the service of Spain—who wielded its power. Richelieu's contempt for the man was shared by all those of his class. Yet perhaps he sensed a hidden affinity between his own ambition and the career of that spectacular lady's man, for he chose the side of Concini.

VIII

Allegiance to the Favorites

TOWARD the end of 1613, M. de Luçon was back in Paris once more. Only this time he did not waste his energies in the palace halls: he went straight to the man on whom he had just wagered. We can only imagine what his feeling were in the presence of Concini, that glib-tongued, blustering braggart who made no attempt to hide his delusions of grandeur: the noble blood in Richelieu must have made him react with a certain disgust to this foreigner whose villainy was universally known; the man of genius considered such a misguided intelligence pitiable; but the ambitious man admired the former "Isabella" [1] of commedia dell'arte fame, now the Queen's lover and almost ruler of France.

He heaped flattery on the Italian, assured him of his devotion and friendship, and placed himself at his service. Concini was delighted at such cooperation, for he had few reliable followers among the clergy and the nobles.

The bishop went next to pay his respects to the Queen's favored lady. Despite a certain amount of domestic strife, Leonora Galigai was the brains of this amazing couple; she served the same function for the Regent. Marie de Medici would not have known how to manage her life had her Aegeria not devoted two hours daily to telling her what to do.

---

[1] Concini had been given this nickname in Florence for having taken the roles (in female dress) of a celebrated actress, Isabella Andreini.

Like a dull-witted Galatea, the Queen's character was actually given life by the intelligence, activity, and audacity of her companion.

Leonora had the gift of captivating weak minds. The power was really controlled by this adventuress, who was said to be in the Devil's hands. Though she had little to do with public affairs, she had a great deal to say about selecting people. Richelieu was aware of this. So he went to confront this strange creature who remained shut up in her three-room lair, filled with gold and silver treasures, except when she visited the Queen for their daily chats. The wife of Marshal d'Ancre did not appear at Court for fear she might fall into a "frenzy," since she suffered from an illness which attacked both her mind and body.

Sometimes they found her bent over backward, so sick that she could not speak. A lump "is tormenting her, the pain rising to her throat, and threatening to strangle her." Leonora suffered from hysteria, and being just as ignorant about this disease as the College of Medicine in Paris, she was convinced it was witchcraft. Then, too, she feared "the evil eye" and allowed no one to look at her, always wearing a black veil to protect her face.

In addition to the useless prayers of monks, she resorted to some bizarre remedies: sometimes a rooster was cut open above her head; at other times she nursed at the breast. She knew that ordinary foods provided evil spirits the easiest entry, so she took the advice of the best authorities on demonology and ate only cockscombs and ram kidneys. These had to be washed first in holy water—also the plates and serving dishes. And all these precautions were useless, for the poor woman continued to feel the Devil attacking her, sending her into fits despite the exorcisms and fumigations in the name of protective virtues.

Then one day a miracle happened: Leonora thought she had been saved thanks to Elian de Montalto. He was a Portuguese Jew, well trained in astronomy and especially in medicine; his knowledge far surpassed that of his French colleagues who literally murdered their patients. Despite the severe (and intolerant) laws of the period, she dared to hide this deicide for several years in the Louvre itself. Finally, in 1613, Montalto thought it best to slip away, and the all-powerful lady-in-favor was lost once more.

When the Bishop of Luçon called on her, she, who was so sensitive to the eyes of others, could not bear his sharp and piercing gaze. Quickly she reached for the black veil to cover her face. From behind it she could still examine the slender, wiry body shaped by M. de Pluvinel's lessons, the pointed face framed by long black hair and punctuated by a severe little mustache and a beard "à la royale," the aquiline nose, heavy eyebrows, high forehead, and, as if to contradict however slightly the gravity of these features, an exceedingly seductive mouth. In this imposing face, the charming smile and sparkling eyes exerted a singular attraction. Leonora felt the spell of it but remained distrustful as usual.

We do not know much more about this meeting, which was a prelude to one of the major episodes in history. But it cannot be far wrong to suggest that Mme Concini thought many times afterward of the handsome young prelate who was too intent on being obsequious, and that Richelieu often recalled the "witch" whose smoldering eyes had frightened Henry IV on his wedding night.

When he was back home, he remembered the rather defensive attitude of the Queen's favorite lady, and Richelieu began to worry that his assurances had not been taken seriously enough. He decided to send a letter to Concini which would dispel any doubts because it would represent an irrevocable commitment:

"Sir: Wishing always to reflect credit on all those to whom I have pledged my service, I am writing you to repeat my assurances, for I would rather prove the quality of my affection to you at an important moment than merely offer you the semblance of it at a later time. . . . I beg you to believe that my promises will be fulfilled and that *as long as you honor me with your affection I shall continue to serve you loyally.*" In the language of courtiers, there was an implicit understanding that this was to be a give-and-take affair.

Results were slow to follow, and the situation remained unchanged for Richelieu when, suddenly, Condé issued a shattering proclamation destined to turn the kingdom against the Regent. All the grievances of the clergy, the nobility, and the people were set forth in a vengeful tone, the coming marriages with Spain were denounced, and a convocation of the States-General was demanded.

Then, Condé and his allies mustered troops while the Duke of Vendôme, an illegitimate son of Henry IV, went off to preach revolt in Brittany. But the people had no desire to see the horrors of the previous century return. The rebellion was too immature to survive, but it had consequences in Poitou which would favor the rise of Richelieu.

With Condé on his way towards Poitiers, the dynamic Bishop La

Rocheposay very properly had the Prince's envoy, La Trie, killed. He stripped of their power all those municipal magistrates who were suspected of supporting the Prince, he forced the Duke of Roannès, Governor of the city, to flee, and he proclaimed a state of siege. The approach of the King's army relieved him of the problem of maintaining the siege, but La Rocheposay's reputation took a great leap. Richelieu had actively supported his friend, so he, too, benefited from the false alert.

The Crown could easily have reestablished order if the doddering graybeards on the Council had had a spark of courage. But they had none. Villeroy wrote to the Queen begging her to arrange a settlement: "Madam: We must have peace at any cost. War would only bring on the disasters we already know, and some we have never seen." Mme Concini, too, was fearful for her husband, their treasures, and herself.

So it was decided to pay whatever price was demanded for the loyalty of the rebellious Princes. The Peace of Sainte-Menehould provided for the convocation of the States-General and, for the meanwhile, postponement of the royal marriages. The rebels could not have cared less what the terms were: all that mattered to them were the new favors and enormous benefices they divided up.

Only Vendôme held firm against the rain of gold. Then Marie de Medici chose just the right means to regain Brittany's allegiance: she showed the rebellious province its King. Louis XIII made the first of many trips that were to span the years of his reign, and wherever he appeared, the magic image of living royalty inspired his people to reaffirm their loyalty.

The experiment was a brilliant success, a little too brilliant for Concini's liking: the King's entry into Nantes and his return to Paris were like an apotheosis. But when the last trumpet had sounded, Louis returned to the Louvre, to his solitude and nothingness. He sensed that his triumph had caused anxiety in the Queen's circle; he remembered his father and the hostile flash, like a bolt from the sky, of the dagger Ravaillac had unsheathed. Marie de Medici and the Concinis shortly were relieved to see him return to his puerile and simple ways. Years afterward, in speaking of this period, Louis admitted: "I acted like a child." He was not even thirteen years old.

Richelieu made the same error as the Florentines: he recognized the power of the Crown but ignored the one who wore it. In announcing the news of the Peace of Sainte-Menehould to his diocese, he had praise only for the Queen.

By this time the bishop had friends in key places and, as a result, he found out long before the public that the States-General would be assembled and that when it came time to elect deputies, the Court would throw all its weight behind its supporters. He was able to exploit this edge. His influence within his own province was already strong, for when the Governor, none other than Sully himself, charged him to convoke the three social classes in his diocese, the reply came back: "I wish to assure you that I respect your honor and friendship as I ask you to respect my own."

His three faithful friends, the Bishop of Poitiers, Duvergier de Hauranne, and Bouthillier, served as electoral agents. Bishop La Rocheposay handled things so adroitly that Richelieu was the only candidate among the clergy of the region. On August 12 each class held a separate meeting in Poitiers, and on the 24th the election took place. Luçon's Bishop was chosen as deputy of three dioceses, Poitiers, Maillezais and his own, while the "peaceful" Dean of Saint-Hilaire was named his adjutant. Their trip was paid for by a tax of 75 livres 2 sous levied on the Saint-Hilaire chapter.

Richelieu took an active part in drafting the *cahier* of the clergy which would be submitted to the States-General. There is nothing in it that foreshadows his policies, except the desire to abolish duels.

As he made his way back to Paris, were the young Bishop's thoughts focused, now that he had opened a breach at last to his ambition, on politics? No one had a more systematic mind than he, and before thinking of France he had to consider his own needs. He was sure of himself and knew his value was far superior to that of the throng of puppets dancing around the throne. At the first possible occasion his ability would prove it.

But ability was not enough in this era of corruption and inconsistencies. He had to find other means, many of them, to attain favor, that master key. But he was confident of finding them and knowing how to use them.

IX

Amid the Chaos of the States-General

ON his thirteenth birthday, September 27, 1614, Louis XIII reached majority. An official proclamation was issued on October 2 but drew little attention compared to what was considered a far greater event, the convening of the States-General. In 1588 the national assembly had all but surrendered the throne of the reigning Valois to the Guises and in 1593 had barely managed to snatch it from the King of Spain, who considered it already his. For a government so weak and so defenseless a prey to foreign powers, a face-to-face meeting with the nation could be dangerous.

Condé, Vendôme, Nevers, and their fellow Princes discounted the last factor. They anticipated a glorious role for themselves: reviving the ghost of Henry IV in the Assembly, promoting his Gallican, anti-Spanish policies against those of subservience to Rome and Madrid, and, if necessary, intimidating Marie de Medici by demanding another investigation of Ravaillac's crime.

Jacqueline d'Escoman, the woman who had accused Epernon of murdering the King, was still alive and in prison, for thus far it had been impossible to convict her of false testimony. Better still, Captain La Garde had just returned to France, barely escaping ambush on the way. La Garde, who had been chosen at first to carry out the assassination and who later had warned Henry IV, had one weapon: a letter from Le

Bruyère, former League member turned agent for Spain, urging La Garde to dispatch the King for a reward of 50,000 écus and a grandeeship.[1] It also contained assurances that the Duke of Nevers would take care of any problems that might arise.

But to stir up a tempest of this magnitude required strong men motivated by genuine ambition, not simply by greed. The Princes had already lost the elections for deputies, having disdained to take any part in them, but the ministers, who were far more clever at this sort of activity, had gone to great lengths to prepare careful lists of candidates for circulation.

The Duke of Rohan was the first to grasp the situation. He told Condé: "Fear and hope are the two principal motives of these deputies. You are in a position neither to make them promises nor to frighten them with threats, while the Queen has rewards and offices to distribute and can cause a lot of trouble for anyone who opposes her. Who will be willing to support you against Her Majesty?" Certainly not the clergy, which was delighted to have such a pious sovereign, nor the nobility, whose deputies were generally as hard up as they were factious.

What of the third estate? There lay the great unknown factor. This group was not representative of the common people, for its deputies were almost entirely magistrates and civil servants, that is, privileged persons. The legal profession, known as the *bourgeoisie de robe*, soon to become the *noblesse de robe*, was at a critical stage in its history. There were two grave abuses undermining its dignity: the system of purchasing from the crown offices which became hereditary property and for which an annual fee was collected by the King, and the scandalous practice of selling justice. But the members of this group had no share in the moral depravity or wasteful follies of the nobles; they outclassed the aristocracy by their university training, their business experience, their strict principles, and their deep interest in public welfare. These dishonest judges were the privileged "clergy of the law," loyal servants of the State to which they were devoted.

But this in no way implied blind submission to the monarchy. On the contrary, the third estate included many independent and reform-minded men.

If the Princes had been shrewd enough to ally with them, they could have imposed their will on the King as they did at the time of the Fronde

---

[1] Cf. Philippe Erlanger, *L'étrange mort de Henri IV*

and as it occurred in England. But they were too arrogant and divided. Besides, de Sillery, the old Chancellor, was a monster of cleverness and expert at sowing dissension.

Richelieu grasped the problem immediately. There were three elements operating: the Crown, the Princes, and the third estate. The question was how they would align themselves. As for the clergy, it was less interested in acting as arbitrator than in extending its own power.

The Bishop of Luçon, in his purple gown, white bands, and doctor's cap, walked in the solemn procession representing all of France, down to her beggars and cripples, who were purposely placed in the lead. The opening session took place on October 27 in the Hôtel de Bourbon [2] amid great splendor and commotion; only the first and the final sessions brought together the deputies of all three classes.

Richelieu gazed at the royal family and surrounding dignitaries, who were seated on a platform which rose five steps above the hall and held the throne, topped by a dais of purple velvet with gold fleurs-de-lis. There, all in white, sat the King; at his right were the Queen, his mother, Queen Marguerite, his father's first wife, and his sister Elizabeth; at his left were his brother Gaston, Duke of Anjou, and his two other sisters. Louis rose and gave a brief address, trying to control his stammer; then his Chancellor took the floor. Richelieu paid scant attention to the child who, just a few days before, had announced his desire to be called Louis the Just instead of Louis the Stammerer. His pale, puffed face, so unlike his father's, seemed to confirm the nasty rumors that had been wantonly spread about this shy, melancholy boy who, apparently, was also a weakling.

The bishop turned from the sad little puppet to watch the real professionals. Condé and his friends had missed their bid for support; the Assembly would not back them. So another contest began.

The clergy opened with Du Perron leading off, reinforced by a group of young bishops among whom Richelieu was preeminent. The latter judged it wise to stay in the background when his colleagues demanded that certain questions, of major importance to their group, be extracted from the *cahiers* and submitted to the King for immediate consideration. Both the Court and the third estate were equally alarmed at this move. They managed to calm the excited clerics.

Then the nobles went into action, opening fire on the commons by

[2] Located on the present site of the Colonnade.

calling for abolition of the *droit annuel,* the annual payment made to the crown for hereditary offices. The third estate came right back with a demand for outlawing pensions. Savaron, its spokesman and president of the bailiwick of Auvergne, spoke passionately in defense of the impoverished peasants, citing that in Guyenne and Auvergne, they were reduced to eating grass like animals. He went on to denounce to the King the whole system of pensions which functioned in "such a reckless manner that some great and powerful nations do not possess the revenues you distribute to buy the loyalty of your subjects. . . . If this amount [5,660,- 000 livres!] went toward easing the suffering of your people, then would there not be cause to bless your royal virtues?"

Henry de Mesmes, a civil lieutenant, came to the rescue: "The three orders are three brothers sprung from a common mother: France. . . . The clergy is the eldest, the nobility the younger, and the commons is the cadet. In consideration of this relationship, the third estate has always recognized the higher rank of the nobility, but at the same time the nobles must acknowledge the commons as a brother and not treat it as if it did not exist."

Unable to reply, the aristocrats declared that they had been insulted and headed for the Louvre to complain to the King that "the children of shoemakers had called them brothers." Indeed, the distance separating the two classes was that between master and servant.

Violence seemed imminent when the clergy intervened, sending Richelieu as delegate to the commons to obtain an apology that would soothe the offended nobles. Savaron's retort was that he had spent five years in the army and was prepared to defend his statements against anyone. It was a curious exchange between the people's champion and the representative of an essentially privileged class, both of whom, in spite of their opposition, believed in absolute monarchy.

At that point Richelieu's talents came into focus, and he was able to extract a mollifying statement that closed the incident.

But then a loud protest was heard from the Duke of Epernon and the more volatile of his fellow Princes who were out to bring the commons to heel. Epernon was in constant fear that one of those insolent lawyers might bring up the murder of Henry IV, the sham trial of the Escoman woman, and Captain La Garde's accusations.

When one of Epernon's soldiers challenged and killed a man, the Duke had the audacity to abduct the guilty hireling from prison. Parliament ordered proceedings against the man, whereupon the Duke sent his rowdies into the law courts to insult and rough up the magistrates.

Far from intimidated, the third estate in an about-face—foreshadowing its action on the night of August 4—made its own motion for abolishing the sale of offices. If it had been sustained, the course of French history would have been altered and the Revolution of 1789 might well have been avoided. But the other two classes were afraid of the sacrifice involved: they risked having to make one, too, in the ensuing public pressure.

The Queen had been uneasy since the scandal involving Epernon; the Duke knew too many vital secrets and had to be appeased. So the young King, acting as his mother's mouthpiece, ordered the commons to apologize to the nobles and Parliament to leave the Duke alone.

The balance of power that had existed for two centuries broke down. Since the time of Charles VII and the famous States-General of 1439, the King and the third estate had been united against the nobles. The reversal of this alliance, which was later to cost Louis XVI his throne, would, from 1614 on, cause unforeseen upheavals.

Aiming to preserve the long-standing pact of unity and to rescue the crown from the little clique of self-interested parasites, the third estate sought to revive that old and ever-smoldering issue of Gallicanism versus ultramontanism. On December 15, it voted to preface its *cahiers* with an electrifying declaration intended as a fundamental law of the land: "If it please the King, he shall proclaim . . . that he is sovereign in France and is beholden only to God for his crown, and there is no power, either spiritual or temporal, with authority to remove it from the sacred persons of our kings." The effect was to put the monarchy beyond the call of obedience to the Pope, to make the King "God's lieutenant" with unlimited power. The commons demanded this in order to stem the abuses of the nobility; despite many setbacks, this demand was to provide the foundation of absolute monarchy.

There was another motive behind it: to raise the King so high that, on moral grounds, an assassination would be impossible.

This veiled allusion to the death of Henry IV sent a shudder through the Queen and her attendants, the nobles flared up angrily, while the clergy, overwhelmingly ultramontanist under Du Perron's influence, was "visibly moved." Now the power factors were back in their traditional positions: the King and the people on one side, the priests and nobles on the other.

"Casing their words in velvet," the prelates tried to make the commons retreat and, failing, they called on Du Perron to try his hand. Flanked by churchmen and nobles, Du Perron went before the inferior brethren and delivered a pathetic speech to the effect that he and his followers would endure martyrdom rather than "take an oath in the English manner." Not only was the attempt a failure, but Parliament handed down a decision confirming the doctrine set forth by the third estate. An uproar broke out, and the clergy appealed the matter to the King.

It would have been sheer folly to expect the monarch to deny his own absolute authority had the kingdom not been already a pawn in the hands of men who valued the interests of Rome, Madrid, and themselves before those of France. Marie de Medici was not in the long tradition of queens, who, like caryatids, held aloft the supreme power of the throne.[3]

The clergy's deputies planned to go to the Louvre with representatives of the nobility. Richelieu was asked to arrange this meeting, and he managed it superbly. Thus, the opportunist aligned himself against a principle he had formerly embraced and which was later to be an essential arm of his government.

The privileged classes expressed their "grief" to the Court with "shocking insolence." Du Perron muttered threats of excommunication and the eternal fires, then outlined a series of reprisals which bespoke the clergy's latent desire for political control.

Hearing this, Condé and the Protestants belatedly sprang to the rescue of the commons.

"You, Sir, are most lightheaded," said the Prince to Cardinal Sourdis, president of the clergy.

"I would not expect to find any lead in your head," retorted the Cardinal.

As this point Louis XIII intervened personally with Condé, his cousin. "I beg you, Sir, say no more, for they reject you now and will reject me also."

This unwonted interference did not seem to surprise anyone, yet it

---

[3] Blanche of Castille, Yolanda of Aragon, Anne of Beaujeu, Louise of Savoy, Catherine de Medici, and even, later on, Anne of Austria.

71

revealed feelings on the young King's part which would prove costly to Richelieu. Beneath the appearance of a timid child, Louis was irritated by the pretentious churchmen; it would be a long time before he accepted the idea of making one of them his minister. M. de Luçon had been a little too clever and had played against his own side.

For the moment, the King could do nothing. The Queen was linked with the Nuncio, the Jesuits, and Epernon. The ministers were only concerned with avoiding any clashes. They had Parliament's decision annulled, then, after a series of delays and excuses, managed to bury the motion put forth by the commons. So it appeared that the latter were beaten now; nevertheless they had implanted the doctrines of divine right and absolute monarchy that Richelieu would apply one day.

The most outspoken members of the clergy failed to grasp the situation and, seeing themselves triumphant, sought to widen their advantage as much as possible. The Bishop of Angers called for inspection of the government's financial records and openly attacked the Queen, finding considerable support for his opinions.

M. de Luçon censured this effrontery. Having weighed the forces in play, he judged Marie de Medici to be the most powerful because of the magic name she bore. He would have to lean on her. Thus, as representative of the clergy's moderate element, he declared that it was "most harmful to seek a separation and division of the King's authority from that of the Queen, his mother, that he would be extremely grieved if Their Majesties were thereby offended, and would wish to assure them of complete obedience, fealty, and devotion." The clergy joined in this manifesto of loyalty and directed Richelieu to include the nobles as subscribers thereto.

Meanwhile, the chaos continued. Condé tried to set himself up as leader of the opposition. The Queen forbade him to show his face to the commons, and, in reprisal, he arranged the murder of Marcillac, one of the King's retainers. This in turn led M. de Bonneval to take his cane to Chavailles, a deputy of the third estate.

The Queen and her circle could not wait to end the session. They were in constant fear of some violent explosion, a sword of Damocles, perhaps a new investigation of Captain La Garde's charges, since he had petitioned the States-General directly for a hearing. This annoying witness had been bought off cheaply with the office of Inspector of Breweries, and his suit was kept dormant in a pile of equally dangerous documents, but supposing Condé or one of the deputies suddenly got the idea of resurrecting it?

The King was told to announce the deadline for turning in the *cahiers*, and the final meeting was set for February 23, 1615—a plenary session during which each order summarized its desires and complaints through an elected speaker. The Queen discreetly informed the clergy that she wished the Bishop of Luçon to be its spokesman. Thus, Richelieu's efforts reaped a reward full of promise. His election as speaker followed as a matter of course; he protested modestly, apologized, then finally said he would "obey."

He spoke for an hour in the Hôtel de Bourbon, pleased everyone and offended no one. There was universal applause, yet his address, which he delivered amid a terrible hubbub and commotion, made less impression on his listeners than on posterity. This much-analyzed speech, in which the future minister took a position for the first time on the principal political issues of his day, was a document he was very proud of and which he had printed and distributed. Rather than redissect this speech, we shall limit ourselves to underlining the passages of special significance.

First, an ardent plea *pro domo* aimed at proving the necessity for bringing the clergy into the government. The Church, said Richelieu, without blinking an eye, was "deprived of honors, stripped of its possessions, denied authority, profaned, cast down" since it had no representative on the Council. Yet the very training of priests "prepares them for such service since it cultivates ability, honesty, and wise guidance, which are the only qualities necessary for loyal service to the State. . . . Since nothing survives them but their souls, the only treasures they may store up in earthly life, while serving their king and country, are those everlastingly glorious and perfect rewards of Heaven."

Joyeuse and Du Perron were among the Cardinals with highly developed tastes for earthly rewards, and Richelieu himself became singularly interested in "building up treasures on earth." However, there was nothing ironic about the statement, nor did his cynical and naïve display of ambition shock anyone. It was the age of plunder, and greed was a perfectly normal vice, even in a priest.

In speaking of the system of pensions, the Bishop cleverly gave the clergy credit for the motion put forth by the third estate, taking care to dilute its substance. In effect, he advocated liberality, "well-ordered and reasonable in terms of the relationship between what is given and what

73

can rightly be given." This was aimed at strengthening the King's independence in such matters.

On the other hand, Richelieu violently attacked the sale of hereditary offices which, later, he wrongly did not abolish when he had the means to do it. Above all, he sought to flatter his own caste, the nobility, "whose purse was as empty as its courage was abundant," to denounce the granting of ecclesiastical benefices to lay persons, as well as to proclaim the solidarity of the two highest Estates. His own government would one day put that solidarity to a severe test.

The essential part of his address, in terms of his personal ambitions, came in the summation. Turning to Marie de Medici, who was listening attentively, Richelieu declared: "All of France, Madam, owes you the tribute which our ancestors reserved for those who kept the peace and preserved order in the land."

He had unqualified praise for her administration of the regency, and particularly the marriages with Spain (exactly the opposite of his future policy): "United, Spain and France have nothing to fear, for the only harm that could come to either is from the other." Finally, he beseeched the King "humbly and ardently" to let his mother wield the power. "You have done a great deal, Madam, but there is more to do. Not to push forward and upward on the path of honor and glory is to retreat and fall."

He could see that his words pleased the Queen, but he was unaware of the scorn they provoked in the young King.

The nobles had no gift for oratory, and their representative, M. de Senecey, spoke briefly and in empty words. After him, Miron, president of the commons, knelt and delivered a solemn address. He pictured the miserable plight "of the impoverished people, stripped down to skin and bones," and lashed out at the warmakers, the nobles, and even the wicked priests. "No words can describe their cruelty. . . . Tigers and lions, even the more savage beasts are kind, or at least do no harm, to those who look after them. . . . And it is the people who provide sustenance to Your Majesty, the ecclesiastic state, the nobility, and the third estate."

After a lengthy discussion of the regime's flagrant abuses, Miron concluded gravely: "Who, then, will answer for this chaos, Sire? . . . You must be the one to do it. . . . What we ask of you is an act of majesty."

Thus the disinherited masses placed their hope in the monarchy. Richelieu had neither love nor compassion for the common people. No one, and he least of all, could foresee that the desired "act of majesty" would come from his own hand.

The King thanked the deputies and affirmed his will to serve God, solace his people, and satisfy everyone.

The Estates then went their separate ways for another 174 years. The Council ruled to reestablish the sale of offices. Louis XIII was rewarded for his fine performance by having Luynes, one of his favorites, made Governor of Amboise. As for Captain La Garde, he was thrown into the Bastille after being compelled to hand over to Parliament the letter—it was promptly consigned to oblivion—which could have shed some strange light on the murder of Henry IV.

X

Impatience and Perseverance

ECAUSE of his success in the States-General and his fine display
of loyalty, Richelieu felt certain of receiving an important post at
Court. The weakness and inefficiency of the ministers was becoming pathetic. Furthermore, Villeroy, chief figure among them, tried to oppose Concini just as the latter was maneuvering to seize power after forcing them to watch the useless comedy he had staged. The Queen and her favorite were in need of a strong man, and none had shown himself at the Hôtel de Bourbon save the clergy's young spokesman.

Sadly enough, Marie de Medici lacked imagination, and Concini resembled her in that respect. Only Leonora had the ability to guide them, but she was too preoccupied by illness and distress to think of the handsome bishop. For her beloved and seductive husband, whom she had pulled out of the mud and lifted to dizzying heights, had broken off their conjugal relations, intending to get along on his own.

Yet she was the one behind his ambition to acquire, in addition to a number of cities in the Somme region whose governments he already controlled, the governorship of Picardy, which would bring the citadel of Amiens under his aegis. At first, Concini did not want to be burdened with a fortress,[1] but the anxious Leonora pressed for a refuge near

---

[1] Command of a fortress often involved equipping and manning it at the noble's own expense. (Trans.)

76

the Spanish border which would put them in reach of safety on foreign soil, hence in a position to threaten Paris.

Concini finally adopted the idea. Without consulting his wife—a singular aberration on his part—he charged Villeroy to offer the Duke of Longueville, Picardy's governor, the exchange of his province for rich Normandy. But Villeroy spotted the danger and, of course, killed this fine project. Concini saw red. Villeroy walked out, expecting to be recalled, but after two weeks had passed without any message, he came crawling back to the Court. When he humiliated himself further by calling on the Italian, the reception he got bordered on rudeness.

"Marshal d'Ancre has absolute power," wrote the Venetian ambassador. Why then did he not get rid of the graybeards and replace them with loyal young men, such as M. de Luçon, who had practically sworn fealty to him? If Concini thought of it, he lacked the courage to act. In fact, once he was out from under his wife's thumb, he sank back to the level of a fortune-hunting mediocrity.

With nothing developing for him, Richelieu again fell into a state of depression and left Paris for Coussay. Fortunately, when these black moods occurred, some hidden mechanism reacted quickly to restore his mental balance, keeping him from the edge of that gulf which was to claim the wits of several family members.

With the return of good spirits, he got off a volley of letters to the group of friends who remained his constant admirers. Duvergier de Hauranne, in particular, was eager to serve him: "I admit to having a mind that ranks below yours." He did not foresee the conflict that would erupt one day between them.

Bertrand d'Eschaux, Bishop of Bayonne, and L'Aubespine, Bishop of Orléans, as well as the Bishop of Nantes, were just as enthusiastic and shortsighted. Through them and through Bouthillier, Bérulle, and many others, Richelieu had a window in his own priory on the spectacle of the decaying monarchy.

"Up to now," complained Villeroy, "we have governed by our purse-strings and our wits, but who knows what will happen next, for we have reached the end of both."

In May, 1615, Parliament, backed by Condé, opened fire on the Queen. Without naming the Concinis, it demanded that administrative posts and government offices be reserved for those "of French birth," and

77

it denounced "the infamous sects that had crept into the Court," meaning Leonora's entourage.

The only result was that the Princes had an excuse to parade their virtuous indignation in front of the unmoved Queen. Condé found a willing ally in the Duke of Longueville, who, despite pressure from Concini, was resolved to hold onto that garden of treason, Picardy. The two of them walked out of the Court once more, followed by the Dukes of Mayenne and Bouillon, and proceeded to raise troops.

Anarchy spread like a brushfire. The Duke of Nevers dressed one of the King's treasury agents as a jester and sent him out on exhibit astride a donkey—the poor man had tried to stop the Duke from paying his soldiers with tax monies collected in Champagne! There was only one element of stability: the confusion and helplessness of both government and opposition balanced each other.

By all rights the Queen should have been panic-stricken, but in fact, she was in her glory. All other matters were trifling now that she was on the verge of satisfying her supreme ambition: by virtue of the treaties of 1612, her children at last would wed the children of Charles V's grandson. The double ceremony was to take place in Bordeaux at the end of the summer.

Condé was vehemently opposed to the marriages, for the birth of a Dauphin would greatly decrease his importance. From his fortress at Coucy he proclaimed his refusal to consent to them unless the government were reorganized and Marshal d'Ancre banished. Uneasy over the prospect of Spanish influence gaining further inroads, the Protestants held a threatening meeting in Grenoble. The boiling point was reached when Concini's henchmen murdered M. de Prouville, a lieutenant of the Duke of Longueville.

But the Queen, for want of forcefulness, could be fearfully obstinate, as Henry IV had found out on numerous occasions. She would not hear of delaying the project that was so dear to her heart. President Le Jay, leader of the parliamentary opposition, was arrested, and two armies were formed, one to protect the King on his journey to Guyenne, the other to hold the Princes in check.

Marie offered her favorite the honor of escorting His Majesty, but Concini declined; his obsession for Picardy made him choose to go fight the rebels in the North. Leonora, whose love for her husband always brought her back to him, made sure to accompany the Queen. There was a serious question that she counted on settling, as usual, according to her own views: what persons would be called upon to make up the future Queen's household?

The office of Chaplain, one of the most important in this new Court, had been earmarked for a close friend of Richelieu: L'Aubespine, Bishop of Orléans. The writ of appointment was already lying on Marie's table when Bertrand d'Eschaux, Bishop of Bayonne, decided that the honor should go to the leader of his own little clan, and he opened a campaign to that end. During the month of August, Richelieu was stunned to learn this in a florid letter from his friend d'Eschaux: "Whatever qualities you may find admirable in me shall be devoted solely to proving my love and esteem for you."

Wisely, the young bishop did not appear too eager; his reticence was such that the naïve d'Eschaux thought he had to overcome his friend's scruples: "I shall never knowingly deal anyone a low blow. . . . When *I* last wrote you about developments at Court concerning our mutual friend, the Bishop of Orléans, at that time, and contrary to my opinion, his cause was taken to be hopeless and lost. . . ."

But it was not so, and the Queen signed the appointment. As for M. de Luçon, he claimed to have rejected temptation, saying that he wished neither to harm dear L'Aubespine nor to change his occupation.

Despite his friend's noble disinterestedness, the Bishop of Bayonne renewed his efforts, aided by the Marquis of Richelieu. And he won out, for one day the Queen, "in an unusual fit of temper," suddenly ordered the writ returned to her. "Only M. de Loménie and I noticed her deep satisfaction," wrote d'Eschaux, "and, if I may say so, her appeased anger as she hastily stuffed it into her pocket, and the only explanation for her rapid change of mood must lie in what the poet said: *'Tantae ne animis coelestibus irae.'* "

There was another explanation, the only conceivable one: her fear of incurring the wrath of Leonora, who wanted nothing more to do with the Bishop of Orléans.

D'Eschaux wrote again to Richelieu to tell him that he was going to act "against his Stoic inclinations." The letter concluded: "And don't talk to me about your building in Luçon. With your permission, we know better than you what is best for you." He was very frank indeed, or else Richelieu was playing his part brilliantly, since the idea of frustrating one of his best friends did not trouble him in the least.

Each at their own pace, the prelates and the Florentines continued their scheming. Weeks passed. Mastering his impatience, Richelieu gave the impression that he was completely absorbed in his theological studies. He ordered several Latin works from his bookseller. He wrote to the Bishop of Langres: "The very air you breathe is saintly and the food you touch is spiritual," the pompous tone of his letter calculated to imply that the image also fitted himself. Poring over his obscure texts, the grave bishop did not even look for news of the Court, which had left Paris on August 17 and was making its way leisurely toward his own province, escorted by one thousand horsemen and three thousand infantry.

But there were times when this cramped existence became stifling, and then the most insignificant incident would touch off his violent and brutal temper. A humble soul who did some pamphleteering work for him later on received an angry blast for a trifling offense: ". . . Since you are obviously in the same offensive mood as when you were here, I advise you to take a dose of hellebore [2] and eat whey for a while to cool the heat and purge your system of the vapors that have gone to your head."

Flattering and obsequious toward persons of rank, but savage toward the common variety of men, M. de Luçon had a most uneven disposition.

On August 31 the King and Queen arrived in Poitiers and denounced Condé for high treason. They were obliged to remain there until September 28 while Elizabeth, the Queen's daughter, recovered from an attack of smallpox.

Richelieu went to pay his respects to Their Majesties. He had many friends at Court, and one of them, whose background gave no reason to expect it, had a wider influence than even Richelieu's brother the Marquis, or Bertrand d'Eschaux. He was Claude Barbin, a "nobody" who had been appointed public prosecutor in Melun under Henry IV. Barbin had used his trips to the Court at Fontainebleau to cultivate Leonora's friendship, and when the all-powerful favorite had set herself up in business, so to speak, Barbin left the courtroom behind and went to serve as her adviser. In 1611 he was appointed Financial Steward of the Queen and rendered outstanding service to her as well as to her confidante. The amazing thing is that in the midst of all the Florentine intrigues he was able to remain indisputably honest. Arnaud d'Andilly, as severe a judge of men as any,

[2] A plant of the buttercup family which was believed to offer a cure for madness. (Trans.)

found that Barbin's "hands were perfectly clean." That gave him a position of strength among the voracious wolves.

In 1615 "he was the strongest figure in Court affairs. . . . His house was the meeting place of financiers, party followers, pension seekers, and people who needed someone to say a word on their behalf in royal ears." [3]

Barbin was in no way connected to the group of Richelieu's admirers, and it is hard to see how their friendship began—and grew to the point where, so it seems, the bishop hoped to marry one of his sisters to this person "of extremely low extraction."

The proud bishop, author of "The Courtier's Breviary," had plotted his course of action without reference to Leonora's business adviser, whom he had met through faithful Bouthillier, and for a number of years he was careful not to mention this acquaintance. At the time of the royal visit, however, there was prestige to be gained from a relationship with Barbin.

Despite their different backgrounds, the two men had much in common. Both aspired to gain power regardless of the means, and since they were not competitors, their twin ambitions formed a solid base—with one important qualification: although Barbin tried to serve Richelieu, Richelieu never served Barbin.

In Poitiers, it was Barbin who helped out the Bishop of Bayonne by conducting Richelieu to the private apartments of the Queen and Leonora. Once again he cast his disconcerting spell over these women, who wavered in "the eagle's piercing glance." But by now M. de Luçon was an old acquaintance who had their friendship and confidence.

One day, quite unexpectedly, Marie de Medici promised him the office of Queen's Chaplain.

It was only a *promise*. For the bishop's artful methods had not fooled those who feared him as a dangerous rival. In a Court where almost any position could be won by sheer fighting, everyone was his neighbor's enemy. In the shadows, a group formed, pledged to expel the intruder, and it had no trouble stirring the fires of Leonora's obsessive fears for her own and her husband's security. But she, too, was a mistress of dissimulation.

When the Court left Poitiers, Richelieu felt all the more certain of his standing, having just been asked a signal favor: to keep the Queen

[3] Brienne's *Memoirs*

informed about her daughter, who was still ill and unable to travel. This gave him the opportunity to establish a direct correspondence with Her Majesty through which began to filter a certain amount of respectful familiarity. While following the progress of the young princess, he paid close attention, naturally, to the course of events.

Concini was on the warpath in Beauvais. He attacked the city of Clermont, which supported Condé, and, thanks to his experienced officers, was able to take it after a short battle. Three lyric accounts of the event exalted the "great Marshal's glory," and he returned to Paris as the monarchy's triumphant savior. Meanwhile, right under the nose of Marshal de Bois-Dauphin, commander of the King's forces, Condé slipped across the Loire and headed for Poitou in the hope of finding Protestant support, but luckily the Protestants were completely divided.

The Court had been in Bordeaux since October 7, and Richelieu was furious at not having received a single word from the Queen. He could have gone there, since Mme Elizabeth was well again, but a combination of anger, impatience, and humiliation so irked him that he returned to Coussay and stayed there, waiting for news and sending out daily packets of letters.

Anticipation only added fire to his chronic fever, but at last, in the beginning of November, the long-awaited letter arrived. He had been appointed Chaplain. Immediately, he sent his grateful acknowledgment, well seasoned with innuendos, to the Regent: "I beg Your Majesty's permission to explain in three lines [!] that since I know no words worthy enough to describe my gratitude for the undeserved honor it has pleased her to bestow on me *in my absence* [subtle hypocrisy], and since she has resisted *by her own actions* [extremely clever] all those who sought to deprive me of the fruit *of her promises,* I dedicate my life to this purpose: may God extend my years so that I may lengthen yours, and, without denying me His grace, *may He heap woes upon me so as to glorify Your Majesty with all manner of prosperity.*"

One can well imagine that this vain and clever man was quite pleased with himself as he wrote these extravagant words.

The Duke of Epernon, medal by Dupré—Paris, Bibliothèque Nationale, cabinet des Médailles (Giraudon)

ie de Medici, the regent on her throne 1610, seventeenth-century engraving— s, Bibliothèque Nationale

LA COURONNE DE JUSTICE.

Celle ie suis qui fais regner les Roys Et maintenir la Paix et la Milice
Qui scay regir les Armes et les Loix En corrigeant des hommes la malice.

The Estates-General in 1614, engraving by Piquet—Paris, Bibliothèque Nationale (Bulloz)

Cléonore Galigaï Concini by François
Quesnel or Thomas Key—Rennes, Musée
es Beaux-Arts (Bulloz)

Concini, Marshal of Ancre, French school
f the seventeenth century—Blois Museum
Bulloz)

Marie de Medici, French school of the
eventeenth century—Versailles Museum
Bulloz)

S. Geneuiefue

Noſtre Dame

S. Iacque

Le Roy

Louis XIII and Anne of Austria on the heights of Belleville arriving in Paris, seventeenth-century engraving—Paris, Musée Carnavalet (Bulloz)

Cardinal Richelieu, by Philippe de Champaigne—Chantilly, Musée Condé (Giraudon)

Louis XIII (detail from a Crucifixion), French school of the seventeenth century—Paris, Church of Saint-Julien-le-Pauvre (Bulloz)

Fantosme de Conchini.

Caricatures of Concini and his wife, seventeenth-century engravings—Paris, Bibliothèque Nationale

Portraict du mauuais demon, gardan Conchini.

Concini's house being pillaged, September 1, 1616, seventeenth-century engraving—Paris, Bibliothèque Nationale

Concini's death and the mutilation of his body by the people, seventeenth-century engravings—Paris, Bibliothèque Nationale

Au Louure entrant il fut pour le bien de la France
Arresté, & tué trop honnorablement:
Car il deuoit mourir au haut d'vne potence,
Et le ventre des loups estre son monument.

Au lendemain matin vn grand peuple en colere,
Cerche le lieu où est de ce faquin le cors:
Apres l'ayant trouué le tire hors de terre,
Qui desia s'apprestoit pour le jetter dehors.

Le peuple courageux le trainant par la bouë,
Exclamoit, le coyon, le traistre, ô le meschant!
Voilà comme de luy la fortune se iouë,
Puis qu'il estoit par trop deuenu arrogant.

Attaché par les pieds au haut de la potence
Qu'il auoit fait dresser, tant auoit du pouuoir:
Il est ards & brusle, ô iuste recompence,
Et le peuple y accourt pour ce spectacle voir.

LE
T...
...
...
...
...

Phœbus eſtant leué Phœbe perd ſa puiſſance,
Les voleurs & brigands perdent tout leur credit
Par les bons librement la verité ſe dit
Et de tous leurs deſſeis en fin ont iouyſſance.

SVR LA DESCENTE DE CONCHINI
AVX ENFERS.

Alors qu'on envoya Conchin dans les Auernes,
Le Diable ſ'oppoſa, & dit Helas grand Dieu
Souffrons nous pas aſſez icy bas dans ce lieu,
Nous ſommes tourmentés aſſez dans ces cauernes,

The rising sun, which symbolizes the king's
power, eclipses the moon, which symbolizes
Concini's power, seventeenth-century engraving—Paris, Bibliothèque Nationale

The king has become more glorious and more powerful by his defeat
of the dragon, which symbolizes Concini, seventeenth-century engraving—Paris, Bibliothèque Nationale

Concini's successor, the Duke of Luynes, seventeenth-century engraving—Paris, Bibliothèque Nationale (Giraudon)

Father Joseph, seventeenth-century engraving—Paris, Bibliothèque Nationale (Giraudon)

Pope Paul V, by Bernini—Rome, Borghese Gallery (Alinari-Giraudon)

Marie de Medici escaping from Blois, 1619, by Rubens—Paris, Louvre
(Giraudon)

The voyage of Marie de Medici to Pont de Cé, by Rubens—Paris, Louvre (N.D. Giraudon)

Louis XIII giving orders outside La Rochelle, 1621, seventeenth-century engraving—Paris, Bibliothèque Nationale (Bulloz)

Louis XIII, seventeenth-century painting—Paris, Musée Carnavalet (Bulloz)

The reconciliation of Louis XIII and Marie de Medici after the Constable's death—Paris, Louvre (Bulloz)

XI

Two Women to Comfort

RICHELIEU'S letter was dated November 6. By a curious coincidence, on November 9 Louis XIII directed Luynes to deliver his first note of congratulations to Infanta Anne of Austria, his fiancée. In the message, he referred to his friend as "one of my most trusted servants," thus raising the falconer to a level far above his rank. The old retainers trembled, their eyes suddenly opened to this newcomer who had already "arrived."

In 1611, Luynes, a former page of Count de Lude, was appointed His Majesty's Master of the Falcon. Having neither famous ancestors, alliances, fortune, arrogance, nor penchant for duels, he was generally considered harmless. When he had to settle an affair with his sword, one of his brothers appeared instead. A good-looking young man, soft-spoken and well-mannered, he was the exact opposite of the braggadocios around the Court.

Louis, in his isolation, turned to Luynes as a plant turns to the sun, and from this contact a strangely powerful feeling began to surge within the young King. Luynes became his light, his refuge, his inspiration. He cried out the name in his sleep, saw Luynes in his dreams, and never tired of describing the experience. To his great delight, the falconer was promoted to captain of the palace guard, with the privilege of lodging directly above his master's apartment. Louis would go up there at all hours to play or have something to eat. When nightmares woke him, he had a mattress taken up to his friend's bedside, and there found peaceful sleep.

Marie de Medici and the Concinis had often discussed this matter and agreed that it was not of any importance. They spoke of it again after Louis sent his letter to the Infanta and again decided that even if Luynes were out of the way, another favorite, unknown and therefore dangerous, would probably replace him. After all, what did they have to fear from this thirty-three-year-old native of Provence whose ambition was satisfied by a few minor offices? And anyway, for Marie, mother-in-law of the Catholic King, the Hapsburg alliance was a solid guarantee of power.

Did Richelieu know about the incident of the letter? He probably did, since he had friendly eyes everywhere, but paid scant attention to it. In his calculations—advanced as they were—Henry IV's son was a nonentity.

Nor did the Bishop show any particular interest in the little fair-haired, pink-and-white Infanta, with her milky skin and rosy cheeks, her soft, slightly almond-shaped green eyes, her delicate and perfect hands; nor in the fairy-tale pageant that unfolded in Bordeaux's Cathedral of Saint Andrew; nor even in the royal wedding night, prelude to so many grim consequences, when those two children of fourteen, who were expected to love each other, had to endure the shame and fright of consummating the marriage under the eyes of nurses and the medical staff.

This detail points out again what limits excessive haste can impose even on a genius of intrigue. Now that he had made important progress, Richelieu should have been doubly careful not to overlook any detail. Under the monarchic system, there was considerable significance in Louis XIII's brutal and premature initiation to love, which numbed his senses, intensified his fear of women, and stimulated what was called the "Italian" element in his sexual instincts. But if the new Chaplain had taken the King's personality into account, he would have been forced to change his plans, that is, fall behind schedule.

Condé's arrival in Poitou gave him a number of other worries. Rebel troops plundered the area mercilessly, and old Mme de Richelieu bore the brunt of it. "I have lived in this house for forty years and have seen all the armies pass this way," she wrote her son, "but never have I heard or seen the likes of these people who bring such ruin among us." The pillage extended to the Bishop's personal property.

The Duke of Rohan had finally succeeded in stirring up the Protestants; the State was disintegrating; and the King, slowed on his return to Paris by difficulties en route, risked crossing paths with Condé, who was now convinced the time had come to "prostitute his loyalty." His chances were good, and he knew his real strength.

The Court arrived at La Rochefoucauld's residence in Verteuil on January 12, 1616, to find word that Condé was prepared to come to an agreement. An "act of majesty" would have sufficed to end the revolt then and there, but, unfortunately, Villeroy, Sillery and Jeannin, the chief ministers, whose combined years totaled 225, were well past the age of heroic action. Also Leonora's fears were back again. The result was, as usual, a decision to buy off the rebels, and in mid-February at Loudun, something called a conference opened, which amounted to a disgraceful carnival for the robber princes.

With Loudun such a short distance from Richelieu and Coussay, the Bishop was furious that he had not been invited and that the fate of France was being decided without him. He asked to attend the conference in order to obtain reparations for the damage to his property. The ruse was too crude; the ministers did not fall for it and slammed the door in the face of their future heir.

For, indeed, the question of succession was in the wind. After signing the treaty, the Queen would be forced to choose between installing a strong government or letting Condé run the show. Well aware of this, Richelieu was working at top speed. He sent Charpentier, his secretary, to Tours, where the Queen was in residence during the negotiations, and wrote him significant instructions: "I have just received word that I may be in line to replace a cold-as-marble colossus [Sillery]. Keep an eye on this. . . . If he [probably Bardin] writes me as warmly as he did in Bordeaux, I'll consider the affair in the bag." As for Bertrand d'Eschaux, "that impossible bore," he found him rather useless and dropped him. Instead of his subtle-minded ecclesiastic friends, Richelieu now preferred the group of energetic men, Barbin in particular, who were beginning to align themselves behind the Concinis.

At present, the ravenous appetite of the Princes had to be satisfied. Under pressure from Villeroy, the Queen yielded, then yielded some more. The fantastic sum of six million had already been distributed, yet most of the arrogant rebels were still unsatiated. Condé obtained Chinon, governorship of the duchy of Berry, a number of important positions, and 1,500,00 livres. He held out for more; demanding withdrawal of the fortress of Amiens from Concini's hands, and, for himself, supreme control of the government: two things which the Queen, leaping, as usual from passivity to violent obstinacy, was resolved not to grant him.

Condé then produced his trump card: he demanded "an investigation of the act of parricide committed against the late King." This was enough to knock over the Florentine beehive. Leonora panicked and ran off to Paris, where she told her husband a thing or two, then returned with a letter in which Concini nobly renounced the fortress in the interest of peace. The Queen wept as she read it, and cursed the Princes as well as her impotent ministers. She had the letter published.

After offering to demolish the citadel with his own hands, the favorite concluded: "I would only add that, regardless of my personal interests, Their Majesties shall always have my total and unqualified obedience, and I would be content if all of France recognized this fidelity in me, a foreigner, and used it as a model. . . ."

With all her artfulness, Leonora could not have written such clever lines; that her husband did it is even less likely. A hand such as Barbin's was probably behind them. In any event, the Marshal's sacrifice was well rewarded, for he received the fortress of Caen and governorship of Normandy.

But Condé still was not satisfied and continued to call up the dreadful ghost. Spurred by Villeroy, who feared a scandal that could rock the throne, Marie finally resigned herself to signing a secret document making the Prince head of the Council with authority to execute official documents.

As of that moment, there was no further mention of Henry IV, and the Prince was once more a loyal subject. Addressing a crowd of disappointed lords, he told them cynically: "Let those who love me do as I do!"

He thought he had won; it was an error, and he was wrong to discourage so many of his confederates. The real victor was behind the scenes: Barbin, who aimed to rule the government from behind the flashy cloak of Concini and the black veil of "the witch."

Leonora had finally grasped the fact that their progress was really a retreat, and the Queen blamed her ministers for it. Sillery was the first to go. Barbin preferred to wait until the sovereigns were back in Paris before taking aim at the others. And fortune smiled on him when the lawyer Dolé, his only serious rival, died quite suddenly.

Two Women to Comfort

Richelieu knew Barbin's plans and counted on being called on to aid him. He waited, restless, but used the time to make sure of success on both fronts. When Condé had come to Poitou, Richelieu had sent him letters full of those flatteries that he dispensed so freely when they did not commit him to anything. At first, Father Joseph, who supported the rebels, served as go-between for the Prince and the Queen.

In Tours, Richelieu saw Marie and Leonora again. Both women were grieving over the absence and desertion of Concini, who, in any event, "suffered a good deal from hernias" and no longer was apt at love-making.[1] Both were badly in need of consolation and completely at a loss to cope with the shocks and threats and last minute stunts produced by the tense situation.

They were nearly forty-three, and the years had marked them in different ways. Marie, whose "wonderfully strong and robust nature" appealed to Henry IV, had once had "a complexion that was very white, though a bit coarse," a majestic forehead, beautiful arms, and an ample bosom which was highly appreciated in those days. What survived was a graceless corpulence, large, dull eyes and heavy features, clumsy gestures and an incurable vulgarity.

Now, in place of the voluptuous Juno, there stood a matron whose dignity was lost in her constant shuffling between extremes of despondency and agitation, who had nothing to compensate for her colossal bulk, her distended cheeks that were alternately purple and pallid, or her shrill voice. Rarely did a face reflect a personality so faithfully: one look made it clear that Her Majesty was stupid, haughty, irascible, opinionated, and indolent.

Her prestige as sovereign had not outlasted her looks, but beneath the fading surface still burned a desire for power, perhaps the one steady flame in her unstable character, a legacy of the Hapsburgs [2] who had no genius to impart. Feeling that her dearest possessions were now slipping away, she struggled to hold onto them; her shifting moods, angry outbursts, panic, tears, and screams exasperated those around her, Concini most of all.

As for Leonora she knew her husband was waiting for her to die in order to marry the illegitimate daughter of Henry IV. Illness and her ungrateful spouse's cruelty tortured her. A description generously pro-

---

[1] Richelieu, *Mémoires*
[2] She was a daughter of Joanna of Austria.

vided by her enemies gives us the following picture of her: she had "a tangled mop of jet-blond hair like the Medusa's; a forehead smooth as a pumice stone, eyes green as fire, an elephant's trunk for a nose, fangs in place of teeth, the hands of a harpy, the feet of a lobster, the slender shape of a buffalo, and a mouth as tiny as an oven door." Actually, she was a small, dark-haired, wrinkled woman with blotchy skin and a nervous and morbid disposition.

Only Shakespeare (who died that very year) could have caught the image of the handsome Bishop, now thirty and in the radiance of his youth, as he labored to subdue these two weird, paradoxical and complementary creatures.

Of all the connivances—either criminal or merely sordid—that bound them closer than any ties of childhood, one in particular was quite special. In 1608 the Queen had made such a public spectacle of her attraction to Concini that one day, at the close of a sporting event, Henry IV's retainers offered to do him the favor of killing the impudent Italian. There is little doubt that, despite her jealousy, the diabolical Leonora pressured her husband to seduce the Queen, just as, on the eve of their wedding, she had encouraged him to seduce Henriette d'Entragues, Henry IV's mistress.

But all this belonged to the past. Marshal d'Ancre was now snubbing his strange harem, since he could no longer play the sultan.

Richelieu was aware of this. Despite his robe of office, the conversations he had with the two women were not just on politics and religion, and what he offered them in the realm of consolation had little to do with Christian teachings.

Marie, in a great flutter, called in her wise men and tarot-readers to find out whether this strange prelate made use of a secret love-inducing spell. The story goes on from there. . . . Leonora, too, was all a-tremble, enjoying every minute of it.

We have no way of knowing how far the courtship progressed, during the last months of that turbulent winter, between the Queen's Chaplain, the corpulent blond, and the withered brunette. What we do know is that by the time spring arrived, he felt sure of them and of the road ahead.

Father Joseph, still pledged to Condé, had gone in another direction. The two friends argued the question of loyalties so heatedly that they parted on the worst terms and ceased to write to each other.

Richelieu was burning his bridges behind him. In April, after Leonora had left the Court and returned to Paris, he decided to go there, too, although he was ill again. By this time he had set up living quarters in the capital on the rue des Mauvaises-Paroles, between the rue des Lavendières and the rue des Bourdonnais.

He moved in even before the Treaty of Loudon was signed. His clever plan was to please the Queen's confidante by coming to her side and, at the same time, to upset the Queen by his absence. One of his letters to Marie, in which flirtation and a rather heavy-handed irony play beneath the surface compliments, reveals how indispensable he considered himself: "I cannot tell you how much I regret it [having had to leave]. But there is comfort in knowing that, in affairs of state, Your Majesty's own mental resources are more than adequate and quite the best to ensure success."

The Queen had always been empty-headed, and at this moment she was nearly reeling. For her predicament was such that unless she surrendered all authority to Condé, she would have to direct Concini to establish a type of dictatorship. The latter was ready and waiting, encouraged by Barbin, who had quietly gathered together a small group of unfamiliar faces from the legal profession, all honest and capable men, especially the lawyer Claude Mangot and Bullion, who was called "the little pig" and was a clownish fellow, deformed, truculent, and sinuous as a snake.

Sillery's successor was Guillaume Du Vair, who was much less intelligent and whose long beard and solemn manner bespoke his cautious attitude.

These people had a program, a good part of which the Cardinal would utilize later on. Briefly, it set out to "strike a blow for the crown" as demanded by the public. But at the same time the people were up in arms against the Florentines and against the Jews who were rumored to be hidden in Leonora's apartment. An incident, rather slight considering the violence of the period, added the final touch to the Marshal's unpopularity and aroused strong currents of xenophobia and anti-Semitism.

To prevent any outbreak of violence, the bourgeois guards were under instructions not to let anyone enter the city's gates without a passport. The Queen's favorite was headed toward his house in the Faubourg Saint-Germain when he was stopped at the Buci Gate and asked to show "his papers." Like a horse gouged by a spur, Concini reared up in protest; his companions started raising a row. The district sergeant, a shoemaker named Picard, stated firmly that they did not know any Marshal d'Ancre and he would have to obey instructions. Concini's escort became threatening, and passers-by gathered at the scene, siding with Picard. In no time the Italian found himself facing a crowd of angry, determined people. He dove into the first house at hand.

"A French nobleman," Richelieu later wrote, "born in a more benign climate," would have let the matter drop. But not this braggart, whose wounded vanity cried vengeance. A few days later, two of his hired ruffians fell on Picard and gave him a merciless beating.

Paris seethed with rage. Parliament ruled against the assailants, who were arrested, condemned, and hanged at La Grève,[3] a slap in the face to Concini and the beginning of his open struggle with the capital.

Paradoxically, the hated Florentine was prepared to surrender his power to the crown in deference to popular demand, but the people's affection went out to Condé, their Prince, symbol of feudal disorder.

Condé was certain that time would work in his interests. So, as soon as the Treaty of Loudun was concluded (on May 3) he went to take over his newly acquired governorship of Berry, letting the public's hatred of the foreigners do the job of clearing his path.

Marie de Medici returned to Paris on May 11, at nightfall and almost furtively. Her retainers could not wait to fill her ears with all their anxieties, for which there was good cause: the Princes had taken up positions in the provinces and were ready to resume fighting; the Parisians had become turbulent and unmanageable. And there was something worse: Concini and his cohorts had got wind of a threat from the King's direction.

But nobody could conceive of any spark of intelligence or will in that "most childlike of children," which was the insolent Marshal's name for Louis XIII. On the other hand, the King's favorite had begun to worry them seriously.

Since his marriage, the monarch had showed much greater affection to Luynes than to his young wife. He had lived with him in complete intimacy at Blois and, during the interminable conference of Loudun, at Amboise. A number of little things reported by the Queen Mother's spies had seemed to indicate a change in the boy, who was becoming in-

[3] An open area on the banks of the Seine. (Trans.)

creasingly melancholy. Was it the work of Luynes? Did Luynes harbor secret ambitions? Did he hope to replace Concini?

The braggart could sneer all he liked, but this idea made Marie de Medici and Leonora tremble. Barbin, Mangot, and Richelieu, the influential men in their circle, convinced them that ministers could not be dismissed without a hearing.

Apparently it was Richelieu, their master in everything, who contrived the plot for a scene which would force the boy-Sphinx to say what was on his mind. The King was due back at the Louvre on May 16. In four days the whole affair was arranged.

XII

An "Unctuous Prelate"

WHEN he was very small, the future Louis XIII adored his father. He admired him, but, having occasion to observe him closely, he also judged him and made no secret of what distressed or repelled him about his father's untidy life.

His mother was no comfort to him: a goddess who dispensed rewards and punishment but seldom a caress. Henry IV liked to be "Daddy"; Marie de Medici was never "Mommy." The languid and lusterless Queen, under the influence of the woman who was her former hairdresser and of a suspicious Court gallant, was astonishingly successful at taking in her husband and her family. Henry's final moment would probably have been different if he had established some authority over his wife.

From his cradle days, Louis worshiped the opulent princess, resplendent in her marvelous jewels.[1] He always took her side in the perpetual clashes between his parents. He was knight to this grim lady who would sometimes launch into lunatic fits of anger, this goddess whose heart he wanted so badly to win.

It was a vain hope, more so after his father's death. For all the tenderness Marie showed her younger son, Gaston, Duke of Anjou, whose ill-wishers said he resembled Concini, she remained harsh, icy, and dis-

---

[1] Of all the queens (not excepting Marie-Antoinette and Empress Josephine), Marie de Medici spent the most money on her wardrobe.

tant to the boy in whose name she reigned. In seven years she did not kiss him once.

As to his education, "He was kept idle, useless . . . purposely divorced from the Court. To come anywhere near his apartment was such an obvious and dreadful crime that only one or two valets were ever seen there, carefully chosen by his mother's servants and instantly replaced if they caused the slightest concern to the persons who ruled the Queen." [2]

The object was to make God's representative on earth an ignorant imbecile.

Imbecile? Louis was never that. The remembrance of his father's death told him what the cost would be if he showed a hint of independence or a spark of intelligence. So despite his youth, he play-acted in secret, for dissimulation is as necessary to kings as to little boys in revolt against their elders.

As Dauphin, he had detested the Concinis for all the horrid scenes they managed to provoke between his parents; as King, he had given up keeping track of the instances of their contempt and insolence. There was the time when one of the royal pages was beaten up by a page of Mme d'Ancre. Another, when the Marshal put on his hat during a billiard game. And once, when the Queen Mother refused to settle a debt involving a miserable 2,000 livres, along came that scoundrel, dressed to the teeth, offering the required amount together with advice that the King should call on him for credit in the future. Then there was the servant of Leonora who asked the King to make less noise because her mistress had a headache. And the incredible scene in the gallery of the Louvre: Louis, with only three attendants, was standing in a window recess; in another stood Concini, surrounded by a crowd of gentlemen who, with their hats off, addressed him as "Your Royal Highness." The Italian did not deign to notice the King's presence, and Louis, flushing with anger and humiliation, was forced to withdraw. Finally, there was the dinner, more like a circus, during which Concini's guests had shouted out to their patron: "The King drinks."

But all these indignities were nothing when it came to the two matters that obsessed him: he suspected that the couple was involved in his father's death, and he had heard the scandalous gossip about his mother's affair with the hated braggart.

[2] Saint-Simon, *Mémoires*.

Shakespeare left his mark on a whole epoch, even in countries where his name was unknown. Louis XIII had never heard of *Hamlet*, but he suffered the same torments as those of the Danish Prince. He, too, wondered "whether 'tis nobler in the mind to suffer the slings and arrows of outrageous fortune, or to take arms against a sea of troubles and by opposing, end them."

Or: "How stand I then, that have a father kill'd, a mother stain'd, excitements of my reason and my blood, and let all sleep. . . ?"

His thoughts, his humiliations, his feelings of impotency, his efforts at dissimulation so jolted the nerves of this boy of fifteen that some people began to believe he had epilepsy. The Concinis could be proud of the results of their work. As for Marie, she rejected her son's love and cared little that it turned to gall.

Yet it would have been so simple to win it back. Subjected first to the cruelty of his governess (whom he always loved), and later of his tutor, Louis had developed a temperament of combined stoicism and masochism. Throughout his life he kept to the rigorous principles instilled in him in childhood and regarded kindness to others or to himself as a disgraceful weakness.

This most sensitive of monarchs would always experience a peculiar pleasure in being dominated and browbeaten; the best way to handle him would have been roughly, but with proper respect for his kingly pride. Malherbe had already noted this in describing the Prince at the age of eight: "He is extremely proud of his greatness."

His mother was completely incapable of making such an analysis. Richelieu did not think of looking for an explanation. He was not familiar with Shakespeare, had no foreknowledge of Freud, and considered Henry IV's son a simpleton, a common loafer, who spent all his time hunting, beating on his drum, or cooking fritters.

On the other hand, he had a healthy respect for the power of a royal favorite, and, contrary to the general opinion, he considered Luynes perfectly capable of winding up the King like a mechanical doll in order to take a shot at Marshal d'Ancre. And this is why he, Richelieu, wound up the Queen to prevent an accident.

*

Veiled in black, the Queen Mother sailed into her son's apartment like a funeral ship. Louis faced her with his usual respect and timidity.

Luynes stood against the wall, immobile and silent, his eyes fastened on his master.

Marie launched into laments, and reproaches aimed directly at the falconer, though she was careful not to mention his name. Her voice, at first plaintive soon picked up the shrill and raucous tones of her former marital quarrels. "I have done my best to see you through to your majority, and now that you have reached it and are married, I consider my duty done. I ask that you come before Parliament with me so that I may be discharged of my obligation to govern the kingdom and allowed to end my days in peace." She added that she was negotiating the purchase of the principality of Mirandola in Italy and intended to retire there, far from slander and ingratitude.

Despite his immaturity and Richelieu's expectations, the King spied the trap. His mother was trying to appear detached, but she watched his reactions like a hawk, anticipating that he would betray his real feelings about the Concinis. If he fell into the snare, some device could perhaps be found to depose him and put his brother, Gaston, on the throne. No, the time had not yet come to unmask himself; he had to continue to act the child (as Hamlet played the madman).

So Louis set up a great fuss, protesting that he would never let his mother give up the throne. She was insistent; he remained firm, praising her wise rule, not breathing a word about Marshal d'Ancre or his wife, and ending on the assurance that "no one spoke of her [the Queen] except in terms most dignifying to her high position."

The huge lady was entirely nonplussed. Slow-witted to begin with, she felt disarmed in a strange situation. Could she demand the dismissal of Luynes? And under what pretext? Nobody had primed her with the answer to this one. Baffled and unable to reply, she decided to burst into tears. Her son threw himself into her arms, and a complete reconciliation took place under the benign gaze of Luynes, after which the black ship sailed off again, laden with pride and confidence.

There was also a mood of confidence among the men who waited impatiently to rake the spoils of office from behind the deposed ministers. On the evening of May 16, Guillaume Du Vair took oath as Keeper of the Seals; a week later Barbin replaced Jeannin as Minister of Finance. When it was Villeroy's turn to go, he resisted, complaining to the Queen that he had held office for fifty-four years; it was *his* office and he did not feel like giving it up. "*Lo voglio!*" (I command it!) was Her

Majesty's way of giving him notice, in Italian, the language she always used when she turned an angry purple.

The old man gave in. He remained the titular Secretary of State, but Claude Mongot held the power of that office.

And what of the Bishop of Luçon? Were they afraid of seeing him in the ministry? Apparently he himself preferred to remain in direct contact with the Queen and her favorites. In any event, he became State Councillor, which opened the door to the Council for him, and Marie's chief adviser. In addition, he was awarded a large pension of 6,000 livres.

Now that his duties brought him constantly into the royal circle, his purple robe became a familiar sight moving in and out between the sovereign, all in black, and her favorite, in a pearl-encrusted gown. Soon, the pamphlet writers were accusing Leonora of having, among her other lovers, an "unctuous prelate."

The unction was mixed with considerable authority; the two women savored one part and yielded to the other. As Richelieu explained it in his diary, they were convinced that sorcery worked its spell in the look of an eye. Though the eagle's gaze sometimes frightened Leonora, it held them both in submission.

Since his influence over the women was likely to offend Concini, Richelieu overwhelmed him with a barrage of flattery, protests of loyalty, and disgraceful obsequiousness. Utterly disdainful of anyone who denied him the right to make whatever alliances he chose, he found it easy to change his opinions in a manner that would have shocked men of lesser pride. Concini was equally cynical, two-faced, scheming, and hard-headed. But he had a weakness, his vanity, which Richelieu exploited masterfully. "I won his confidence" he wrote in his *Memoirs*, "and he began to respect me the first time we met. He told some of his intimates that he was cultivating a young man who could teach the graybeards a thing or two."

The valuable young man was soon to have an opportunity to show his talents.

A strong government remained impossible as long as Condé, now entranched in Bourges, could cry rebellion at any time. The new ministers discussed ways to neutralize him; a few hardy voices advocated using the King's troops in Berry to capture the troublemaker. But this alternative frightened the Queen and Leonora who much preferred treachery to violence.

So they decided to lure the Prince to Paris by dangling an olive branch decked out with false promises. Once he was back at the Court, they would take him into the government, ostensibly; then, at the first sign of trouble, they would pounce on him.

But how to lure him? Richelieu, from whom the suggestion probably came, had stayed on excellent terms with the Prince and had showered him with flattery at the outcome of the Treaty of Loudun. So the task fell to him of using this friendship as bait for the trap. He accepted it without the slightest hesitation.

First, he got off a number of honeyed letters to the Prince, styling himself as both the Queen's ambassador and Leonora's messenger. Condé's reply was cautious. Richelieu came back with proof of the good feelings shared by these two ladies: "I have transmitted the contents of your letters to the Queen and have assured her once again, as strongly as I could, of your sincere affection. . . . Mme d'Ancre continues to press for settlement of pending matters and desires wholeheartedly, as always, your presence at Court. . . . I can safely assure Your Highness that you will find Their Majesties more favorably inclined than you could imagine and that Mme d'Ancre has served you well and faithfully in this respect, as she no doubt wishes to do at every opportunity."

Condé was not shrewd, but he was hesitant and shifty. Barbin and the Concinis decided that the tempter should be on the spot to entice his victim, so they dispatched Richelieu to Berry.

As soon as they met, Richelieu turned his charm on the Prince like an expert. The Queen desired only peace and unity; she wanted the prodigal son to return and would keep her promise to make him head of the Council. If Condé had the slightest doubt about Her Majesty's good feelings, Mme d'Ancre stood ready to back them and to use her influence to maintain harmony. She and Concini were making it a point of honor to regain the Prince's good grace. Provided His Highness took an oath of secrecy, he would have full knowledge of State affairs, and nothing would be decided without his consent.

It was an incredible soft-soaping, complete with oaths and reminders that the bishop's miter was a guarantee of the high level and good faith of these negotiations. The pathetic Condé was snowed under and completely bewildered. Without even consulting his allies, he promised to return to the Court. A triumphant Richelieu returned before him to the open arms of the Queen and her favorites, who compared him with the wily Ulysses.

XIII

A Clay Giant

IN no time they were singing a different tune. From the moment Condé entered the gates of Paris on July 17, the entire nation welcomed him as a savior and flocked to his banner. Nobles, Parliament, the populace, Catholics and Protestants alike—everyone was on his side.

When the Prince went to call on the Queen Mother, he arrived with a throng of followers large enough to make a second Court, only more arrogant than the real one. The King came by and felt ill—because of the heat, the official story went. Actually, this boy, whose real precocity was hidden, had a foreboding that France would be torn apart by the two men he hated equally: Condé, the unworthy descendant of Saint Louis, and Concini, the former idol of Florence's foulest dregs.

Condé worked hard in the Council and surprised everyone by his able leadership. Du Vair, Keeper of the Seals, promptly switched camps. In their efforts to be clever, the Queen's advisers and Richelieu foremost, had brought a wolf into the sheepfold.

The Prince saw himself as lord of the realm. He wallowed in the most sordid debauchery—which gave him "the Neapolitan disease"—and went about with the airs of a potentate. "The Louvre was deserted; his house was like the Louvre of old. You had to cut your way through the crowds to reach his door. Everybody with any sort of business came to him."

He seemed bound for success and would have had it if his own mediocrity had not puffed his ambitions too high. Throngs of admirers flocked to his banquets, which were more splendid than a king's. When he entered the Court amid a mob of liegemen and petitioners, it looked as if he were on the verge of a *coup d'état.* Soon he began to stir up new rumors casting doubts on the legitimacy of Louis XIII—the King was a bastard if Henry IV's divorce were not valid—and let it be known that "the next step was to depose the King and put him [Condé] on the throne."

"Barrabas!" shouted his friends during the course of a banquet. What did it mean? Was it simply an insult to Barbin, or was it an ominous pun? *"Barre à bas!"* (Down with the bar!) could have indicated that in the Condé coat-of-arms the symbol of the younger branch ought to be removed and the Prince regarded as the head of the Bourbon dynasty.

The Dukes of Vendôme, Bouillon, and Mayenne made no effort to conceal their intrigues. The Duke of Nevers, clinging to some wild notion inspired by his distant relationship to the Byzantine emperors, called for support in starting a crusade, and Father Joseph encouraged him, since the idea of freeing the Holy Sepulcher was one of his pet obsessions. The Duke of Longueville stirred up revolt in Peronne against the governor, none other than Concini, and seized control of the province.

The Princes no longer had any use for the protection of the favorites; in fact, at every opportunity they denounced the couple publicly, as if waving a red cloth in front of the bull. In the Queen Mother's circle there was terror and consternation. Toward the middle of August, for the first time, both of the Concinis showed signs of weakening simultaneously. "They told Barbin they had lost hope and realized that everything was over for the King and themselves, that they both wanted to slip off to Caen and from there take a boat to Italy. They only wished they were already aboard and halfway back to Florence!"

Despite some polite protests, Barbin did not hold them back. Their unpopularity stood in his way, and he hoped to get rid of them now that their usefulness was ended. A secluded spot in Normandy was chosen, but at just the moment she was about to step into her traveling litter, Mme d'Ancre fainted. After that, she refused to budge from the Queen's side.

A strange attitude indeed. Of the two Concinis, Leonora had always been the more anxious and determined to safeguard her hoardings, the less preoccupied with politics.

What accounted for her change of heart? It could only have been one man, the one who, for just a short time, had completely dominated this gloomy creature, seeking to fulfill his ambitions through her, and who, without her might have become just a shadow of Barbin. So it is not a rash judgment to attribute Leonora's about-face and her sudden spurt of courage to Richelieu. It is one of those grains of sand that can alter the course of history.

*

In the Cardinal's words, "The Council was made up of persons who were passionately dedicated to the establishment of central authority." Barbin and he were prepared to do anything rather than lose the power which was almost in their grasp.

While they stood firm, there was panic in the Louvre. Sully came out of retirement and went to call on the King and the Queen Mother. Dressed in the fashion of Henry IV, he confronted them with a terrifying picture of the situation and an endless list of sinister predictions. Barbin was present and asked what means he would suggest for saving the kingdom. The former minister had only one solution in mind: to take over the government himself. But despite his proverbial abruptness, he did not dare come out with the thought and marched off in a vile temper. In the doorway he turned and fired his parting shot: "Sire, and you, Madam, I beseech Your Majesties to think about what I have just said. My conscience is now clear. Would to God you were in the midst of 1200 stampeding horses! I see no other remedy."

Marie de Medici was almost wild with fear and, like a huge bumblebee, zoomed from one noble to another, defending her good intentions. Next, she cried out for relief from her responsibilities and pleaded with the stony-faced King once again for her quittance.

They managed to calm her down, and Barbin went off to see what was going on in Condé's quarters. He found the Prince intoxicated with his own fantasies and vainglory. The two men quarreled and separated.

A decision had to be made. Both Barbin and Richelieu despised Condé and had no fear of him. They persuaded the Queen and the Concinis to strike first. Within a few days they arranged everything, swore Marshal de Thémines and seventeen trustworthy retainers to a

116

special oath of secrecy, and smuggled arms into the palace in cases which were supposed to contain Italian silks.

On the evening of August 31, the Prince, accompanied by a single servant, was on his way to M. Chercaut's establishment, a brothel located near Saint-Martin-des-Champs where they "entertained him royally," when warning came of his imminent arrest. Shrugging his shoulders, his only reply was: "The animal is too big for the trap!"

The next day he went to see the Queen. Louis XIII, siding firmly, for once with his mother, put on an act of friendship. But as soon as the King left, Marshal de Thémines called on the Prince to hand over his sword, and Condé, thinking he was going to be killed, acted like a true coward. They locked him up first in the Louvre, then in the Bastille.

As soon as they heard the news, Vendôme, whom Louis XIII would have liked to see behind bars (he hated this bastard brother), Mayenne, Bouillon, Longueville, and La Trémoille took to their heels. All the other lords came running to the palace to bow and scrape and register their fealty.

Only the dowager Princess of Condé took her cry "To arms!" into the streets of Paris. But the response was scant until a personal enemy of Concini, the shoemaker Picard, joined in. A group of commoners gathered and, with a little encouragement from Condé's men, they headed for the Hôtel d'Ancre on the Rue de Tournon.

The Governor of Paris tried vainly to halt the mob of angry marchers who invaded the house and ransacked it steadily for two days. To their astonishment, they found some of the Queen Mother's dresses there.

Concini had damages estimated at 150,000 écus and received an indemnity of 175,000.

No other incident occurred. The giant turned out to be clay, making it evident that the sole strength of the rebel factions lay in the weakness of royal authority.

The last of Condé's confederates surrendered at the beginning of October, except for Nevers, who, angered at getting no support for his crusade, was mustering troops. Reims almost fell into the hands of this eccentric. At which point, the great charmer, the Bishop of Luçon, was sent off to take care of the Duke. After a long talk, Nevers seemed willing to come to terms, and Richelieu, too confident of his own eloquence, returned to report success to the Louvre. Such zeal and ability surely had to be rewarded and utilized.

Since Condé's fall, the general feeling at Court was that a new reign had begun. However, it was a little too much the reign of Concini, meaning Barbin. If the Marshal and the financier really wanted to strengthen the government, they would have to find outside support against the troublemakers within.

Only six years had passed since Henry IV had been Europe's arbiter and had set out to humble the House of Austria, take over Spain's leadership, and bring Germany and Italy under French influence. But now this seemed like a legend from the distant past.

Although Spain was on the threshhold of decline, the signs of which were not yet visible to foreigners, she dominated the Continent: the Hapsburg in Madrid and the one in Vienna could have crushed France in a vice. Spanish power was supreme territorially, politically, and, owing to the gold from the Indies, financially. In addition, the fact that she fostered an ideology gave her an excuse to keep agents all over the world, especially in Paris. The day was near when the wars of religion, after having torn apart so many lands, would take on international proportions, and the Spanish-Catholic bloc seemed to have the upper hand over the Protestant camp.

On the eve of the storm, the Dutch and the Venetian Republics as well as the small states and Protestant princes of Germany, all former allies of Henry IV, turned once again to France. Knowing that Marie de Medici was Spain's servant, they had hoped to see Condé reverse the policy followed since the beginning of the regency.

But the old allies were abandoned with fewer scruples than usual. The Queen Mother, the Concinis, and Barbin all agreed that their only hope of holding out and controlling the Princes was in becoming integrated with the Spanish network. To strengthen the ties with Madrid, they decided to send there, as ambassador extraordinary, the man who had just given ample proof of his talent for diplomacy, none other than M. de Luçon. The bishop accepted.

At this point the historian, if not the psychologist, may well pause in confusion. During his lengthy meditations and his solitary walks in the Poitou country, did not Armand du Plessis form "a particlar conception of France," or was it merely a certain idea of his own destiny? How is it that this brilliant man, whose tireless efforts were later to bring Spain to her knees, was now prepared to surrender his country abjectly to Spain? Perhaps in his haste to gratify his ambitions he had not bothered to map an over-all political strategy or, even worse, was quick to shed his convictions if doing so promised to enhance his career.

The truth cannot be so simple. The key may lie in his immense pride. At thirty-one, this extraordinary man had surely sized up the world scene and envisioned France as the leader of Christendom, with himself as leader of France. And since he believed he was the sole person capable of accomplishing such a feat, everything became subordinated to his pursuit of the requisite power. A few deviations or retractions, a false testimony now and then, a bedroom intrigue, or a fleeting betrayal—how important were these when it was all part of the unpleasant road to power?

Nothing could prevail against power. And when it finally was his, the tremendously egocentric bishop would feel no shame or twinge of conscience in using it, whether he shocked and alienated those who made his fortune or had to break the ties that were his own making.

XIV

An Adventurer in Office

THE new ambassador's appointment had not yet been signed when an unforseen event threatened to upset the chessboard: Louis XIII, whom no one took time to think about, had a convulsive seizure. He had been ill since October 16 and grew increasingly pale, thin, and withdrawn. Dysentery was wearing him out; apparently this was the price he had to pay for excessive hunting and gluttony. Héroard, his doctor, was not alarmed and merely increased the number of purges and bleedings. It came as a complete surprise to him on the night of the 31st to learn from Beringhen, the King's personal servant, that His Majesty had lost consciousness and had a rattle in his throat.

They forced him out of bed, massaged and shook him. His teeth were so tightly clenched that in trying to pry them open with a knife, they gashed his gums. The seizure lasted less than ten minutes. "A convulsion due to an intestinal vapor" was Héroard's diagnosis.

Louis ate supper in public that same evening, but he looked terrible. In no time rumors went round that he was going to die, and all the factions began scheming in preparation for the event. Richelieu thought it best to delay his departure.

Marie de Medici was not overly upset at the prospect of having her favorite son, the Duke of Anjou, succeed to the throne, and she sounded out Parliament to get its reaction to a second regency. She would have done better to think about what had caused the mishap. Surprisingly enough, her advisers gave no more thought to it than she.

The fact was that Louis could no longer put up with Concini's affronts. The adventurer did not bother to remove his hat in the King's presence and even took his seat at the Council table! He intended to have himself appointed High Constable of France,[1] was equipping an army of several thousand men at his own expense, and went out of his way to offend the Duke of Guise and the ambassadors. He would brook no criticism, even from the Queen Mother herself.

Despite his cocksure arrogance, there were times when the look on the King's face made him anxious, not that the King himself worried him, for the only one he felt the slightest reason to fear was Louis's favorite.

"*Alberti*," he said one day to Luynes, "the King looked at me *con occhi furiosi* [with a glare]. You must answer to me for it!"

Beneath his charming appearance, Luynes, in Richelieu's estimation, was "a mediocre and timid soul, with little sense of honor and no trace of magnanimity." He would have answered willingly for his master had there been anything in it for himself. Bartering his honor came more easily to him than overthrowing the government. He petitioned the Spanish King for a pension of 1,000 écus. After his run-in with Concini, he thought it politic to ask for the Marshal's daughter in marriage!

Leonora made the mistake of countering Luynes with a haughty refusal, which he took as an affront and a declaration of war. He determined to stake his life on destroying the little clique, but, for the moment, neither the King nor he could make a move.

When things had quieted down, the Bishop of Luçon received his diplomatic credentials for the visit to Spain. Just then, the grave-mannered Guillaume Du Vair, whom the Princes and his colleagues in Parliament criticized for serving the Concinis, came out in defense of the Duke of Nevers when the Council was again discussing the latter's actions. There were bitter words between Du Vair and Barbin, following which the Queen dismissed her Keeper of the Seals.

This was the last obstacle blocking the strong and homogeneous government which Barbin hoped to control through Concini. Claude Mangot replaced Du Vair. Then, suddenly, the major post [2] of Secretary of State,

---

[1] Supreme commander of the King's army. (Trans.)

held by Villeroy, became vacant. On behalf of the Queen, Marshal d'Ancre offered it to Richelieu.

Richelieu already knew that Barbin wanted him to have this office. Reverting to his customary tactic, he pleaded modestly that the temporary post of ambassador was more suitable for him than a permanent ministry. However, since Her Majesty's desire was his command, he had no choice but to accede. And in his *Mémoires* he added: "I confess that few young men could refuse the attraction of an office promising both favor and high position." Indeed, his position would turn out to be singularly glamorous, since it included control of two ministries: Foreign Affairs and War. War in the hands of a priest! Everything was already so topsy-turvy that one more surprise made no difference. Only the Protestants complained.

M. de Luçon took his oath of office on November 26, and then a second time—we don't know why—on December 2. It was both a joyous and a sad occasion, for he had just learned of his mother's death on November 14. So unlike her son in sweetness and tact, so like him in her courage and tenacity, Mme Richelieu was one of the few people to evoke tenderness in the Cardinal. There is no doubt that he was deeply moved.

His mother's body had been placed in the chapel of the château so that her youngest son could pay his last respects when he found the time. But the new minister never did find the time: at the end of three weeks, the funeral took place without him.

From a psychological point of view, it is both strange and interesting to compare two letters written by Richelieu at approximately the same time, one in which he pours out his grief to his brother Alphonse, and the other expressing gratitude to Leonora following his appointment to office. The first is highly instructive: "In death, God bestowed on her [their mother] as many graces, consolations, and comforts as she had received in a lifetime of frustrations, afflictions, and bitter experience in life. . . . For myself, I pray God that, in the time ahead, her good example and yours will guide me to a better life."

And here are his thanks to his protectress, at once excessive, cynical, and too familiar: "You show great favor to those who serve you when you *feed them according to their appetites* as you have done with me at this time, and since my greatest desire is to be honored by your kind

---

[2] There were four such offices.

remembrance, I am indeed gratified. . . . The favor you have shown me
is all the greater since *it comes to me from a beautiful lady* [!] in the
midst of my distress, which shall end when it please God."

*

The distress did not last very long, for he had the deep satisfaction of
having reached safe harbor after so much casting about on rough seas.
Except toward the Queen, the favorites, and Barbin, he was through
with bowing and scraping, mouthing platitudes, and begging for favors.
Now he could be himself: decisive, bold, and scornful. He immediately
claimed that his bishop's robe entitled him to rank above the other Secretaries of State. One of the latter, Brienne, retorted that if he were indeed a bishop, he belonged in his diocese.

This incident took place in Council in the Queen's presence. Afterward, Barbin brought the two antagonists and the Marquis de Richelieu
together. On many past occasions, M. de Luçon had showered assurances
of his devotion and friendship on Brienne, as he had done with countless
others. Brienne had acted as intermediary when Richelieu corresponded
with the Queen during her trip to Guyenne. This did not stop the
Bishop from declaring, in a menacing voice, "that for a long time he had
been aware that a number of persons close to the King had little regard
for the Church."

"My reply was mild," wrote Brienne in his *Mémoires*, "and I merely
commented that I regarded him as a bishop, and upon finding him in
the Royal Household, I had nothing to say to him, but that I would not
advise his brother to use such language with me."

Concini insisted that Richelieu have precedence, an important victory
in that Court, where the smallest incident assumed enormous proportions.
Assured of his favor, Richelieu felt it was safe to dispense with his ecclesiastic unction, his theologian's pedantry, even the garb of austerity
that had served him so well. He no longer wore his purple robe except for
ceremonial occasions. Now it was a handsome gentleman dressed in black,
slender, wiry, and wearing a dapper little mustache, who was often seen
hard at work, exhausting his secretaries, dictating, writing, carrying on
endless discussions—or at other times, strutting about at parties and
masked balls.

Though he no longer had to flatter the people around him, the new

Secretary of State felt he must ingratiate himself with the Spanish faction. He completely won the Spanish ambassador, the Duke of Monteleone, who wrote home to Madrid: "He is my close friend. . . . I have actual proof of his devotion to our cause."

The Papal Nuncio was also delighted with "this favorable change," while the Venetian ambassador announced sadly to his Senators: "This minister cannot be considered to favor the interests of Your Lordships. . . . He is a frequent visitor at the Spanish Embassy. It is even rumored that Spain is paying him a pension."

Despite his great activity, Richelieu's movements were quite restricted. The government, a curious caricature of his own future rule, was entirely under Concini's control, with Barbin in the background lending his vigor and talents. Nothing was done without Concini's authorization, and he received daily reports of all affairs. The Council often met in his rooms.

Concini was not a man to rise from a gutter to the heights and keep a cool head. One day when Louis XIII wandered into a Council meeting, his mother, seeing the look on her favorite's face, sent the King away, telling him to go play somewhere else. Yet the King's authority was the very thing this adventurer and his aides were bent on restoring by pitting all their resources against the conspiring Princes. Perhaps they would have succeeded if they had held out longer; it would have spared Louis XIII countless rebellions.

Curiously enough, Barbin and Richelieu did not realize that their plans could not materialize under a patron who was so discredited. Even they were forced to put up with some outrageous treatment: if they disagreed with him, he threatened to throw them out, and soon there was serious friction. But as far as the indignant public was concerned, the country was yoked to the combined tyranny of the Concinis, Barbin, Richelieu, and Mangot.

Richelieu resolutely accepted Concini's affronts and the people's hatred. In fact, he would have accepted anything in order to win control of France's foreign policy.

*

And which policy was this? The Gallican policy of Henry IV, or the ideological one of his widow and the Concinis? The first consisted in raising barriers wherever the Hapsburgs had enterprises afoot and in making France the protectress of small nations and the guarantor of Europe's balance of power. The second sacrificed every thing to the triumph of the Catholic Church and reduced His Most Christian Majesty to a satellite of the Hapsburg Emperor and the Spanish King.

It is unlikely that Richelieu did not yet realize the absolute necessity of reviving the policies of François I and Henry IV. But his mission was taking him in the opposite direction and, awkwardly for him, a conflict arose involving Spanish hostility to Savoy and Venice which forced him to make a choice then and there.

It was an old conflict that had now reached a crisis. The House of Austria wanted to extend her hold over the last few Italian States remaining outside her orbit. Her troops were on the march. The Duke of Savoy and the Venetian Republic called for aid to their old ally, France.

Of course, the Court had no intention of answering the appeal, but the feudal anarchy that had persisted for six years produced an unexpected result. Marshal de Lesdiguières, the Protestant Governor and Viceroy of the Dauphiné region and a former companion in arms of Henry IV, set off on his own to make war against the King of Spain, who was the father-in-law and ally of the French monarch. Lesdiguières led a force of 7,500 men across the Alps while, in Grenoble, a royal edict was issued ordering him to halt. Savoy was saved.

Louis XIII was delighted, thinking it would bring the Spaniards down a peg or two.

Richelieu, too, was secretly pleased with the Marshal's initiative. After consulting Béthune, the French Ambassador in Rome, he decided it was an opportune moment to review Italian affairs and proposed that a conference be held in Paris to iron out the numerous political problems involving Italy. The Pope, the Emperor, the King of Spain, Venice, and the Duke of Savoy would be invited to send ambassadors. "May God favor my most ardent desire to maintain peace for France and to establish it throughout Europe," were the words that Richelieu wrote above the signature of Louis XIII.

It required a certain naïve enthusiasm to venture such a plan. In 1609 they had begged Henry IV to hold a similar conference on German affairs. Now, in 1616, Richelieu was boldly seeking to restore France's faded influence, not realizing that it would take thirty years of struggle to do it. Of course, this betrayed his lack of experience, but, more important, it also revealed the vision which was to occupy his whole life and bring him glory.

Negotiations had just begun when the Venetian ambassadors asked the Queen not to oppose an alliance between their Republic and the Republic of the Grisons. This tiny State constituted one of the focal points of Europe, since its territory included the alpine passes over which the armies of the two Hapsburg branches had to travel in order to join forces; it was also the route of Swiss mercenaries bound for Italy. Henry IV had maintained a close alliance with the Grisons to assure France sole use of these passes. Now, however, the mercenaries Venice had hired in Bern and in Zurich would never reach her if France were opposed.

Since these Swiss troops were destined to fight the Spaniards, Richelieu could not satisfy the Venetians without overturning the Queen's policy. He made the mistake of playing too shrewd a game, first offering hope to Venice, then trampling it in a most brutal fashion. "The alpine passes," he informed the furious ambassadors, "remain closed to all armies except those of France, whose passage is assured even against the Venetians."

It was a clumsy error to thus offend the old Republic, whose agents subsequently saw to it that all the invited powers refused to come to Paris, expressing preference for a meeting in Madrid. As it turned out, instead of mediating Italian affairs, France found herself excluded in the most humiliating manner.

Angry and resentful, Richelieu vented his spleen, a sure sign of youth, on the jeering ambassadors. But the failure was not a total loss, for it taught him some valuable lessons.

Later on, as Cardinal, he would try to erase all memory of this humiliation. On the other hand he always prided himself on having worked to revive good relations with England, Holland, and the German princes. The Dutch rejected his advances; James I of England was more friendly. As for Germany, who knows what the results might have been if Schomberg, the new Ambassador and a Protestant, had had the time to implement his instructions.

Schomberg's first job was to foil the conspiracies of the German princes. He also had to discredit actively the widespread "slander" that "our [the King's] interests lay with Rome or with Spain rather than with our former allies" and to play down the political implications of the marriages with Spain. "We are thus mistaken to fear that the union of these two powers will divide France."

But the Secretary of State went a step beyond these justifications. "We must take the opportunity to show them [the German princes] to our credit *that we do not desire to further the interests of Spain but to assist them* [the princes] *discreetly against the intrigues of the King of Spain intended to make, in due time, the crowns of Hungary and Bohemia and that of the King of the Romans as well as the imperial crown fall on the head of one of his children.*" And, in fact, less than two years later, the designs of Spain would be one of the causes of the Thirty Years' War.

Unfortunately, the instructions given to Schomberg, whom the Cardinal brings into his *Memoirs* so as to defend "wherever possible the conduct of government affairs since the late King's death," ended with a vindication of Marshal d'Ancre, "a foreigner who is so intensely French that he shares his fortune only with Frenchmen." It is obvious that Schomberg's instructions, like everything else, passed through the hands of Concini, a tool of Spain.

And what game was M. de Luçon playing? The same as Concini's, trying to take away from the French Princes their German support? Or was he deceiving the Florentine, in true Machiavellian style, in order to revert to a policy of nationalism later on? We will never know.

XV

Hamlet's Triumph

THE Duke of Bouillon, a shrewd conspirator, had capitalized on the Duke of Nevers' foolish dreams, and once more the provinces were in flames. The Council met in January, 1617, and deliberately ruled out the traditional remedy, appeasement, adopting instead the same methods that Louis XIII and Richelieu would later use.

The Venetian ambassadors, always on top of the news, hastened to advise their Senate of the revolution in progress: "If necessary, they will resort to force and violence, but they intend to compel total submission. . . . We have this assertion from the Bishop of Luçon himself."

The Secretary of State had plunged into domestic politics, and in that area there was no question what his aims were. The letter he sent to the Duke of Mayenne, again in the King's name, could have been written ten or twenty years later: "The desire to find peace of mind in harmless acts, which you expressed in your letter, would give me good cause for rejoicing if the results did not seem to contradict your words. . . ."

Taken aback by the firm tone, the Princes came out with another violent denunciation of the Queen Mother, the favorites, and the ministers. Again, it was Richelieu who answered them in a royal Declaration that outlined his future policy to combat sedition: "If no motive will compel them [the rebels] to perform their rightful duty . . . His Majesty, acting with the concern of a true father and the courage of a great king, will be obliged, regretfully, to punish all those who disturb the peace of his realm."

The bishop moved rapidly when the new civil war broke out in March. A large army commanded by the Duke of Guise was sent into Champagne, and another one was dispatched to the West. "The King," wrote Richelieu, "is prepared to bring to reason those who have departed from it."

It was imperative to destroy the multifaced and self-perpetuating monster of revolt, yet the government appeared to be acting not in behalf of the King but of the Concinis. The Queen had grown tired of her favorite's insolence and even confided to the Papal Nuncio "that the Marshal intended to ruin the Princes in order to achieve his ends, that is, to become High Constable and sole ruler of the Court."

Richelieu did not seem to be worried about this. His main concern was to raise additional troops so that the royal armies could restore order in the province of Maine, then lay siege simultaneously to Nevers, Rethel, and Soissons. Spurred on by Richelieu and Barbin, Concini threw all his energies into the fray. He ordered fifty gibbets set up around Paris, confiscated the weapons of the hostile bourgeois guards and built up Normandy's fortifications. His order sending the King's guardsmen to join the army and those of the Queen to duty at the Louvre gave the impression that he intended to lay hands on Louis.

Though it was one in a long series of conflicts, this war presented a different sort of threat. To all intents and purposes, it was fought to reestablish the King's sovereignty; but it was bound to end in disaster, since the only possible outcome was either the dictatorship of Concini or the triumph of feudal anarchy.

*

At this point the King's position was extremely insecure, so low, in fact, that the future champion of absolute monarchy hardly knew the monarch! Richelieu had been borrowing his name for use in presumptuous letters, but during the first three months of his ministry, he did not give a thought to the person whose will he was constantly citing. He never tried to approach the young man and never reported a thing to him.

It is amazing that a tinsel-wrapped package such as Concini so fascinated the bishop that he lost sight of the Lord's Anointed. Had he known how much resentment Louis XIII was storing up against him, he would have been terrified. But his own haughty attitude was not the sole cause. Because of Louis's pathetic and jealous love for his mother, the boy naturally hated any man who was accepted into the Queen's intimacy. Furthermore, the stories involving the "unctuous prelate" were no longer about his relations just with Leonora.

After flattering, charming, and captivating so many people and spending so much energy in the name of his career, the ambitious Richelieu, without even knowing it, had become as odious to the King as Concini. It was an inexcusable error, and France would have to pay for it.

Of course, the favorites had erected a solid wall around the boy. The King of France's entourage consisted of a motley crew: Luynes and his two brothers, Brante and Cadenet; the Baron of Modena, a cousin; a lawyer named Tronson; Marsillac, a would-be gentleman with an uncertain reputation; Dubuisson, keeper of the birds; the guard Deplan; the Tuileries' gardener; Travail, a Capuchin friar of low morals known as Father Saint-Hilaire; and finally Guichard Déageant, chief clerk in the Ministry of Finance.

This Déageant, a rather shady fellow who perhaps had the makings of a Fouché, was the only strong man in the group and, like so many others, was playing both sides of the table. He had won the Queen's favor and paid a daily visit to Barbin, ostensibly to give him information, but in reality to gather whatever news he could—he himself "fed poison" to the minister. He then turned around and reported to Luynes, briefing him on whatever plans were afoot.

Luynes had hopes of maneuvering Concini as he pleased, but the favorite was not a man of action either. After Leonora's snub, Luynes, still looking for a way to come to terms, proposed a sort of alliance to Concini. The Italian was too drunk with his own importance and rebuffed him jeeringly. Nothing developed further between these two.

Nevertheless, it was not Luynes who provided Louis with the impetus to break his chains. He was not even the unwitting instrument since the affair would not have succeeded without the active support of a handful of dependable men. The sole significance of his role was in the young King's devotion to him. This ardent friendship, a motive for survival that Shakespeare's hero never had, gave the crowned Hamlet strength to conquer his doubts and break the shell of his isolation.

*

Louis XIII dreamed of escape from the moment his guardsmen received orders to prepare to leave Paris. First, he had thought of going to Amboise, where Luynes was Governor, and gathering his loyal troops there. Reports said that Sully, Montmorency, Lesdiguières, and Alincourt, all powerful lords, enemies of Concini although loyal to him, stood ready to aid the King. To forestall this danger, the ministers proclaimed that His Majesty would personally attend the siege of Soissons, and ambassadors were advised to prepare for the trip.

Louis XIII immediately saw his chance: as soon as he was with his army and had the protection of his guards, he would declare his will to rule in person. But rumors leaked out; the Marshal sensed something was wrong, and the King's departure was postponed. Louis was sick with anger.

At this point Richelieu woke up. Violent quarrels between Barbin and Concini, and the possibility that the favorite might appoint new ministers, finally convinced him how dangerous his own situation was. He looked for a way out, or, better yet, insurance coverage that would guarantee maintaining his position against all risks.

"This chap will turn out to be a first-class scoundrel," Paul V predicted. And, at this moment, he proved himself a master-schemer. Yet we can scarcely condemn his deceit—which was worthy of a combined Talleyrand and Scapin—knowing that this extraordinary man's intense self-interest was tied to the best interests of France.

His first move was to layer the Marshal with another coating of blandishments and fawning attention. Richelieu's letters during this period are those of a servant to his master. But that did not stop him from seeking out Bentivoglio, the Papal Nuncio, ostensibly to pour out his heart and confess the fears, the weariness, and the disgust with political intrigues that were plaguing him. The "unctuous prelate" went on to say that he wanted to return to his church duties—at the highest level, naturally, where he could best serve the Holy Father. He mentioned the Archbishopric of Reims and a cardinal's hat.

Next, he turned to Marie de Medici. He knew this lumpish woman was in his power and coldly denounced Concini's faults and unpopularity to her, pointing out the dangers to which the braggart was exposing her. Finally, he asked her permission to leave the ministry.

The Queen was frightened rather than angry as much by her own weak position as by the prospect of losing her bishop. She told him she would give her answer in a week.

It is possible that in his search for all available reinforcements, Richelieu may have visited Jacqueline d'Escoman, the woman who nearly saved Henry IV's life, in her horrible prison cell, and that he was able to get some valuable information from her.[1]

His last move was particularly dangerous and bordered on treason: he directed his brother-in-law, M. du Pont de Courlay, to establish secret contact with Luynes.

*

The King's departure, originally scheduled for the 12th of March, put off until the 20th, then the 31st, was finally canceled completely. It was Concini who left Paris instead to supervise and speed up the fortification of Quilleboeuf in Normandy, a bastion whose governorship he had just seized. Richelieu openly opposed his plans for the first time and persuaded the Queen to write to the Italian urging caution. Concini blew up at the cheeky bishop and, of course, did exactly as he pleased.

The King's little clique decided to take advantage of the Marshal's absence. Louis was brokenhearted at having lost the chance to regain his kingdom at the head of his army. Well then, his advisers told him, if he could not imitate Henry IV, he ought to follow Henry III's example, when the latter escaped from the clutches of the Duke of Guise.

It was Msgr. de l'Estang, Bishop of Carcassonne, who lit the fuse by pleading with the Queen Mother to get Marshal d'Ancre out of the way. The news reached Concini in Normandy, and back to Paris he dashed, fuming and hurling threats in every direction (April 17). In reality, he was as weak-kneed as Luynes and could already see the writing on the wall.

By now, the King had become an insomniac, although his behavior gave no hint of the state of his nerves—this, at the age of fifteen! Yet historians still continue to assert his weak and puerile character.

On April 19 or 20, the crucial Council took place between His Most Christian Majesty, his favorite, and a handful of adventurers who counted on reaping the spoils of this affair. At Luynes's suggestion, they agreed to get Concini into the King's *salle d'armes* and arrest him there. What if he resisted?

"He must be killed," said Déageant.

"No," protested Louis.

"Then get ready to flee," warned the financier, "for you cannot risk

[1] A number of reputable historians, such as Jean Héritier, accept this for fact.

failure after arresting him. His death is the only thing that will save you, your servants, and the kingdom."

The King did not answer. Full responsibility for the execution lay on his shoulders.

Execution or assassination? Louis XIII's overscrupulous and wavering conscience was never to trouble him about Concini's death. His honor as a gentleman made him almost duty bound to punish the beneficiary of his father's murder; as sovereign, he alone had the right to condemn a dangerous subject and sentence him according to whatever means he possessed.

Recurrent civil wars had kept such questions very much alive. Yet many honest men were loath to face them, and Lieutenant de Mesmes, the first to be sounded out, refused to serve the King in the same way that Crillon had refused Henry III. Henry IV always avoided such extreme methods, but he was the exception in his century, and, furthermore, since he was not in direct line to the throne, he did not share to the same degree as those who came before and after him the unshakable conviction that the King could do no wrong.

His son, however, was born and bred with this belief. Obviously it would have enhanced Louis's "glory" if he had allowed the Marshal a trial, even though such a proceeding would have been a pure formality. But the King was isolated and unable to gauge his real strength, convinced that his life was in jeopardy and that by not following the advice of his retainers he might lose everything.

In any event, he showed no hesitancy or remorse—"whether or not my thoughts are bloody," as Hamlet put it—but at this point the two characters begin to separate. Circumstances alone made Hamlet take action; Louis XIII had to break through his natural timidity to do it, just as Henry IV struggled with fear as he went into combat. "Tremble then, thou flesh!"

Who would take charge of the operation? The father of Dubuisson, keeper of the birds, went to fetch Nicolas de L'Hospital, Baron de Vitry, who was Captain of the Royal Bodyguard. Stammering slightly, Luynes ordered him, in the King's name, to arrest Marshal d'Ancre.

Vitry was a violent man, greedy and fearless, with a deep hatred of the Florentine. He understood what was wanted: "If he resists, Sire, what would His Majesty have me do?"

Luynes was about to reply, then reconsidered and fell silent. Instead, it was Déageant who gave the instructions in a steady voice: "The King intends to have him killed!"

Vitry looked at the young sovereign, who remained perfectly calm and said nothing. The silence in itself was a judgment. "Sire," said the Captain, "I shall execute your command."

The operation was set for Sunday, April 23.

Meanwhile, Richelieu was now on the alert; he felt the wind of change and knew a storm was brewing.

On Friday, April 21, the King was strolling in the Tuileries gardens when M. du Pont de Courlay suddenly appeared and made a prearranged sign to Luynes. The two men went off to a secluded spot via one of the narrow paths where Catherine de Medici had had her final argument with Coligny just before the Massacre of St. Bartholomew.

Du Pont de Courlay delivered a message which left Luynes completely flabbergasted. Richelieu had declared (finally!) his loyalty to the King and proposed to keep him minutely informed of all affairs, particularly those concerning the Marshal. Luynes reported this discreetly to Louis and to his own brother, Cadenet. The offer seemed like a gift from heaven. If the King had someone spying on Concini, the Italian would be at his mercy. So, then, why chance such a risky venture?

Cadenet objected that since Vitry was now involved, the plan would surely leak out. Therefore, to do nothing at this stage would present even greater problems. Moreover, Louis XIII had no intention of retreating, for he hated both Concini and Richelieu too much. So nothing was changed, except that the King not only loathed but was now disgusted with the bishop for his readiness to knife the Queen and her favorites in the back—his benefactors, on whom he had lavished such praise.

On the morning of the 23rd, Cadenet, anxious to test his master's resolution, informed him that undoubtedly Concini had received a warning and was massing supporters at his house. What would His Majesty's attitude be if the Queen Mother tried to obtain a confession? Louis's reply was: "I am so firmly resolved to remain silent that, were I about to die, they could not pry one word out of my mouth."

"Were I about to die": no fear or pity would ever deter him from a decision he had made. Reassured, the conspirators could sharpen their weapons.

All morning long, Louis waited. Finally, near the close of midday mass, Dubuisson gave the alert: Concini was with the Queen Mother. A page was immediately sent to say that the King awaited him. Too late. While the beater approached from one side, the game made off on the other. Louis went to dinner with a broad smile on his face.

Luynes, however, was tearing his hair out and almost ready to attack the Marshal's house. His cohorts managed to calm him down. Certain details of the operation had been changed, upon Vitry's advice, and they decided to postpone the whole affair until the following day, the 24th. Instead of in the King's *salle d'armes*, the job would be done on the bridge of the Louvre, between the Bourbon Gate and the Philippe-Auguste Gate, both of which could be blocked to form a trap for the victim.

That evening, Richelieu was already in bed when he received word that the Marshal would be murdered the next day. Shoving the letter under his pillow, he went off to sleep. Thus did he turn his back on the sinking ship that could no longer serve his purpose.

*

Louis remained unperturbed and kept to his normal schedule. He went to bed at ten; sleep, as usual, was hopeless. This night, in a sense, was the eve of his birth: the old shell was falling away, and tomorrow, in place of the child scorned by everyone, a man would emerge, a king. Or, possibly, only a broken puppet.

His Majesty was up at dawn on the 24th, announced that he would go hunting, and ordered the hunt party to assemble at the end of the Tuileries gallery. A carriage and six was also to be in attendance just in case he needed a quick getaway if the plan should go awry.

The morning crawled by. While Vitry lined the Louvre's courtyard with his men and then camped himself on the main floor, the King found one excuse after another to delay the hunt. A game of billiards kept him busy until ten o'clock, then he went back up to his bedchamber. It was raining. A heavy, leaden sky seemed to be crushing the city, and everywhere the nauseating stench of mud hung in the air.

*

It was exactly ten o'clock when Concini left his house, with a princely escort of gentlemen, bodyguards, and courtiers—some sixty-odd persons in all. He wore brownish-gray velvet breeches with wide knee bands in the Milanese fashion, a black cloth doublet embroidered with gold, and a black velvet cape trimmed with braid. His handsome face was partly hidden under a black felt hat ornamented with enormous white plumes, and over his boots he wore clogs to keep out the insidious mud. In one hand he held a petitioner's letter, in the other, a large bouquet for the Queen.

The procession made its way down the Rue d'Autriche and reached the Bourbon Gate. Concini passed through with part of his retinue. As soon as he was well ahead, several guards under the command of M. de Corneillan quickly shut and bolted the gate.

Absorbed in the letter he was reading, the Marshal did not notice what had happened. He moved onto the bridge where his escort formed a small crowd.

Vitry had been waiting it out for some time in one of the lower rooms of the palace. As soon as word reached him of the enemy's arrival, he set off with five officers and strode rapidly across the courtyard and the drawbridge, but then ran into a group of people who, along with Concini's men, usually hung around the palace. Not knowing what he and his lieutenants were up to, they greeted him good-naturedly in their normal fashion and tried to draw him aside to exchange the latest gossip. With some difficulty, Vitry finally extricated himself and dashed ahead, right past his prey. "Where is the Marshal?" he demanded wildly. Someone pointed him out. Vitry turned around, found Concini, and grabbed him by the right elbow, shouting: "I arrest you in the name of the King!"

Stunned, the Marshall drew back, so stupefied that the French words failed him: "A *me?*" he asked.

"Yes, you!"

Did the Florentine move for his sword? It is doubtful that he had time even to try, for the five officers, drawing pistols from their doublets, unloaded them instantly at their victim.

Three bullets struck Concini, the first between the eyes, the second in the cheek, and the final one in his neck. He sank to his knees, his back to the parapet. The five officers, and others who joined in, fell upon him with their swords. He was dead long before they finished stabbing him.

"Long live the King!" cried Vitry. And he kicked the corpse that was now a human wreck fit for the spoilers. Who would get the diamond worth 6,000 écus, the silk scarf, the jewel-studded dagger, or the 2,000,000 livres (several times a billion in present-day francs) that were in his pockets?

There was a great uproar; in the King's apartment it sounded as if the affair had failed and Concini were attacking the palace. Louis called for a gun just as M. d'Ornano ran in with the news: "Sire, it is done!"

They threw open the window, and d'Ornano lifted the King into view for the frenzied crowd below; at the sight of him, there was a roar of adoration. "I thank you," he called to them, "I thank you very much. At this hour I am King!"

Word spread quickly, and all the Princes of the realm headed straight for the Louvre. Louis savored at once the exaltation of victory, liberation, vengeance, the conquest of power, and the idolatry of his people.

*

The uproar found Marie de Medici in her "closet," a handsome room filled with statues, paintings, engravings, medallions, coffers, porcelain, and gilt mirrors. The walls and chairs exuded a heavy scent of perfume, relic of the days when the Queen resorted to this method of contending with Henry IV's body odors. Since then it had become a habit.

Catherine, the Queen's personal maid, entered the royal bedchamber and opened a window overlooking the palace courtyard.

"What's going on?" she called down.

Vitry himself answered: "Marshall d'Ancre has been killed."

"Who did it?"

"I did, at the King's command."

Catherine ran to find the Queen as others arrived with the news. Marie was aghast, but at first there was dignity in her reactions. She sighed: "I have reigned for seven years and look forward to nothing more than a crown in heaven."

But the panic of her retinue soon caught up with her, and this obese, haggard, and disheveled matron began to tear around the room like a madwoman, wringing her hands, and clawing at her face. Over and over she groaned: "*Poveretta di me* (Woe is me)!"

When they had calmed her a little, one of Leonora's servants, La Place, approached the Queen to ask how he should broach the news to his mistress. He, poor fellow, assumed that Her Majesty wished to be of comfort to her dear friend. How mistaken he was, for Marie had ears only for the voice of self-preservation: "I have others things to think about," she snapped. "If you don't want to tell her, then sing it to her!"

La Place had to return alone to the Concini house, where another shock awaited him. Not a tear, not a murmur of grief escaped Leonora when she learned of the death of the man she had idolized. All she could think of was the wreckage of her own fortune and how she might escape ruin.

Despite pressure from his entourage, Louis XIII would never consent to get rid of his mother; his pathetic love and reverence for her were too strong. If the Queen had played this to her advantage, she could have saved herself and those who relied on her. But once again this dull-witted Juno allowed herself to be influenced by her scheming confidante.

Leonora knew she must see the Queen immediately and sent La Place to ask Her Majesty to receive her "so that they might console each other."

The request could not have come at a worse moment. Having made three efforts to obtain an audience with her son and been rebuffed each time, Marie now saw herself in imminent peril. Look where she had ended up, thanks to the woman who had been her eyes, ears, and brains, the creature she had set above her husband and her children! La Place was cut short in the middle of his message.

"I have enough worries of my own!" roared the furious Queen. "Don't speak to me about those people! I told them often enough that they should have gone back to Italy long ago!"

And that was the funeral oration ending one of the most extraordinary friendships in history.

When the hapless La Place reported the results of his mission, it was clear to Leonora that the end was near, something she had feared and predicted all along, but somehow had never accepted. Could she accept it now? After so many miracles, what more could she expect from life? Love and happiness had left her long ago, and each day her illness became more unbearable. The Queen's rejection broke the last link between Leonora and the rest of humanity. Why, then, should death frighten her?

Because death utterly strips its victims, forcing them to part with all their worldly goods. Leonora had not flinched at crime for the sake of her husband's career and the immense wealth they had won. Concini was gone now; she could not face losing her fortune also.

The weird creature turned wildly hysterical. Rushing to her coffers, she flung out sacks of gold coins, jewels, streams of diamonds, some of which belonged to the Crown. She carried them over to her bed and frantically shoved them under the mattress, then undressed and lay down atop her treasures.

When the guards entered, they found her groaning as if in final agony. Paying no attention, they ordered her to get up; she became furious, clinging to the bedpost and hurling the choicest insults inspired by the Florentine rabble. To subdue her, they had to push her onto the floor.

The guards turned the magnificent room inside out in their looting. But it was not her treasures—which they knew they would find anyway—that drew a triumphant shout from the captain; it was the discovery of astrologic documents attached to horoscopes for the Queen and her children.

Now they could burn the witch!

The guards rode throughout exultant Paris crying the news: "Long live the King! The King is king at last!"

XVI

"This Funereal Splendor"

T HE Bishop of Luçon was visiting one of his friends at the Sorbonne when the news reached him. He put on an air of appropriate astonishment, having known about it since the night before, and left immediately for the Louvre. In the Queen's apartment there were only tears and confusion. Barbin and Mangot were hiding in the stables, where he joined them for a moment. The two men asked him to confront the King alone, since his position would protect him. Nothing could have pleased him more.

In the midst of a throng that filled the great gallery, he saw, hunched over a billiard table, a new Louis XIII, wildly happy yet perfectly controlled, who was informing everyone: "I did what I had to do."

And to Parliament's delegation, he offered: "Serve me well and I shall be a good king."

To the commandant of the Bastille: "You are responsible to me alone."

To Villeroy: "Stay by me, good father."

Seeing the bishop, he called him over. "Well, Luçon, I'm out of your clutches at last. Come now! Start moving and get yourself out of here!"

But Luynes intervened, and M. du Pont de Courlay's mission bore fruit. Still unsure of himself, the favorite thought they should not pass up the free services of a spy close to the Queen Mother. He told the King that M. de Luçon had asked to leave the ministry and had had numerous "disagreements" with the Marshal. The bishop then gave a brief speech which, according to his *Mémoires*, was "ingenuous," a masterpiece of duplicity and a tribute to his courtier's training. He pointed out that there had been little love lost between himself and Concini and that the latter never trusted him. So he could not have known the wicked intentions of the Florentine. As for himself, he would rather die than fail in his duty to His Majesty.

The King softened. He said that the office of Secretary of State should revert to Villeroy, but that M. de Luçon, after turning in his portfolio, would still be privileged to sit in Council. He could even keep his salary. Afterward, Richelieu took Luynes aside and thanked him for his help, assuring him of "his affection and *his service*"—meaning that he still stood behind the proposal made through his brother-in-law whereby he would do what he could to spy on the Queen Mother for the King.

So he broke his fall by clinging to a strong branch. While Mangot's fate was prison and Barbin was kept under house arrest, Richelieu was able to retain a position of major importance. The cost of the operation fell on his benefactress, but it was a success.

Thus strengthened, Richelieu made his way to the Council. In the doorway stood old Nestor himself, Villeroy, brimming with rancor, barring the way, and demanding to know what Luçon thought he was doing there. The other ministers—the 1615 vintage who had been returned to office—glared at him. Richelieu understood; he remained near the entrance for a moment without saying a word, then, as he later recorded it, quietly went away.

The next day he set out to visit the Papal Nuncio. On crossing the Pont-Neuf he met up with a howling mob that had just strung up Concini's corpse on one of the gibbets that had been erected at his order. The populace was indulging in its customary practice of dismembering the body, gouging out the eyes, hacking off the nose, ears, and arms. Each district in Paris would receive a fragment of this tragic gallant, who, for a moment, had been Henry IV's successor. On the eve of her era of enlightenment, France still had a population of near-cannibals.

When the bishop's coachman went after one of the mob, it nearly ruined his master, who escaped being torn to pieces only by tongue-lashing his servant and shouting: "Long live the King!"

That scene on the Pont-Neuf was engraved in his memory. Even when he became the mighty despot, the terror of Europe, he never forgot that a sudden change of the King's mood could turn his most powerful minister into a disjointed puppet.

Now, on April 25, 1617, he retraced the capricious events of the past and congratulated himself for having handled things so well. Barbin was headed for the Bastille, Concini's followers were being thrown out of Paris, Leonora faced death; he was the sole member of the defunct party to remain free and, as it were, well regarded.

All this he owed entirely to Marie de Medici, a virtual prisoner in the Louvre, but who, as a widow and a mother of kings, was still a person to be reckoned with. Since childhood, she had been accustomed to having someone else do her thinking and now felt completely lost. She pledged herself to obey the counsel of whatever adviser they wished to send her, and Luynes had excellent reasons for giving the job to Richelieu.

Five days later, after being authorized to resume contact with the Queen Mother, M. de Luçon was welcomed as a savior. And another scene took place that belonged on the stage.

The bulging, slow-witted, sentimental matron came to life at the sight of her dear friend, the only one who could bring her consolation and guidance. The remarkable and charming young bishop assured her of his devotion, his protection, and his loyalty. But in reality, it was she who provided the shield; her confidence and complete surrender were his most important assets in this complicated and desperate game. Indeed, he relied on the decrepit and emotional woman to advance his fortune.

Naturally, Richelieu was the Queen's spokesman when Louis XIII agreed to hold talks, just as Luynes represented the sovereign. He protected the disgraced Queen's interests so well that she was allowed to reside first at Blois, then, when it was ready to receive her, in her château at Moulins, where she was to have complete authority; she could retain possession of all her property and take her entire staff with her. The agreement guaranteed that Barbin's life would be spared; he was one of the few people to whom the future Cardinal had any sense of gratitude.

On the 3rd of May, a meeting, rigidly outlined in advance, took place between the new Marie de Medici, now humble and tearful, and the new Louis XIII, resolute, icy, and impassive, already the symbol of the State.

The Queen Mother read a rather long statement which Richelieu had prepared: she had done her best to carry out the regency and was indeed regretful if it had not worked out as she had hoped; it was not for lack of good will on her part, but rather because the King had not made his own wishes clear; she was pleased that he had assumed control of the State and prayed that he would act toward her as a dutiful son and a just monarch.

Louis replied: "Madam, I come to say farewell and to assure you that, as my mother, you shall always have my regard and protection. I am resolved to be the sole ruler in my kingdom. Farewell, Madam. Love me, and I shall be your dutiful son."

Marie burst into sobs. She rushed forward and, without embracing him, kissed him on the lips—she who had not put her arms around him once in seven years! A few weeks earlier, such a caress might have changed the whole situation.

Louis, in turn, began to cry, but the tears came from deep within him, from memories and regrets of a ruined childhood; they were not the tears of self-pity.

Taking courage, the Queen ventured: "Sire, I have sent you pleas on behalf of Barbin. If any harm has been done during his ministry, it is not his fault. I beg you to set him free."

The King pulled himself together and replied, curtly: "Madam, I have already informed you that I shall see that you receive satisfaction in regard to him, as is my intent in all other matters."

When young Gaston d'Anjou took leave of his mother, she burst into tears again. And to Luynes as he bid her farewell, she pleaded: "Monsieur de Luynes, you know I have always loved you. Keep me in the King's good grace." The favorite was intent on being most tactful with her, but before he had a chance to reply, the impatient voice of his master rang out: "Luynes! Luynes! Luynes!"

The Queen had definitely lost the match.

Her carriages, with the Bishop of Luçon riding in the last one, moved slowly across the city, heralded by trumpets and escorted by light cavalry. The mocking Parisians jeered them mercilessly. Richelieu's *Mémoires* have left us his impressions of the event: "Anyone with an ounce of humanity was moved to compassion at the sight of this funereal splendor. To see a great princess, yesterday's absolute ruler of this great kingdom, abandon her throne and, not furtively or hiding her disgrace in the night's protective cloak, but publicly and in broad daylight, before the eyes of her people, pass through the center of her greatest city, as if on display, leaving behind the empire that was hers—the sight of this was so moving that it left one speechless."

Thus, even the power of a queen crowned in the Cathedral of Saint-Denis was at the mercy of the King's humor. This notion of "disgrace" haunted Richelieu and became an obsession. Over and over he retraced the incredible rise and sudden downfall of the Concinis, searching for the slips and errors that cause the ruin of royal favorites.

But there was no trace of discouragement in these morose reflections, no suggestion of his turning back from the conquest of power. The ambitious prelate was simply intent on distilling from this first defeat some useful lessons for the struggle ahead.

XVII

The Perils of Double-dealing

THE seven years that followed were a "journey through the desert." At the end of it, Armand du Plessis was in complete command of his extraordinary gifts, which even his enemies were forced to recognize, but the self-control prerequisite to controlling others and the supreme skill which turned an unscrupulous politician into the greatest statesman of his era were not achieved without countless mistakes and failures. His personality would often play tricks on him, and it is interesting to see how his remarkable intelligence acted as a kind of conditioned reflex to rectify errors resulting from brash deceit, impatience, and fear.

The first stage of this long journey was his appointment to the newly created post of head of the Queen Mother's Council. It was in this capacity that M. de Luçon arrived at Blois after a very tiring trip. The château had scarcely been lived in since the murder of the Duke of Guise and the death of Catherine de Medici. Despite its beauty, it was a reminder of sinister events.

The little Court-in-exile settled down as comfortably as possible. A Court it was, indeed, with the strangest assortment of members. There was the lengendary Mme de Guercheville, reputed to be the only woman who had been able to resist Henry IV; gentlemen such as Bressieux and Villesavin, the latter a personal enemy of Richelieu; Bonzi, Bishop of

Béziers, who would have been delighted to replace Luçon faithful retainers, as well as a hive of truculent, greedy, and scheming Italians, including Tantucci, "an incredible fellow, a genuinely dedicated traitor."

The most dangerous person was Abbé Ruccellaï, former confidant of Concini, whom the favorite at one time had wanted to appoint Secretary of State. Through his wealth and cunning, Ruccellaï was now in favor with Luynes and made frequent trips from the Louvre to Blois and back again. He, too, was playing a double role and also coveted Richelieu's position, taking care to mask his hatred of the Bishop by a lavish display of good feelings.

Richelieu went to work to please his new masters. He worked too hard, as a matter of fact. The day after his arrival at Blois, he sent Luynes and Déageant reports boldly claiming "that she [the Queen] no longer remembers the events of the past," and a procession of letters followed in this same vein. "I shall stake my life," he wrote to Luynes, "on satisfying the King's wishes, and yours especially, with regard to the Queen Mother's conduct and *on convincing you one day that I have acted honorably toward her.*"

And how, in his eyes, ought an honorable man to act? Why, he must be in constant attendance on the woman he is committed to spy on and keep her completely under his influence. In the evenings, after supper, the two of them would disappear into her private apartments and stay there alone for hours. What went on is anyone's guess.

There were repercussions in Paris. Richelieu had enemies who accused him of deluding the King and stirring up the Queen Mother so as to remain indispensable. He was even implicated in the trial of Leonora. In turn, Marie de Medici received a warning. Richelieu's strategy, now quite obvious, reduced Machiavelli to the level of a double agent.

"He has already had a falling-out with the Queen Mother," wrote the Papal Nuncio, "having taken it upon himself to spy on her and report all her movements to the King. The poor man has certainly lost a measure of his reputation and authority."

On June 11, the Marquis of Richelieu warned his brother, based on information which later proved to be false, that the King intended to send him back to Luçon. That evening, the Queen did not appear at supper. Neither did the bishop. The next day, before sunrise, he left suddenly for Richelieu.

The Perils of Double-dealing

We must assume that, during their last conversation, he convinced Marie de Medici of his innocence without disclosing his design. Perhaps he told her he would be away for a week. Whatever was said, as soon as she learned of his disappearance, the impossible woman took to her bed from furor and despair. As one of her physicians expressed it, she had an acute "tempest in the soul" that called for immediate bleeding.

The Queen's letters to her son and to Luynes were like "the roars of a wounded lioness." Such loud laments had not been heard from her even when Concini died, and it is hard to believe that they were inspired purely by an adviser for political and religious matters. No, the roaring was an echo of feelings that lay deep in her heart—so deep, in fact, that her passion turned against its object when the perfidious Bishop of Béziers, on a mission to Paris, revealed the truth of the situation: M. de Luçon, without taking the time to verify his brother's facts, had panicked and fled, abandoning his patroness.

The Queen deluged her ungrateful confidant with letters of reproach. She commanded, she begged him to return—Mme de Guercheville's carriage was ready to come and fetch him. But Richelieu would not leave his château. He was in one of his depressions, and the image of Concini's butchered corpse haunted him. Realizing that in trying to be too clever he had stumbled into a hornets' nest, he now wanted to extricate himself.

He wrote like a demon; the letters piled up on the desks of the Queen Mother, the King, and Luynes. To Marie, he sent confused apologies; to Louis, a request that the monarch designate a residence where he "could live free from calumny." For Luynes, he put on a show of sorely offended dignity: "They seek, Sir, to strip me of my honor. I placed myself under your protection with no thought other than to serve the King, the Queen his mother, and you."

Finally, he won out. On June 15, the King sent his ironic congratulations to the "man of honor" for having returned to his diocese and ordered him not to budge from it. M. de Luçon answered that he was resolved to "live in a little hermitage among his books and his duties."

Indeed, under these circumstances, it was far better to disappear than to betray everyone.

The forsaken Marie, however, could not be expected to understand this. Her intimates cast the worst suspicions on the cold-hearted bishop; still, she felt compelled to write him. She thought of him much more often than of Leonora, her life-companion, who would soon go to her

147

death "for the crime of treason, both divine and human." In July, she complained bitterly at having had no word from him, so Richelieu decided to send her a letter that would leave no doubt as to the nature of their relationship: "Madam, since the days seem like centuries when I do not have the honor of seeing Your Majesty, my devotion to her will not allow me to postpone any longer [!] expressing my assurances that *although I am apart from her, I never cease to think of her as it is my duty and my obligation to her graciousness* [the euphemism is well chosen] . . . Your Majesty would be most kind if it pleased her to release me from my duty to her *until such time as I may have the happiness of being in her presence . . .*"

Neither one seemed to care about Leonora, the woman who had brought them together. If Richelieu ever mentioned her, he made it clear that his "civilities" toward Mme d'Ancre were of a purely anodyne nature.

During the trial, Leonora had been tempted momentarily to ruin the Queen, who had so savagely dumped her overboard, when the judges, Jean Courtis and Guillaume Deslandes, asked her whether she had been warned of the plot against the late King "and whether she prevented action being taken on the basis of this warning,[1] thus rendering herself guilty of a most evil murder." But she settled instead for a bout of weeping.

On the scaffold, before the blindfold was tied, one of the judges called on the "witch" to reveal how she had got possession of the Queen's mind. And Leonora's reply, with a last faint smile, was: "By the spell that a strong will exerts on a simple-minded clod."

*

After three eventful years, Richelieu was now back in retirement and involved in religious pursuits, wiser for his experience and with the reputation of being a man "of great ability," which is to say, one to be feared.

He corresponded with a great many people and made it known that he intended to devote himself to his house, his books, and his church

---

[1] From the cell where she had been imprisoned since 1609, Jacqueline d'Escoman had been able to warn the Queen's apothecary of the plot against Henry IV's life. The apothecary passed the information on to Leonora, who "buried" it.

duties. So as not to be forgotten, he wrote frequently to the Court. In September, 1617, news that the Queen Mother was under the thumbs of Rurcellaï and Bonzi brought him new anxieties. He begged the King, Luynes, and Déageant for their patronage, then realized that he was wasting his time. But he had another idea, which turned out to have far-reaching consequences.

Father Joseph, who was now the Capuchin's Provincial of Touraine, had been extremely active in the interval following the near breach in their friendship. He observed his own personal system of mystical rites; he had had visions as well as revelations and had experienced religious ecstasy. While preaching, he would have cataleptic seizures, much to the edification of the faithful.

But he was unable to contain his holy fervor within the limits of purely religious causes. Father Joseph abhorred the Turks and had espoused the Duke of Nevers' fantasy, adding his own peculiar slant to it. In that area of the world where Nevers, a descendent of Byzantine emperors, sought only a crown, he saw all of Christianity assembled and united in the cause of exterminating the infidels. It was a way of avoiding the horrors of an impending war between the Catholic Princes and the Protestants.

Father Joseph imagined himself as Peter the Hermit in this twice-holy crusade and began to preach it everywhere. He was a great writer of verse and had composed an epic poem on the Turks containing a pledge to liberate Greece first from the Ottoman yoke:

> If, to assist you, the world I'd spin round,
> It would not match the strength of my vows;
> In an ocean of blood I should wish to be drowned
> The fires of my anger to dowse.

Since no sea of blood could be released without the Holy Father's blessing, he went to Rome and obtained Paul V's sanction, as well as letters from him that could be used to break down Spanish resistance, for Spain was extremely hesitant about such a project, which was a little too French for her taste.

He returned to Paris in June, 1617. His ardent eloquence, his fanaticism, his keen mind and, above all, his fame as a visionary made a deep impression on the King. Richelieu, always watching for an opportunity, learned about this and immediately reached for his pen: "Father, this letter brings you assurance of my confidence in you, for though we have not seen each other in more than a year and a half, I am writing to you with the same candor as if we had never drifted apart."

The candor was entirely relative: M. de Luçon opened his heart and presented a somewhat magnified picture of the trials he had undergone in recent months, "protesting before God" that he was guided solely by a desire for peace of mind; then—a stroke of cleverness—he casually mentioned a lengthy treatise destined to silence the Huguenots, who were already using slander to get back at him for it. Finally, he asked the priest for his help and patronage.

Father Joseph was moved; he had always liked and admired the young bishop. They resumed their friendship, but it was too late for it to bear fruit. By now, the King had built up an extreme hatred of his mother's too-intimate confidant, and Luynes was too fearful of such a superior rival.

Richelieu sought consolation in work and did indeed prepare a reply to four Protestant ministers who had jointly published A *Defense of Confession in the Reformed Churches of France Against the Accusations of M. Arnould, Jesuit.* This type of controversy continued to fascinate the public.

The rebuttal, which M. de Luçon prepared over a period of three months, was far superior to run-of-the-mill disputations. A masterpiece in its own category, the work was entitled: A *Defense of Principal Points of Faith of the Catholic Church Against the Document Addressed to the King by the Four Ministers from Charenton.* In his very opening words, the author dared to preach the suggestion of tolerance, which, for many, was still equivalent to treason. He rejected the use of force and called for peace. Then, as a practiced theologian, he went to work refuting his adversaries. But soon the statesman took over from the priest, and his argument turned political: "You attribute to the people much greater power than that which you deny the Pope, and this is indeed a disadvantage to kings; for it is generally agreed that there is far more risk in being committed to the whim of the people, which sometimes imagines itself mistreated and is a multi-headed beast usually guided by its own passions, than in submitting to the correction of a father who is full of love for his children."

Finally, after lamenting the Church disunity which the Reformation had brought about, the Bishop accepted it as an accomplished fact. A passionate believer in order, discipline, and cohesion, he called on the State to restore at least the nation's unity and to end the strife. The Cardinal's entire policy towards the Protestants was there in a nutshell: freedom of conscience, provided it did not interfere with the King's sovereignty. Basically, this doctrine was not so different from that of Luther and of Calvin, both of whom, in rejecting the medieval ideal, had sought to win the feudal lords away from Rome's domination.

The book had an enormous success the moment it appeared, which only added to the fears and jealousy of Richelieu's enemies. Luynes, who already had more power than he could handle, saw all too clearly which of his rivals intended to succeed him. He was responsible for an order forbidding the bishop to reside at Coussay and requiring him to remain amid the noxious marshes of Luçon.

At this time, Marie de Medici gave her son the opportunity to patch up their relationship. She had been foolish enough to correspond with Barbin in the Bastille and, upon his advice, to write to several of the Princes. Luynes gave the impression that he was facilitating such contacts as a gesture of reconcilation to the exiled Queen; then, without warning, he showed the intercepted letters to the King and convinced him that a conspiracy was in the making.

The commandant of the Bastille and his lieutenants were arrested, a new trial began for Barbin, and the pamphleteers in the Queen Mother's hire were put out of business.

Richelieu had no part in the affair, but Luynes made the King believe otherwise. On April 17, 1618, the bishop, his brother, and his brother-in-law were all ruthlessly banished to the papal city of Avignon.

In his *Mémoires*, Richelieu commented: "I was not surprised to receive this dispatch, since I have always expected acts of cowardice from those in power, every imaginable form of unjust, cruel, and unreasonable treatment."

And how many people would say the same things about him one day!

XVIII

Luck Returns

RICHELIEU was not cut solely from politician's cloth. He had
also the temperament of a writer and the compulsion to get things
off his mind by putting them on paper. *The Courtier's Breviary*
had been a product of his preoccupation with winning the King's favor.
In Avignon, brooding bitterly over his disgrace, he plunged into the draft
of a *Caput Apologeticum*, a work which would exonerate him in the
eyes of the world and especially of his own family.

Though this vehement self-defense contains irrefutable arguments, it
is not uniformly candid. His "civilities" toward Leonora, for example, once
again are claimed to be perfectly innocent and natural remarks, and his
"solemn declaration before God" that Marie de Medici had deep affection
for Louis XIII and never sought to displease him is equally extravagant.

The exile recalls—and reminds himself—how highly esteemed he was
by Henry IV and the Pope, as well as the Sorbonne and the deputies to
the States-General. Disillusioned, he asserts "A man in misfortune is
wrongfully blamed for everything. . . . The virtues of a man in favor are
deemed vices when he is in disgrace."

The most interesting fact is that he prides himself for his toleration
toward the Huguenots while disclaiming any sympathies with the Spanish
cause. Yet, Luynes had made a switch to the Hapsburg orbit, leaving Pope
Paul V almost the sole champion of the expatriated bishop.

Certain historians have inferred that Richelieu's definitive self-awareness came at the beginning of his exile in Avignon. And indeed his notes have a personal character, and the *Caput Apologeticum* was never published. From the time he first dreamed of ruling France, he envisaged restoring her to world leadership, and the path to power as he had conceived it was capable of satisfying both his pride and his patriotism.

In 1618 it was becoming increasingly difficult not to choose sides. In Germany, the long-predicted storm was brewing which would either destroy the House of Austria or raise it to supremacy upon the ruins of the Reformation.

There had been peace since 1555 as a result of the Pact of Augsburg which Charles V had concluded with the Lutherans but not with the Calvinists. These aggressive newcomers were spreading their doctrine throughout the Palatinate and looking for foreign allies. They ran up against Catholic resistance to which the Counter Reformation had lent increased vigor and stubbornness.

The upheaval came in Bohemia, a hopelessly divided State not covered by the Treaty of Augsburg, where Emperor Matthias sought to impose Catholic-oriented Archduke Ferdinand as his successor. All it took was the destruction of one Protestant church in Klostergrab, whereupon armed Protestants attacked the château in Prague (which the Emperor had lately chosen as a residence over the one in Vienna) and defenestrated three of his ministers, whose fall was broken by a dung heap. There followed thirty—nearly forty—years of the worst butchery civilization has known.

Richelieu, Paul V's protégé and Marie de Medici's favorite, had every reason to espouse the cause of the Hapsburgs, who had now become practically a secular arm of the Church, and to place his hopes in a movement of Christian reunification free from the divisive peril of Protestantism. Father Joseph shared the same attitude as did Luynes and the Catholic party, whose opposition had been the basic cause of Henry IV's death.

Since the end of Charlemagne's empire, History has proffered, with seeming amusement, occasional opportunities to "create a united Europe"; the expression is of our century, which has also confronted the problem. France, in the sixteenth and seventeenth centuries, had been obliged to choose between this ideal and her national interests, since a Hapsburg triumph unquestionably would have reduced her to the posi-

tion of a satellite. To the amazement of the Catholic world, François I
of France, "Emperor in his realm," had preferred to keep his kingdom
independent—even going so far as to ally with the Turks against Charles
V when the latter was threatening to draw all the Western nations into
a crusade. Henry IV continued this policy. In turn, it appealed to the
mind and aspirations of Richelieu, who, during his somber days in
Avignon, had all the time in the world to think about the fate of em-
pires. Nationalism, which he was to carry to its utmost limits, was already
rooted in his thinking and ready to assume a political form when, once
again, the world situation became critical. In disgrace and misfortune,
great statesmen often forge the doctrines that will bring them glory in
their day of power.

The unhappy bishop had no taste of power at all in that foreign city,
where he knew he was being watched. When the Pope made overtures
in his behalf to Louis XIII, the reply was stinging. Puisieux, Secretary of
State for Foreign Affairs, wrote to the French Ambassador in Rome: "It
appears to us that His Holiness is exceeding his authority. . . . If M. de
Luçon had been content to remain a good bishop in his own parish, he
would not be where he is today. . . . But men like him wander from their
line of duty and become a dangerous public menace."

Extremely dangerous, too, in the eyes of their small-minded successors.
So there was no ray of light on the horizon. The young Marchioness of
Richelieu, who had remained behind in the family château, died in child-
birth at this time, and her husband obtained permission to return to the
family home along with Pont de Courlay.

M. de Luçon stayed on alone in Avignon, in the worst state of depression he had yet known. Like all highly emotional people, he managed
to aggravate his despondency as thoroughly as he had stoked the fevers
of his ambition. Thinking his life was over, he drafted his will in the form
of a letter to the canons of Luçon. "The world is only a deception," he
warned them. "The sole satisfaction and profit to be had is in serving
God who does not fail those who do so."

But events were to prevent him from finding this kind of satisfaction.

*

Only one of the Princes did not share in the general enthusiasm
which, following Concini's death, snuffed out the fires of civil war and

reunited the entire kingdom around the throne. It was Turenne, one of Henry IV's lieutenants, who, thanks to that monarch, became Duke of Bouillon and sovereign prince of Sedan and from there rose to leadership of the Protestant party; he was one of the dangerous troublemakers in European politics and the stubborn opponent of law and order in France. His saying: "The tavern is the same; only the cork is different," caught on, and in a country such as France where images produced an immediate reaction, it began to shed discredit on the first signs of sovereign authority, as we see from the biased *Mémoires* of Richelieu. Like most overly neat aphorisms, it did not do justice to the facts. The tavern was not the same, but the young master who intended to run it needed training, and it was in the nature neither of his subjects nor of events to allow him time for this.

Nothing except his own determination had prepared Louis to shoulder world responsibilities. He began by doing what appeared sensible, seeking support from his father's ministers, but they, poor souls, were well on in years, worn out, and timid. Furthermore, the key man, Villeroy was soon to die. The ship needed a strong hand to stay on course, but if the Princes took the helm, there was only trouble ahead.

Louis's mistake was to listen to his heart instead of his reason, and, because of his affection for him, to imagine that Luynes was a great man. In an ordinary adolescent, the error would have been inconsequential, but on the part of an absolute monarch, it was to affect the destinies of France and Europe for the next ten years.

Not that Luynes was incompetent (as Richelieu insistently maintained). He was clever, hard-working, and conscientious, a skillful manipulator able to adapt to or adjust obstacles in accordance with his own purposes. What he lacked were courage and inspiration, the two qualities indispensable to the leadership of France during those tumultuous forty years between Henry IV's death and the end of the Fronde.

It was normal for the new favorite to be unpopular, for the people's dislike of him complemented their idolatry of the King. It was also to be expected that he would amass a mammoth fortune. Under Valois and Bourbon rulers, no chief minister neglected to do so, and Richelieu and Mazarin probably brought the practice to its apogee.

Luynes and his brothers set about feathering their nests without the slightest hesitation or modesty. "If the whole of France were for sale," the saying went, "they would buy her from herself." For his own account, the former falconer made off not only with Concini's hoard, but with forever coveted Picardy, Ile-de-France, Boulogne, and Calais, then with a dukedom and the peerage that went with it, and finally had himself decorated with the Order of the Holy Ghost. His younger brothers soon ranked among the lords of the land. But the economy minded and scrupulous Louis was not disturbed; he enjoyed rewarding his friends and saw justice in remunerating those who had to face the almost insuperable task of running the government.

Luynes was unable to arrange a match for himself with one of the illegitimate daughters of Henry IV—his aspirations were in line with Concini's in this respect—but he married Marie de Rohan-Montbazon, who turned out to be the most dangerous Circe of that era. No sooner were they wed than the young girl of sixteen tried to seduce the King. But the greenhorn, who had not slept with Anne of Austria since he had been forced to do so on his wedding night, refused to go along.

The young siren took her revenge by becoming the neglected Queen's favorite. Anne, forgetting her jealousy, could not resist the newcomer's bouncing good spirits, and soon the palace corridors resounded with their squeals and merriment. It was just the sort of thing Louis disliked, and once he had put in his required appearance, he rushed off to be with Luynes.

The King had none of the boyish enthusiasm of either François I or Louis XIV. Each morning after his riding lesson, he would preside over the Council, grave, tense, impassive, both a student and a supervisor of the bearded old men around him. Then he would go off hunting, rarely returning before nightfall.

His enigmatic personality troubled and confused those who served him. The less they understood this silent youth, the more they feared offending him; and the constant anxiety, in which Luynes also shared, discouraged any display of initiative.

It was equally impossible to revert to the former regime's policies or to return Concini's enemies to power. Condé remained a prisoner. Luynes, rather than openly oppose his rivals, preferred to serve their designs. Seeking a moderate position, he tried to conciliate the different parties, leaning heavily on the Catholics for support. The King's and his own religious convictions sent him in that direction, which promised safety but which also had a very restricting effect on the nation's policies.

If outwardly the Catholic front seemed less tightly knit and somewhat counterbalanced by a treaty with Savoy, inwardly the rightest elements were regaining ground: heresy was severely fought, and, despite the protests of Parliament and the Sorbonne, the Jesuits reopened their boys' schools. It was a good way to flatter the Queen Mother and prevent her from forming an opposition.

For Marie de Medici, lurking behind the walls of Blois, continued to be an obsession with both her son and his ministers. The château, with its many tragic memories of the Holy League, seemed to harbor infernal machines.

Luynes had made two errors in removing Richelieu from Blois: he had provoked Marie's anger, and he had left her a prey to some treacherous schemers.

Torn between conflicting emotions, the King tried vainly to appease his mother. Out of pride and avidity more than political ambition, Marie sought to regain her seat in the Council and to install herself, as Catherine de Medici had done before her, as the kingdom's permanent arbitrator. She would hear of nothing less than that. Anxiously, Luynes made one concession after another, stripping himself of his best weapons in an effort to win her. The Escoman affair, which had been muffled for a number of years, was regenerated, and the poor woman, sealed away in her cell, was condemned to end her days in the unspeakable hell of the Institution for Wayward Women.

What was more, a fire broke out in the Palace of Justice, and in destroying the great hall it also obliterated certain documents relating to the trial of 1611 which had so upset Chief Justice de Harlay that they had been sealed mysteriously into the wall: that was the trial of Jacqueline d'Escoman, who accused Epernon of Henry IV's murder and against whom they were unable to bring a conviction of false testimony.

With these things to his credit, plus the fact that he had Anne of Austria under his thumb through her close relationship with Mme de Luynes and that he had at last managed to bring about a proper consummation of the royal marriage, Luynes felt strong enough to attempt a reconciliation with the Queen at Blois. Then the fireworks started. The principal cause was the fidgety Abbé Ruccellaï, a frail gentleman who was forever avoiding drafts and, in hot weather, was subject to fainting spells, but who was in spite of this an ambitious soul and perennial conspirator. Using quite different tactics from Richelieu's, he came to Blois a number of times in fanciful disguises and urged the Queen Mother

157

to escape and place herself under the protection of the Princes. Marie de Medici listened to him although she had sworn "before God and the angels" not to leave the château. Actually, Louis XIII had written her an ill-advised letter asking her to forget the past, thus making it appear that she was free to go wherever she wished.

Ruccellaï decided that the Duke of Bouillon would serve his purposes and, again in disguise, went to ask whether he would look favorably on Her Majesty's presence in Sedan. Bouillon avoided the question, pleaded ill health and advised Ruccellaï to approach the Duke of Epernon.

Epernon, the great favorite of Henry III, remained one of the most powerful and wealthy men in the kingdom, Colonel-General of the Infantry, Governor of Metz and Loches as well as the provinces of Angoumois, Aunis, and Saintonge. At the age of sixty-four, this feudal lord, grandson of a notary, was an eager hothead, arrogant, cruel, and vindictive, with the makings and outlook of a statesman once his personal interests ceased leading him astray. Unscrupulous as he was insensitive, miserly or munificent according to the circumstances, he was a man who seemed to have lived several different lives. Under Henry III he gave countless proofs of his loyalty to the Crown, but after the death of his beloved King, he turned rebel in the cause of Spain; under Henry IV he was a conspirator and appeared to have plotted the regicide, after which he instigated the half-successful *coup d'état* that brought Marie de Medici to the regency. Taken in by the Concinis and denied the power he had anticipated, he did not become the least fearful or docile. From time to time he enjoyed unleashing a bit of terror, such as the incident during the States-General, and again in 1618 when a quarrel over precedence led him to insult the Keeper of the Seals in a Council session.

He detested Ruccellaï, who was able, nevertheless, using cloak-and-dagger methods, to get to the Duke a letter from the Queen Mother. It was pure foolishness for the old warlord to join in such an enterprise. Marie de Medici was already in his debt and, in 1610, had treated him most ungraciously. Finally, however, the lure of adventure and perpetual mirage of power won him over.

On January 22, 1619, despite the King's interdiction, Epernon left Metz with a princely escort and traveled across the country to Confolens, where he was safe. From there he sent his closest aide, M. du Plessis, to Blois and an insolent letter to the King: "I thought the laws of this kingdom and the privileges of my rank entitled me to common liberties. . . ."

En route, du Plessis managed to persuade the commander of Loches's citadel to receive the Queen Mother. After a series of melodramatic adventures, he finally reached Blois and saw the prisoner. Epernon's letter had put the King on guard; so they had to act quickly. Marie de Medici decided to leave the next morning.

During the night of February 21, with her jewel box clasped to her rolling bosom, she hoisted herself through a window, clambered down a ladder, slid down an enbankment on her back, and landed in the street together with du Plessis and another conspirator, Count de Braine. A carriage awaited them.

There had been panic for a moment when the Queen's jewel box could not be found and she refused to leave without it. Luckily it turned up, and the coach-and-six set off at a good pace for Montrichard.

Epernon and 150 horsemen were camped in the village of Liège; as soon as the carriage stopped, the Duke rushed up to the Queen and kissed the hem of her robe. The two of them looked at each other and burst out laughing: once again they had pulled off a good one! If luck were with them, they could needle the perpetual rebelliousness and discontent of the French and restore a fruitful state of anarchy.

At this time the King was celebrating his sister Christine's marriage to the Prince of Piedmont, heir of the Duke of Savoy. The Queen Mother had been neither consulted about the match nor invited to the festivities which had been going on since the 10th of February.

On the 24th, a spectacular hunt was to take place in the forest of Saint-Germain. It was there that two messengers turned up unexpectedly, bearing a letter from the Queen Mother and one from Epernon which was well larded with cynicism and irony. The hunt was canceled, and the Court rushed back to Paris. All the provincial governors were alerted, members of Parliament were summoned to the Louvre and informed of the situation, while the Spanish ambassador announced to Madrid that civil war was about to resume.

And, in fact, as soon as she had made her triumphant entry into Angoulême, Marie de Medici sent off a wave of dispatches to the Princes and to the Huguenots. It was the unfortunate weakness of the monarchy to be caught between a combination of ransom-demanding feudal lords and a separatist minority which, under the terms of the Edict of Nantes, had its own army, over a hundred strongholds, and foreign allies. Fortunately, the moment was ill-chosen, and the Queen found little support.

In the Louvre one Council meeting followed another. The King wanted personally to take on the task of bringing his mother and her band to reason. But Luynes, "always timid" according to the Papal Nuncio who was constantly preaching moderation to him, showed little enthusiasm for the idea. Jeannin, President of the Council, showed even less. Then someone had the strange inspiration to consult Bouillon, as if he were an expert in rebellions, and the good apostle recommended "gentle and benign methods."

Louis ended up writing his mother a letter in which prayers replaced reproaches: "I beg you for your own sake, for the sake of the Queen whose name you bear, for the sake of the mother you are to me . . . to return to your senses a little, to think of what you are doing and what the consequences may be."

On the other hand, he denounced Epernon as a traitor and rescinded his offices and governorships. At all costs he had to rescue Marie de Medici—an ogress with a will like melting wax—from the influence of that terrible lord. At the same time, he sent two men who had won her esteem, Count de Béthune and Bérulle, to soften her up. Whether or not they could do it was another question.

Then Providence showed its hand. Father Joseph was traveling far and wide—on foot, according to the rules of his Order—preaching the crusade to the Spaniards—whose mulish opposition he would never forgive—or inspecting convents in Poitou, or organizing missions to convert the Protestants. By chance, he happened to be in Paris at the time of the Queen's escapade.

He advised sending to Angoulême immediately the Bishop of Luçon, the only one capable of taming the Fury and prying her out of Epernon's clutches. Luynes did not think much of this. But Déageant, whom Luynes was trying to eliminate, favored it all the more since he had had word from the exile and thought the plan would be his own means of returning to grace.

Did Richelieu know of the plot? It is unlikely, since Epernon and Ruccellaï made every effort to keep him away from the Queen. It was not until after the event that the discouraged "hermit" felt a resurgence of his hopes and ambitions.

Déageant no longer carried any weight, but Father Joseph went straight to the King. Louis XIII was convinced by the mettlesome priest's reasoning and made a sacrifice of his personal feelings to the public interest.

On March 7, 1619, Richelieu had a visit from Charles du Tremblay, Father Joseph's brother, who handed him a dispatch from His Majesty containing a number of polite remarks and commanding him to rejoin the Queen Mother immediately. It was bitterly cold and snowing; the bishop was obviously ill. All the same, he started out the next day at dawn, "drawn by inclination and my duty," he later wrote.

His passion for politics and for power also drew him—urgently.

XIX

"A Swarm of Angry Wasps"

THE trip took twenty days and was hazardous and uncomfortable, History providing the raw ingredients of the bishop's adventures. Time after time, he barely missed getting bogged down in the mud, drowned, frozen to death, or attacked by robbers or wolves. He was arrested on the outskirts of Vienne because Lyon's Governor, M. d'Alincourt, had been misinformed about the conspiracy and thought he would win Luynes's favor by turning in such a fine catch. Du Tremblay had a hard time straightening out the situation.

In Limoges, Schomberg, commander of the royal army, had received false reports; thinking the traveler was the Archbishop of Toulouse, Epernon's son, he organized a manhunt. Fortunately, bad weather kept him from locating his prey.

While his carriage jolted in and out of ruts or careened over frozen stretches of roadway, Richelieu was deep in thought. Destiny was offering him a second chance, probably his last, but this time it was more complex and evanescent than the chance he had had in 1616. At that time, the object had been to please the Queen and her favorites, serve as their tool before dominating them. Now, he still had to please the Queen, then control her, but he also had to serve the King; and his experience of 1617 had proved how dangerous such an awkward double game could be. The "unctuous prelate," whom Louis XIII had resigned

162

himself to trust, could win out only if he succeeded in bringing mother and son to some kind of terms.

It would be a difficult task, and Marie's entourage had a major interest in opposing it. Richelieu realized that the nucleus of resistance was the Queen's own party, which, though scarcely organized yet, nevertheless could count on Epernon's temerity and Ruccellaï's activity to recruit the power-hungry Princes as well as the Catholic *dévots* and, paradoxically, the Huguenots.

As the creaking and swaying carriage jolted along, the bishop felt prepared for the first time to come to grips with the Protestants, a struggle that would last the rest of his life.

On March 27 he arrived at Angoulême and called on Epernon, the Governor. It was a strange meeting of the past and the future. The man who had come to Henry III's aid just in time to save the country, then had worked to undermine it, welcomed Richelieu quite civilly. He took him to the Queen, who was presiding at a Council meeting which she did not seem at all anxious to end. This was not encouraging to begin with, and during the session Her Majesty was warned to be extremely careful in dealing with one suspicious person in particular who was surely out to advance Luynes's interests.

In the meanwhile, the visitor looked around him and encountered a sea of stolid, unfriendly faces. Only Mme de Guercheville seemed pleased to see him again.

Finally, the Queen came out and motioned the bishop to stay, dismissing the others. Only then did he heave a sigh of relief, for all signs of the ogress, the Fury, melted away. Here instead was a woman obviously dying to see him who gazed rapturously at the face of her long lost friend and anxiously inquired about his health and his affairs. She reeled off all her adventures since their separation, asked his advice, put herself in his hands.

Richelieu was evidently happy to be at the Queen's side once more, but he made it clear that the rebels must be left to handle the problem they alone had created. Dull-witted as she was, Marie understood and burst out laughing, promising to cooperate.

The next day she announced that her former Secretary would not seek a seat in Council. This so neatly answered the hopes of her little Court that they were stupefied, then alarmed. No question about it: M. de Luçon wanted to keep his hands clean and feel free to cast all the blame elsewhere! No, he must be made to assume his responsibilities!

Richelieu bowed to their wishes and took his place in Council, but remained silent until called on. Then, very gently, he told those worthy gentlemen that his opinion differed from theirs: the wise course was to make peace with the King, not to goad him, for there was no way of fighting him. Neither the Princes nor the Protestants were budging, but Schomberg's royal army was advancing.

Thus, Richelieu's good fortune was to be able to serve both parties, for in Paris there was rather feeble opposition to the Queen's intransigence, and the moment seemed ripe for reconciliation.

Bérulle, always faithful to the Queen, served as intermediary between the Court and Angoulême and was joined by Cardinal de La Rochefoucauld, also a friend of the bishop's. They both found it natural to consult their colleague, from whom the Queen hid nothing, so that Richelieu, as he had hoped, came into position to conduct the negotiations.

The conspirators had pulled his chestnuts out of the fire and were furious when they realized it. Epernon's gratuitous comment to the bishop was that he would do better to go back to his diocese than to make so many enemies for himself. Richelieu replied that he was there at the Queen's request that she was mistress and he would stay as long as she commanded it, that he did not seek to impose his friendship on anyone but could be helpful to those who wished him well.

In any event, his adversaries came nowhere near to presenting a common front. The Duke and Ruccellaï hated each other and were constantly trading threats and insults. The Abbé boldly suggested to Marie that she turn over the unbearable Duke to the King in order to improve her bargaining position. Richelieu stood firm against such treachery and, on another occasion, prevented Epernon from striking the priest.

So he kept his two rivals from each other's throats and molded the swooning, temperamental Queen to his own specifications.

The Duke of Rohan was furious at Richelieu's role as moderator: "The Bishop of Luçon," he wrote, "who would not allow the Queen Mother to go where her forces were strongest for fear he might lose control over her, convinced her to make a timid stand in a useless city . . . placing her in a shamefully conciliatory position from which he could make his peace and then enter into secret communication with the King's party."

It is likely that Richelieu did wish to reestablish this contact, but, under the circumstances, he cannot be accused of acting against the Queen's interests.

La Rochefoucauld and Bérulle returned from Paris laden with undreamed of offers, which the ministers had extended solely to stall off Marie de Medici and open up new bargaining sessions. For Schomberg's army was approaching, and once it opened a siege of Angoulême, the King would not be so accommodating.

Richelieu foiled this plan. To everyone's astonishment, the Queen accepted her son's terms unconditionally, announced that peace was restored, and ordered the *Te Deum* sung. It was a master stroke which left both Luynes and Epernon dumbfounded.

The Treaty of Angoulême was signed several days later and left Marie de Medici free to reside wherever she wished and to name her household officers. It exonerated her administration during the regency and legitimized her appeal for help to Epernon. Most important of all, it gave her sovereign rights in Normandy, not just nominal governorship, but exclusive control of the province and its strongholds. This provision was of supreme interest to Richelieu who thus would exercise power in the heart of a quasi-independent principality.

Another clause of the settlement was also extremely significant, though it remained unwritten. La Rochefoucauld and Bérulle, in their determination to make a success of the affair, had implicitly promised their friend a cardinal's hat. The ambitious Richelieu was dazzled by the prospect, and from then on the scarlet image became almost an obsession.

While waiting to enter the Sacred College, M. de Luçon had become a person of considerable distinction, in fact a party leader. Epernon's sole prize from the whole adventure was a diamond worth 36,000 écus, a gift from the Queen Mother, but Richelieu gained the experts' esteem both in France and abroad. "You have no idea how much he is praised," wrote the Papal Nuncio. His brilliance and his power, which came from domination of the Queen, were very apparent.

From prison, Condé sent his remembrances to proud Epernon; there was no trace of spite in the letter—at least none that met the eye— and the writer's tone was inordinately polite. The Prince had not yet reached the level of Sully, who "stewed in the bitterness of his disgrace" and conceived the idea of a match between one of his family, the proud and illustrious Béthunes, and the modest du Plessis.

Richelieu took this opportunity to weed out potential opposition in the Queen's circle. The Bishop of Béziers was dismissed, and the Bishop of Chartres turned over his office of Royal Chaplain to the devoted Bouthillier. Only Ruccellaï still held on, intriguing as usual and trying to salvage some fruit from all his efforts. M. de Luçon simply laughed at him.

Less amusing, however, was a measure the Queen insisted on taking and which he could not oppose: the release of Barbin. Anything might happen if his former protector suddenly reappeared. Fortunately, Louis XIII loathed Barbin, Concini's prime minister; as for Luynes, sowing discord among the enemy did not occur to him. Barbin was sent into exile.

His letters to Richelieu were full of bitterness. Here was the Bishop, his protégé, rising like a meteor while he, Barbin, faded out of sight, forgotten and destitute. M. de Luçon gave freely of his kind words and assurances: "God knows that I have treated you as I would have treated myself. . . . I shall always share with my friends the few worldly goods I have."

He shared nothing at all. Destiny had already made the choice between these two associates who were equally capable of ruling the country —and Richelieu was not a man to ease the rules of the game.

In this period he was fortunate in attracting the attention of two very different people. One was La Valette, Archbishop of Toulouse and Epernon's second son, whose admiration for the bishop was the source of a devoted friendship that was to leave its mark on history. The other was Fancan, Canon of Saint-Germain-l'Auxerrois, a priest of another cloth. He was an exceptionally shrewd politician, a pamphleteer with a barbed wit, and a double agent, who, using his robe as a shield served the Protestant cause while on the secret payroll of the Catholic Princes. He was active chiefly in rebellion-torn Germany.

This expert schemer also controlled the interests of a very excitable princess, Anne de Montafié, Countess of Soissons, who had joined the Queen Mother at Blois. Her brother was Dorval-Langlois, administrator for the Bishop of Luçon's diocese. This link brought him in contact with the future Cardinal in whose career he was to play a shadowy and important role.

Richelieu also made the acquaintance of Matthew de Morgues, Abbé of Saint-Germain, a gifted disputant who preached for and ardently supported the Queen Mother. For a while he worked closely with the bishop, but it was a temporary friendship, and later he became the Cardinal's most vociferous critic.

*

"It was clear already that he [Richelieu] wanted to govern and that there would be no rest until it happened."[1] This was sufficient cause for an opposition to gather, offering a rallying point for all of Luynes's enemies. Richelieu was in no sense a man who transcended his era— at least not yet—and with the same logic that had guided the nobility for over a century, and Concini as well, he set about building a fortress of his own power that would enable him to intimidate the Crown. For this reason he argued heatedly over the choice of cities which the Queen Mother would control.

Nantes, providing access to Spain and England, would have suited him, and Amboise, a stronghold on the Loire which in case of need would serve to keep the royal armies at a respectful distance. Luynes was not fool enough to accept; in the end he conceded Anjou, the fortresses of Angers and Chinon, and control over Ponts-de-Cé, another key point on the Loire. An entire feudal appanage was established in behalf of Marie de Medici and, especially, of the Richelieu family, whose eldest son the Marquis was appointed Governor of Angers.

It was too much of a good thing. Ruccellaï was furious and cynically offered his services to Luynes, then began plotting revenge by stirring up his friend Thémines, son of the Marshal, who had thought he was assured the post that went to the Marquis.

Thémines started spreading scurrilous remarks about his rival and, as was customary, on July 8 they met in a duel outside the Château d'Angers. The Marquis of Richelieu was stabbed straight through the heart.

His brother was inconsolable. Admittedly, an ambitious churchman was greatly advantaged by having a relative's sword to defend him, but the depth and sincerity of his distress is beyond question. For once, Richelieu reacted like an ordinary human being. He wrote that "the separation of mind and body cannot be effected without an immense effort of nature, and the separation of two minds so intimately linked

---

[1] Fontenay-Mareuil, *Mémoires.*

is not accomplished less painfully." And again: "Never was I so grieved. The loss of my own life would not have been as hurtful."

Unfortunately, the lament pictured in his *Mémoires* is somewhat marred by obvious hypocrisy: "I cannot describe the state of mind to which this mishap has brought me nor the grief which is beyond my pen; then and there *I would have ended everything had I not felt the interests of the Queen outweighed my own.*" M. de Luçon did not hold such unselfish devotion for the Queen.

His brother's death had two important results: it was the source of his hatred for dueling; and it proved to him, to use Talleyrand's expression, that he must build himself "a vast and massive fortune."

The fact that the Marquis left a debt-ridden estate and an incoherent will caused Richelieu considerable anxiety, for it compelled him to act in a humiliating fashion. He had to obtain an annulment of the wretched will on the grounds that its author was mentally disturbed. This is how we know that the head of the family suffered from the mental disorder that also showed up in his brother, Alphonse, and later in one of his sisters. The proud bishop must have found it agonizing, not only to have to admit such a blemish on the family honor, but to be called on to prove it. He resolved to avoid the pitfalls of poverty and began to take an interest in financial matters.

For the moment, his only treasure consisted in the person of Marie de Medici, and he took every precaution to protect her precious bulk. Governorship of Angers passed to his uncle, La Porte; his brother-in-law became Captain of the Guard; and one of his loyal adherents, Bettancourt, was made Governor of Chinon.

Henry IV's widow was his captive. Was her blind trust in him justified? There is proof that Richelieu favored his own interests above those of his patroness and was prepared to resume double-dealing if it could win him his scarlet hat. Apparently, the Court was unaware of Bérulle's promise, and the bishop was growing impatient.

When Luynes did not extend the hand of friendship, Richelieu attempted to thwart him and pulled the rug from under his feet by pressing the Queen to call for Condé's release, which Luynes planned to oppose. He renewed the ties between Marie and the Princes and even brought her closer to the Huguenots.

Above all, through a combination of brutal and subtle maneuvers, he posed objections to a meeting between mother and son. Luynes was most eager to have them publicly reconciled, having plenty of other problems on his hands, and for several months he made unsuccessful attempts in this direction. Strangely enough, it was Richelieu who gave way first, so exasperated was he over the delay in his promotion.

He left rather suddenly for Tours, where the King was enjoying a brief and euphoric honeymoon with Anne of Austria. At the end of five days, a meeting of reconciliation was arranged, to take place at the Château de Couzières, owned by the Duke of Montbazon, Luynes's father-in-law.

We do not know whether or not the scarlet hat was mentioned. In any event, while Richelieu's hopes grew, his impatience was in fact working against him once more, for by becoming dependent on Luynes he provided a weapon the latter was determined to use.

Marie de Medici arived at Couzières on September 4, 1619, Louis on the following day. Weeping, they embraced. The King confessed that he had longed to see her and gave free rein to his affection, believing he could satisfy it at last. All the bitter scenes of childhood became blurred. The first conquest of his manhood was his mother's love, which he had sought so long and so vainly.

"Heavens! You have grown up!" remarked the Queen.

"If I have done so, Madam, it is in order to serve you."

Marie cried but was unmoved, still rancorous and scheming. Suddenly she turned to Luynes: "Tell me what happened when Marshal d'Ancre died."

And at Vitry, now holding a Marshal's baton, she fired: "You, Sir, have always been most obedient and faithful to the King."

Soon other things began to irritate her. She found it especially unbearable to see the reigning Queen take precedence over her on all occasions, evidence of who was first lady of France. This was enough to turn the selfish, unsatisfied woman into the most spiteful mother-in-law.

Relations between Luynes and Richelieu became tense immediately. When Saint François de Sales passed through Tours where the sovereigns were staying, he noted: "It is like a swarm of angry wasps over a dead body."

Marie de Medici had summoned La Valette, Archbishop of Toulouse, who was Epernon's son and Richelieu's admirer, and she presented him to the King, singing his praises. Nothing could have pleased Luynes more, and he pounced on the opportunity: since this was the way things stood, the King, in deference to his mother, would solicit a cardinal's hat right away for . . . La Valette.

Richelieu was tricked. He concealed his bitterness and congratulated the Archbishop but, privately, he declared total war on Luynes. Henceforth, politics in France would reflect the rivalry of these two men.

In two weeks the meeting was over. The Queen Mother had been denied a seat in Council, and she refused to return to Paris, setting out instead for Angers. At Ponts-de-Cé she stopped to review an army of 10,000; after this show of force, she took up residence in the Logis Barrault, a magnificent private house where she held Court and managed to attract a good number of malcontents.

Luynes took revenge by having Condé released from prison. A Royal Declaration submitted to Parliament denounced "all those who would further destroy our kingdom by ruining our cousin." The Queen Mother protested loudly, and hostilities broke out again.

Luynes's insatiable greed furnished the opposition daily with new members. It was not enough that he and his brothers became dukes and peers; honors and pensions, governorships and fortresses, regiments, benefices—all these devolved upon his clan. "You would think," muttered Richelieu, "that France exists only for their benefit."

In fact, Luynes was building every possible defense against the man whose obloquy and rivalry he most feared.

XX

The Quest for a Scarlet Hat

DURING the winter of 1619–1620, the Court of Angers was a beehive of activity. All sorts of people poured into it, some bearing olive branches, others looking for trouble. Communications with the Louvre were intentionally hypocritical; sometimes there were honeyed messages, sometimes threats so layered with ambiguities that their content was scarcely recognizable.

The main question was whether or not the Queen Mother would return to Paris, Luynes favored it, and Richelieu seemed to concur, but neither believed in the other's sincerity. As always, M. de Luçon was after power which, in his eyes, had become inseparable from the cardinalate. His hope was that the Queen Mother would sit in Council and that he would be a prince of the Church. As long as these two conditions were unfulfilled, he intended to keep the fires of discord burning.

His attitude may appear extremely low-minded and egotistical in terms of Europe's destiny and the unity of France. But it is our belief that M. de Luçon sought pre-eminence in order to play the important role he envisaged as uniquely his. Meanwhile, he had to keep abreast of Court intrigues, Protestant agitation, and the machinations of Condé.

After three years of imprisonment, Condé was not cured even partially of his shameful diseases, his debauchery, his extravagances, or his avid and frenzied ambition. Soon he was behaving like a demagogue,

171

calling for violent application of the policies that Luynes would have preferred to impose in more subtle and insidious ways. Once the hope and security of the Protestants, he now attacked them with seeming fanaticism, deliberately inciting civil war, which events in Germany threatened to reinforce. Thus the weakness of the substructure—monarchical authority—caused the collapse of Henry IV's edifice of power. The situation was already at the chaotic level it had been before 1598, and France, after watching her international prestige crumble, now saw her internal peace threatened by old, half-forgotten hatreds.

Where did the responsibility lie for such a disaster? Some of it with the ultra-Catholics, too eager to give the impression that their aims had swung into line with Hapsburg policies. A good deal with the Protestants, whose ideal was a republic similar to the United Provinces of Holland, and who, in 1611, had begun to publish provocative manifestos. "The King is a minor, let us be majors!" was the challenge hurled by old Duplessis-Mornay.

Sully's voice rose even louder. But the graybeards would have acted more cautiously had they not been pressured by Bouillon, La Force, and Duke Henry de Rohan.

Rohan was rich and powerful, a man of heroic purpose, a good general, able diplomat, and excellent orator; with his immense following at home and abroad he ought to have been a top servant of the Crown, but, like so many of his class he preferred the tumultuous role of rebel chieftain to the more prosaic honor of being a loyal subject. Furthermore, should the direct heirs of Henry IV die out, Rohan would come into possession of the late King's native province, Béarn, the principal source of discord between the Court and the Huguenots.

Béarn had remained Calvinist since the time of Jeanne d'Albret,[1] and the Edict of Nantes had not been applied there with regard to restoration of Catholic worship or restitution of Church property. A proclamation of June 25, 1617, ordering implementation of these measures had caused serious disorders. The young King, extremely sensitive to any breach of his authority, was thus very ill-disposed to the Huguenots, an attitude shared by his confessor and other influential priests such as Father Joseph and Bérulle. Luynes, siding with the Catholic party, was no more friendly. Not a single minister, not even the venerable President

[1] Henry IV's mother. (Trans.)

Jeannin, seemed to recall the important lessons that emerged during Henry IV's reign.

In this general atmosphere, the King of France was called on suddenly to take a stand in the conflict between the two religious groups. Since the defenestration at Prague, the Protestants' anti-Austrian campaign had progressed very slowly. They were awaiting the signal for an all-out battle at the death of Emperor Matthias. This half-civilized ruler, who had completely despoiled his brother Rudolf, spent his last days bemoaning the legacy of disasters he predicted. He died on March 20, 1619.

With that, the Protestants unleashed an offensive labeled an international conspiracy by the Jesuits. A giant wave swept from Navarre to Germany and from Holland into England. Bohemia, refusing to recognize Ferdinand of Austria, proclaimed as sovereign the Elector Palatine, Frederick V. Hungary turned to the Transylvanian Prince, Bethlen Gabor. The entire edifice of Hapsburg power would have crumbled had it not been for the efforts of the Jesuits and their disciple, Ferdinand, who succeeded at the last moment in making himself Emperor.

Another Catholic noble, Maximilian of Bavaria, formed a league, gathered an army and promised support to the new Caesar. But he could not meet the combined opposition of Bohemians, Bethlen Gabor, and the Evangelical Union of the German Protestant princes, with its troops under the fierce Manfeld's command.

Ferdinand called for help to the entire Catholic world and sent an ambassador to the French king whose father had struggled so long against Ferdinand's family. Frederick V remembered this and hastened to do the same. France was once more the arbiter between nations.

Unfortunately, we do not know what Richelieu's attitude was in this situation. Had he been in power, would he have challenged the Catholic front and dismantled the Austrian fortress for France's benefit as well as the Protestants' and the Ottoman Empire's? In any event, he alone would have been able to evaluate the consequences of a decision whereby the inexperienced Louis XIII was to involve all of Europe.

The King first sent contradictory assurances to Ferdinand. Then his Council examined the three possible solutions: to reverse current policy, by reverting to Henry IV's strategy and polishing off the House of Austria (which would have opened the door to French supremacy and a Protestant triumph); or, as advocated by Bouillon, to propose, meaning impose, a settlement; or to behave as a purely Catholic power and support the Hapsburgs (which would avoid risks and maintain a principle at the cost of an abdication).

The myopic ministers who had to solve this problem were both cowardly and fearful of irritating Luynes. President Jeannin summarized the French position: "His Majesty is forced to aid the House of Austria against the host of her enemies whose triumph would endanger greatly the religion she professes." The Duke of Angoulême, illegitimate son of Charles IX, was chosen to act as ambassador and try to work out a peaceful settlement, that is to say, try to save the Hapsburg Empire.

On hearing this, the Papal Nuncio exclaimed: "It is a miracle, a manifestation of Divine Will!"

The miracle led to a century of lunatic wars—and also to Richelieu's glory.

*

"You know Sir, that I am neither inclined nor in a position to deceive anyone [!]" wrote Luçon's bishop to Luynes, "and since it is my ardent desire to serve the King as well as the Queen, I am truly your servant. The Queen's purpose is to live in peace and harmony. . . . I beg you to believe this because I know it is true. *But it is impossible for her not to resent acts which she considers prejudicial to her interests.*"

The tone was becoming more strident. With the Duke of Angoulême on his way to Germany, Luynes was convinced he had made a shrewd political move; actually, he had outfoxed himself and was standing on the edge of an abyss. Everyone was against him and, at the same time, against the Crown: the Queen Mother, public opinion, Parliament, the Sorbonne, the Protestants, the Court, and the Princes, whom the clever Countess of Soissons had agitated because of her anger at Condé's return and her ambitions for her son.

This dangerous woman persuaded her lover, the Duke of Mayenne, who was the most popular member of the Guise family, as well as her son-in-law, the Duke of Longueville, and the Duke of Vendôme to leave the Court and prepare the way for revolt in their provinces. All of them pledged loyalty to Marie de Medici, who rapturously watched her power grow from day to day.

Her Councilors were pressing her to make an open break, all of them except her confessor, Father Suffren, the austere Michel de Marillac, and the Bishop of Luçon.

The latter took care to leave posterity a record of his wise council. We are reluctant to accept it, for in fact the Cardinal often resorted to this method of defending a thesis which he knew in advance would not find approval. Such was the case in 1620.

Certain writers have maintained that Richelieu carried his double-dealing to the limit and, while appearing to serve the aims of the Queen, actually worked for her defeat. This is hypothetical, and we prefer to rely on the statement of Marillac. "All the plans and preparations were made under M. de Luçon's direction. . . . Upon his shoulders rested the entire responsibility of managing affairs and handling all persons, both the good and the bad."

For he had reached the point where he was willing to seize the power and honors that Luynes refused to grant him. This attitude clearly places Richelieu in the context of his era, the period of great disorder preceding the great order of Louis XIV, when anarchy was a prelude to unity and reckless passions left France prey to the crises of a sort of daredevil, tormented adolescence.

In 1620, using somewhat refined tactics, Richelieu was acting against the King just as the feudal lords had been doing since the Middle Ages, and had gathered a coalition which was altogether menacing: Marie de Medici, mistress of Anjou; Bouillon and Rohan (who together represented the Protestants and the provinces of Poitou, Béarn, and Sedan); Epernon (Metz, Angoumois, Guyenne); the Vendôme family (Brittany); Mayenne (Saintonge); Longueville (Normandy); Soissons (Perche)— all of them threatening the King and Paris. Marillac pledged an army of 50,000.

Luynes wavered and shuffled, to Condé's great indignation, and finally could make up his mind only to send an embassy consisting of a duke, a cardinal, and some monks to Angers in search of a compromise. On June 29, after learning that the Countess of Soissons and her son in turn were leaving the capital, thus giving the signal for civil war, Luynes still hesitated and consulted Jeannin. The old man's baleful advice was not to lift a finger.

So Mme la Comtesse [2] departed undisturbed on July 1—whereupon

---

[2] *M. le Comte* and *Mme la Comtesse* were titles reserved for the Soissons family.

a section of Normandy rose in revolt and one of Vendôme's lieutenants seized Caen. Even Paris seemed unsafe. Never had the monarchy been in such great danger since the advent of the Bourbon dynasty. For its defense there were barely two hundred cavalry and three thousand foot soldiers.

Once again the Council had to make a decision which would affect the entire course of French history. As usual, it responded faintheartedly, ready to capitulate to the nobles as it had done with the Hapsburgs. The King had no choice but to entrench himself in Paris and try to halt the insurgents with the same methods that prefaced the Treaties of Sainte-Menehould and of Loudun. Besides, the Councilors were not agreed as to how to begin the cowardly procedure and argued about it pitiably. Then, to everyone's astonishment, the voice of the nineteen-year-old sovereign rang out: "Among all the dangers facing us, we must deal with the greatest and most pressing ones, which are in Normandy. My opinion is to make straight for there and not sit about in Paris waiting to see my kingdom torn to pieces and my faithful subjects oppressed."

Such was Louis XIII's first manifestation of his own will in the conduct of national affairs. It completely changed the face of things. On July 7, 1620, the son of Henry IV, wearing his suit of armor for the first time, struck out for the rebellious province with a handful of men. On the 10th he entered Rouen; meeting no resistance he then attacked. Caen was alerted and did not prove so easy a prey. It was a well fortified and stubborn city which had once dealt a stunning defeat to Henry IV. A repetition of the event would ruin His Majesty's prestige, dissolve his army, and open Paris to the troops of the Queen Mother. Louis silenced the graybeards and, without a single stammer, raised the cry: "Forward to Caen!"

He was at the gates of the city on the morning of July 15 and attacked the château at three. Caen fell on the 17th. That very day, solely through his own efforts, Louis resurrected the monarchy.

The King's personal victory had a tremendous effect and evoked broad popular enthusiasm. Richelieu, already anticipating a siege of Paris, was amazed. He compared the strength that the King's determination inspired in his subjects, even the lowliest ones, to the confusion spread among the rebels by their rivalries and personal ambition.

On August 2 Louis had reached Le Mans, his white standard, symbol of supreme command, floating above the troops led by Condé. On the

7th, in torrid heat, he opened his first battle—against his mother—at a quarter to two in the afternoon. By eight that evening, Ponts-de-Cé, key crossing on the Loire, was taken; the rebels were in headlong flight and the civil war was over.

Louis's campaign had two important results. Foremost, France discovered that she had an intrepid king "whose enemies would have to face his tireless energy and unflagging courage." Second, Richelieu learned a lesson that he later recorded: "Those who combat lawful power are already doomed to defeat, for they confront the enemy with a vision of the executioner before their eyes, and the odds are against them."

At Angers, "Fear was in command and left no place at all for reason." In the midst of the "terrifying terror" that paralyzed the Queen as well as her women, the priests, and the nobility, M. de Luçon alone was undismayed. He was the only one to realize what an opportunity awaited the losers for Luynes was as petrified as the rebels by Condé's success and the King's martial spirit. Vittorio Sirri has missed the point when he states that "Richelieu was really responsible for the destruction of this powerful party as well as the ruin of the Queen, his mistress." On the contrary, he saved Marie de Medici, for as he later explained her victory would have brought her downfall.

The day after the rout, Marie sent her beloved bishop as ambassador to her son. Louis, Luynes, and Condé received him with open arms. Luynes could not wait to draw the curtain on this "amusing episode." From the start, Richelieu spoke as if the Queen's troops had triumphed, and no one countered him. The preliminaries were signed on August 10 and simply confirmed the Treaty of Angoulême. Not a single rebel suffered for his treason. The King even paid his mother's debts, while she simply pledged to keep the peace.

There was only one seeming victor, Richelieu himself, for Luynes promised him the scarlet hat that motivated the first civil war since the end of the Holy League.

On August 13 Louis met his mother at Brissac. Both were overjoyed, she at having paid no penalty for her foolish acts, he at the discovery of his gift for leadership. The conflict proved to the young King, still suffering the effects of his childhood and painfully conscious of his failings, that he could triumph as a sovereign and a soldier. He was elated.

Similarly, the two favorites met and made their own settlement, guaranteed by their mutual fear of Condé. Again, Richelieu had an advantage over Luynes, for the latter was in greater fear of the newly emerged King than of Condé. Overnight, Louis XIII had taken a liking to cross-country rides and battles. The question was whether he would remain devoted to his peaceable and cautious friend, who, though a great hunter, had no penchant for the glories of combat.

So Luynes sought a means of neutralizing his rival. During their meeting he spoke at great length, deploying all his charm; and, as if wooing the friendship of a neighboring monarch, he offered to seal their pact by the marriage of his nephew, M. de Combalet, to Richelieu's niece, Mlle de Vignerod du Pont de Courlay—a suggestion that had come from Father Joseph. As for the cardinal's hat, at this very moment a messenger was galloping toward Rome with a letter from Puisieux to the French ambassador, Marquis de Coeuvres, advising that "His Majesty had named M. de Luçon to the cardinalate" and instructing him "to pursue the matter with all possible haste."

Richelieu responded with a flood of fine sentiments, and Luynes was already pocketing his triumph when, to his dismay, the bishop added: "But to insure a lasting covenant each of the parties must occupy his rightful place, and it is only fitting that those who ought to be in the front rank of government shall be there."

He was intent on reseating the Queen Mother in Council and, by extension, himself. If Luynes conceded, he would be committing political suicide so he dodged the question. After all, theirs was only an armed peace.

Richelieu had been wrong to test "how far he could go." His impatience was always betraying him.

On the heels of a rebellion that by all standards ought to have ruined him, his position remained extremely strong. Apart from the Huguenots and himself, the entire opposition had been wiped out. It was general knowledge that he represented a challenge to the government, whose every error and abuse would serve him as springboards to power. In the same way, he planned to exploit the violence of Condé, who was discredited everywhere save in the King's eyes.

With all this, his main weapon remained his cleverness at sidetracking others. Deluding the amorous Juno was child's play. On the other hand, the churchmen and the legal profession were always groping their way in the dark, yet even they were able to see that he championed their cause, "Catholicity."

Father Joseph had had to resign himself to the failure of his crusade. Still eager to do battle for the Church, he now opened an assault on heresy with all the fury he had once leveled at the infidels. In his estimation, Richelieu was the only one capable of destroying the kind of Protestant State which the Edict of Nantes had engendered. Henceforth, he attached himself even more closely to the bishop, became "his confidant, his adviser, his spy, and his protector."

And protection was of enormous value to Richelieu not only against his enemies but against his own weaknesses. He was high-strung and needed a calming influence, hypersensitive and wanted the outlet for candor which a trusted friend could provide. There was no such friendship to be found among the beasts of prey at Court, the schemers whose second nature was to betray, the narrow-minded priests, or even the courtiers who, despite their loyalty, had no loftiness of spirit.

Father Joseph with his intense convictions, his unselfishness and discretion, his penetrating knowledge of humanity, his great intelligence and courage, seemed to have been sent by Providence to aid and encourage Richelieu's ambitions and never to offend him. It was his good fortune to be associated with this monk who was also prophet, ambassador, secret agent, and hatchet-man.

"*Ezechieli! Tenebroso! Cavernoso!*" was the future Cardinal's jesting invocation to this bristly bearded visionary in whose company he found enjoyment, even laughter, which was rare for him.

XXI

Luynes's Strategy

W HILE Louis XIII was snuffing out civil war in France, the
Duke of Angoulême arrived at Ulm, where a parley was in
progress between representatives of the Emperor, the Protestant Union, the Evangelical Union, and the Elector Palatine whom Louis
had refused to recognize. Emperor Ferdinand summoned Duke Maximilian of Bavaria to send reinforcements, without which he had no hope
of resisting the Bohemian insurgents, but the Duke did not budge, fearing
that his own States would be invaded immediately thereafter by the
armies of the Protestant Union.

The French embassy bent over backward to solve this problem for
Maximilian, bringing the Protestant princes round to signing a treaty with
their Catholic compatriots, excluding the Emperor, Bohemia, and Frederick. Seeing the latter completely isolated and Bavaria saved, Maximilian
sent forces to aid Ferdinand.

Spain, for her part, had been manifestly slow to intervene, but now
she sent 25,000 soldiers to the Palatinate. Bethlen Gabor, the Transylvanian was getting nervous, and he, too, received a word of caution from
Paris, so he halted his movements.

Such was the situation when the naïve ambassadors of His Most
Christian Majesty, after concluding the Peace of Ulm, moved on to bring

the olive branch to Vienna. They were laughed at. After providing what was expected of her, France came off with only a "lukewarm and ineffectual influence." The idea was to pay off her good services before she offered any more. They were promptly forgotten. Quite by chance, a maneuver on the part of Luynes and Jeannin turned the mission into a diplomatic defeat.

In Valtellina, nerve center of Europe, the House of Austria gained an even greater victory. There, as in Germany, Protestants and Catholics were fiercely opposed. With the support of Milan's Spanish governor, the Catholics massacred Huguenot families, threw out the Grisons, and put the valley under Spain's control.

This was the dreaded great offensive launched by the two-headed Hapsburg eagle which, shortly before his death, Henry IV had wanted to avert by striking first. Venice, frantic at finding the route into Italy exposed, called to France for help, but France herself was threatened in the Hapsburg squeeze.

There was still time for change. Spain, short of funds and alarmed by a revolt in Naples, did not have the means to wage a large-scale war. Ferdinand II's throne was becoming shaky, and the Bohemians were threatening Vienna.

The Huguenot nobles, whose principal spokesman, Bouillon, was serving as adviser to the Elector Palatine, should have pressed the King to intervene and tip the scales of power. But theirs was the fatal mistake of collaborating in the intrigues of Spanish agents instructed to paralyze Louis XIII. "Rome's and Madrid's emissaries did everything possible to raise the revolt in France. . . . In their view, the surest means was to induce the King to attack his own subjects." [1]

The Huguenots had supported Marie's foolish adventure, and when civil war broke out, "the factious majority [of the party] took control, some acting out of rash fervor, others in the hope of exploiting the chaos for their own gain." [2] This was especially true in Béarn, where Governor La Force envisioned carving himself a little sovereign state as Lesdiguières had done in Dauphiné.

Following his victory, Louis XIII had a fine army and reserves of energy at his command. If he directed these against Spain by turning toward the Alps and reoccupying Valtellina, he could foul the grand

[1] Levassor, *Histoire de Louis XIII.*
[2] Bouffard de Madiane, *Mémoires.*

design of the Hapsburgs and restore the influence and prestige that France had not known since his father's reign.

In his *Mémoires* Richelieu states that he advocated this action, which conforms to his future policies. In any event, he could not support it openly, for his Catholic friends—above all, the Queen Mother and Father Joseph—were begging the King to stamp out heresy. Louis himself, not yet able to grasp the enormity of events on the European scene, was intent on teaching a lesson to the insolent province of Béarn: "I have borne this contempt too long," as he put it.

He left Brissac for Poitiers where the Huguenots, terrified lest he bring the army to Pau, sent emissaries to him. "We protest our readiness to receive Your Majesty's commands. to respect your will, and to restore the property [of the clergy] which has been in our possession until this time."

Would the young sovereign be satisfied with this, forget the rebellious province, and seek the path of greater glory that his father had outlined? It was the last thing in the world the Catholic faction wanted. Bentivoglio, the Nuncio, came running to remind the King that the interests of the Church must be maintained. Condé promised that nothing short of annihilation would keep Béarn's Huguenots from rising again. Churchmen preached a holy war. Bérulle proclaimed: "God himself beckons the King not to leave the task unfinished. Since Providence has brought peace to the land, the King, in gratitude to God, must restore the true faith and its ministers in a province where for sixty years heresy has outlawed the Catholic religion."

Luynes alone could have checked the current and shown Louis the path to grandeur. Unfortunately, if indeed he was able to see the situation clearly, he was fearful of Condé's demagogy and even more fearful of offending his master, who was impatient to ride out at the head of his troops.

In the end, this last consideration won out, and the expedition to Béarn was decided upon. No one could imagine its effect on world history, the seas of blood that would flow, or the tremendous effort that would be spent in erasing its consequences.

*

Even if M. de Luçon had glimpsed the terrible days to follow, he certainly would have hesitated to intervene, for on the eve of his cardinalate, he was careful to avoid offending the King or his favorite. "The reconciliations are complete," he wrote, "and I believe that since they were dictated by reason, they will endure." A surprising naïveté. The bishop was forgetting that by having bared his weapons inopportunely, he had rekindled the vengeful distrust of Luynes.

Before starting out on the campaign, Luynes took advantage of the Nuncio's presence in Poitiers to arrange a secret meeting at which Puisieux was the only other person present.

Luynes told Bentivoglio that the King had designated Luçon for the cardinalate and that the idea so enchanted the Queen Mother that she would brook no opposition. But, he went on to say confidentially, it was to be understood that the honor was only a formality. Even the French ambassador was unaware of the true situation, and they were allowing him to go ahead with the usual overtures. "But now that you know the truth," he continued, "tell Rome about it. The King intends to prevent this appointment at all costs. . . . The bishop is really mad! It is he who has turned the kingdom upside down and has caused all the trouble. . . . And now he would be the one to profit by it!"

Bentivoglio detested Richelieu and was delighted to hear all this, but also curious to know the speaker's real motives, so he questioned him further. Luynes fairly exploded, calling the bishop an ungrateful wretch. After he, Luynes, had gone out of his way to help him, had saved him after Marshal d'Ancre's death and had kept him close to the Queen Mother, Richelieu was still his worst enemy. They were going to have him watched. If he had really changed his ways, they would see; there was plenty of time to make him a cardinal. For the moment, let him wait! The King was fed up with always rewarding the biggest muddleheads among his subjects. But Richelieu's exclusion from the cardinalship must remain secret, a top secret.[3]

The elated Nuncio found this highly edifying and grabbed his pen to dash off the news to Rome. Meanwhile, the impatient bishop did his best to rouse Marie de Medici from her usual listlessness, sometimes cajoling her, sometimes raising a storm or brooding in despair. The Queen Mother summoned the Nuncio and made a fuss over him, begging him to make efforts on her friend's behalf. Bentivoglio found this game very entertaining, the more so when M. de Luçon himself came to peti-

[3] Based on letters of Bentivoglio dated September 6 and 7 and October 13, 1620 (*Nunziatura*, vol. IV).

tion his favor and to declare his complete obedience to the Holy Father. "The Queen must be out of her mind," he wrote to Cardinal Neveu. "As for this bishop, his ambitions are uncontrollable. God will bow his pride. What a rebuff it will be when he finds himself excluded!"

Even as he rode towards Béarn, Luynes continued to feed his rival's illusions. "I am very happy," he wrote Richelieu, "that you realize how hard I have worked to help your affair in Rome. . . . We shall keep up the same pressures we have brought heretofore." And later: "I would die rather than fail in my promise to you!"

However, the Bishop of Orléans, friendly to Richelieu and bearing no grudge despite the fact that he had done him out of the office of Chaplain, was charitable—or perhaps malicious—enough to warn him that "a knight of the Order told me yesterday your promotion was not yet certain and that the Pope has been advised of three things which can harm you: when you were in Rome you took an oath that you were of age when you were not; while you were Secretary of State you did everything you possibly could against the Holy See; lately you tried to incite the Huguenots to take arms in support of the Queen Mother."

Torn between hope and anxiety, Richelieu watched from afar while the King led his expedition across Protestant-controlled provinces. Once again he realized the astounding effect of the royal presence. Wherever the King appeared, Frenchmen fell into a sort of ecstasy, forgetting their perverse fondness for discord. This fervor constituted the real security of the nation, a bond of unity. Nothing could take its place.

As hard as he tried, La Force could not prevent Louis from reaching Béarn, the Huguenots' impregnable bastion for sixty years. "La Force," the King told him, "it is to your interest that I enter Pau in order to bolster your failing strength."

Where, now, was the timid boy, the most childlike of children?

On October 15 he made a solemn entrance into Pau, restored Catholicism, abolished the province's sovereign councils, and at last reunited Béarn with the monarchy. Remorselessly he destroyed the life work of his grandmother, Jeanne d'Albret, a disciple of Calvin, whose puritanism, tenacity, and narrow sense of duty seemed to have rubbed off on her.

On November 7 the King was back in Paris, drinking in the wild acclamation that greeted him; it was like the total approbation of a fond parent he never had, a justification of his use of gentle persuasion instead of violence.

Two days later, Bohemia was in upheaval. The imperial army under its mercenary general, Tilly, seized Prague after crushing the Bohemian forces in the battle of the White Mountain. It heralded "the restoration of the House of Austria, Spanish control of the Rhine, the gradual defeat of the Elector Palatine in his own States, and the growing shadow over Europe of a restored Hapsburg Empire." [4]

It is a curious fact that the Duke of Angoulême, head of the deplorable mission whose success had brought on the disaster, was the first to recognize its gravity. He immediately wrote to the King begging him to revert to his father's policies: "For if the House of Austria were to succeed in dominating the Empire, it would be a blow to the entire Christian world. We must guard against the ambitious and fanciful goal of world domination. We must prevent this fearful thing from happening."

Richelieu could not have stated it better. But Richelieu never said a word, so absorbed was he in the growing suspense and anxiety over his promotion. Instead of taking Luynes to task, he sent him renewed vows of devotion and friendship. And the favorite's reply was full of cunning irony: "You need hardly reassure me of your affection, for I have no doubt. . . . Henceforth let us act, and say no more."

The action he had in mind was allowing the Pope to take sole responsibility for the refusal so as not to incur Marie de Medici's wrath, for, as time for the promotion drew near, she tormented him like some enormous wasp. He also spoke to the Nuncio in an ambiguous manner, and Bentivoglio, smelling a trap, pressed him for an explanation. Exasperated, Luynes "clarified" his point: if the bishop became cardinal, it was all right; if not, it would be even better.

Such was the cynical craft of Luynes. Louis XIII was not yet twenty and was totally inexperienced in politics. Although he had restored the Crown's authority and was now determined to take the nation's responsibilities on his own shoulders, he left the solution of critical matters to his older friend, who continued to exert a strong attraction on him.

Unfortunately, this agreeable gentleman, whose responsibility it was to regulate the Court, was not equipped to guide a kingdom under stress.

[4] Gabriel Hanotaux, op. cit.

Despite the haunting fear of disgrace, he still hung jealously on to the power that terrified him. "You tried to grasp his intentions but they were beyond his own understanding."

After the events in Bohemia, Luynes tried to maneuver, and with more ability than is usually attributed to him. England was up in arms on hearing of the battle of the White Mountain, the Catholic triumph, and the desperate flight of Frederick and his wife, daughter of King James I. Luynes began negotiating a marriage between the Prince of Wales and Henrietta, Louis XIII's youngest sister, with a view to restoring a European balance of power. He laid the framework for a pact of friendship between Venice and Savoy. Bassompierre, French ambassador to Spain, was able to conclude the Treaty of Madrid, under which the Grisons were to regain control of Valtellina. When troops were suddenly called up, there was general confusion as to whether they would occupy that valley or fight the Huguenots.

For at this moment France was in the grip of a new crisis. Alarmed and angered by the events in Béarn, the Protestants had called an Assembly in La Rochelle. The King's interdiction was ignored, and the Assembly met on December 25, 1620.

It was all too evident that the Edict of Nantes, with its ninety-five open articles and fifty-six secret ones, was a Trojan Horse installed in the very heart of the nation.

No modern State could heap such advantages on a group of its own nationals as those enjoyed by the Huguenot subjects of Louis XIII: their own law courts, the right to organize into "circles" or assemblies, political institutions providing a built-in nucleus of rebellion, 150 strongholds commanding half the nation's territory and manned by troops paid by the State Treasury yet responsible only to Huguenot generals.

In addition, 3,500 nobles were in a position to raise an army of 25,000 against the Crown; yet of that number there were scarcely 200 who were willing to give their lives for their faith.

But in 1620 religion was not the cause at stake. Despite the exalted preaching of a Du Perron, a Bérulle, or the Jesuits, Louis XIII had no intention of restricting the freedom of belief or of worship guaranteed by the Edict of Nantes, and he repeatedly affirmed this. What he did want was to force the Protestants to recognize his authority and end their political divisiveness. Later on, Louis XIV sought to complete the unity of his kingdom through uniformity of religion, but this was not his predecessor's aim.

As Cardinal, Richelieu's policy reflecting toleration and a horror of disorder was actually the doctrine of Louis XIII, but in 1620 the bishop wisely avoided defending it against his ultra-Catholic friends.

The Assembly of La Rochelle established a type of government resembling an authoritarian democracy. Its executive branch was a staff appointed for periods of three months. In the legislative arm, the deputies were not free to vote as they pleased but had to conform to instructions from their churches; this favored the radical-minded communes over the great nobles who were less uncompromising. A military budget was drawn up and defenses reinforced. In Montauban, the Protestants turned the Catholics out of the city.

This is how things stood when, on January 11, 1621, the promotion of cardinals was announced. La Valette was among them; Richelieu was not.

It was a great blow. Never, however, had the ambition-driven man, so emotional under his armor of ice, controlled himself so well. This time he did not give into discouragement and despair. He even resisted the temptation to unleash the Queen Mother and break with Luynes. A direct attack on the favorite would have stirred the King's hostility; it was safer to let the wretch founder in the quagmires of European and domestic affairs. And, while waiting for that to happen, he would remain perfectly serene.

His letter mentioning the event to Father Joseph was philosophic: "In France the best solution is patience."

The patience of a tiger.

XXII

The Eagle and Juno

OULD France confront the Austrian menace and leave the Protestants free to spread chaos at home? Could she afford another period of civil war when danger beyond her borders was so great? Public opinion, which can always be relied on for contradictions, was equally hostile to a pro-Spanish and a pro-Huguenot policy, as was the King.

The entire responsibility for a decision fell upon Luynes, who was not equipped to handle increasingly complicated issues and whose nerves showed signs of wear; his irritability and arrogance were reminiscent of a Sully or an Epernon. His conduct was scarcely becoming, and Louis XIII began to take offense, but the King was persistently loyal to his friend and still wanted to give him a fair chance.

Luynes was trapped between Condé, still eager to destroy the party he had formerly led, and the Queen Mother, his implacable enemy since the affair of the cardinalate. Richelieu steered clear of conflicts—at least for the moment—while Marie de Medici made sentimental overtures to obtain a seat for herself in the Council "saying that a mother understands best the interests of her son."

One of her pamphleteers, Chanteloube, came out with the *Comtadin Provençal*, which took Luynes to task and concluded with an echo of its patroness's complaints: "The names of mother and son cannot be separated. The prosperity of Luynes and his relatives rests upon maintaining the division of Their Majesties. And this is the root of all the trouble."

Long before the existence of newspapers, press campaigns were carried on through the medium of these lampoons, called *"bleuets"* because of their blue covers. Richelieu understood their importance through his acquaintance with Canon Fancan. This secret agent doubling as pamphleteer had a fantastic scheme which impressed the bishop very much. Fancan was one of the few persons whose advice he sought, and received in quantity—cynical advice, his critics assert, though his admirers say he had an apostle's ardor and the vision of a great statesman.

Fancan was pensioned by the Catholic princes of Germany but was working for the Protestant cause. He pressed Richelieu to advocate European intervention as against civil war. Naturally, Father Joseph preached the opposite view.

The Council of Ministers reflected the same divergence, with the balance shifting back and forth. As on countless occasions in the previous century, the Protestants took it upon themselves to aggravate the mounting disorder. Pressured by outbreaks of violence, their Assembly issued a "general directive" which, by providing for division of the kingdom into eight military zones, made this senseless war inevitable. Twenty-five years after the last holocaust, Frenchmen were ready again to spill each other's blood and turn their backs on the rest of Europe.

Luynes was not happy about this policy since the King had developed a hearty appetite for military exploits and intended to ride out at the head of his troops with all his generals in the front rank. Yielding to some wild fancy, the favorite had himself appointed Constable, that is, commander-in-chief of the army. The Court wits agreed that he picked the right moment, for war would teach him his trade.

Richelieu was pleased. He advised the Queen Mother to tread softly and to join the expedition. She must remain near her son. Indeed, the King had made it a habit again to see her regularly.

The Queen Mother and her inseparable counselor thus seemed to be supporting Luynes's policy. But at this time a pamphlet appeared, entitled "The Salutary Discourse and Advice of Dying France to the King." In it, France beseeched the King "and all good Frenchmen" to open their eyes, recognize their real enemies, the Spaniard and the Austrian, and not to coerce the Protestants. "Souls and consciences cannot be shackled; they pay no heed to the sword, the gibbet, or the fire."

It went on to say that Henry IV would have wept to see the state of his kingdom and the wretched condition of his widow, dragging along with the army "like a camp follower for some German foot soldiers." Luynes was denounced as having sold out France to Catholic Spain.

This manifesto outlined the tenets of a new party, the "Good Frenchmen," whose program closely resembled the Cardinal's. It is difficult to believe that Richelieu was a stranger to the movement which developed through Fancan's efforts.

It took considerable audacity, even if the purpose was only to discomfit the new Constable, to support a cause that was odious to both the Queen Mother and the clergy. But if M. de Luçon had Fancan behind him, he also had Father Joseph, his reliable guarantor vis-à-vis the Catholic party, to serve as a shield while Fancan did his work. Later, he disavowed the trouble-making canon, sent him to the Bastille, and may have had him put to death there. The *Mémoires* accuse him of having been a traitor, a spy, and a republican.[1] Meanwhile, the bishop applied Fancan's "maxims" and encouraged him to follow up the "Discourse" with "Protests to the King" and a "Chronicle of the Favorites," which were no less explosive.

Historians such as Gabriel Hanotaux take the year 1621 to mark the conception of Richelieu's achievement, a great monument of classic order, majestic proportions, and Cartesian logic. During the first twenty years of that prodigiously fantastic century before losing even the notion of fantasy, Richelieu seemed to have codified French policy just as, in the theater, the rules of drama had been systematized. He, too, observed three unities, order, authority, and national independence, as basic to his triple goal: to humble the Princes, to destroy the Huguenot party yet leave the Protestant faith intact, and to replace Hapsburg leadership with Bourbon hegemony so as to make the King an absolute monarch in France and a predominating influence in Europe.

As Gabriel Hanotaux noted: "This is the policy conceived by Richelieu when he was still among the opposition. He wanted to harness all passions to his chariot and make their collective ardor serve the common good. Religion, whether Catholic or Protestant, became both whip and rein for him. He would guide them all with a steady hand, as he expressed it himself, toward the goal he projected for the nation's welfare."

Actually, Richelieu's thinking had none of the rigidity that his *Testa-*

[1] Admittedly, this passage may be apocryphal. Richelieu's *Mémoires* are not an entirely reliable source.

ment Politique seems to suggest. Watching the upheavals in France and in Europe, he understood the vital necessity of challenging Austrian ambitions as well as tripping an embittered minority of its means of warring against the Crown. The two statements appear to contradict each other; his discernment told him that, despite hardened opinion, both were true. This was already a great step, and it is doubtful that he went beyond it.

Mignet asserted, and others have often repeated, that Richelieu "intended to do everything he did." Perhaps, but his intentions were neither simultaneous nor parts of a preordained system; they grew out of each other or out of circumstances. Richelieu was a pragmatist, not a doctrinaire.

In 1621 his path was strewn with obstacles. First, he needed power; after that, there would be time to maneuver and avoid the pitfalls, even "to reach a goal, as oarsmen do, by turning your back to it."

If Richielieu was able to distinguish this goal, he had no idea yet what was beyond it. He was like an archaeologist about to dig for treasure, unaware that before finding it he would have to construct a whole subterranean city.

Even in these terms, the scope of his vision is scarcely imaginable considering that he had only one tool to work with. The fact is that despite his recognized abilities and several useful friendships, the Bishop of Luçon was hated by the King, was a rival of the all-powerful Constable, and would have been entirely isolated had the Queen Mother not been at his mercy.

The sole instrument of Richelieu's ambition was that enormous, dull-witted matron, with her moods and languor and violence, her bigotry and capacity for the lowest acts, her lack of feeling and hopeless inability to understand anything around her. Because she was the wife and mother of kings and had been consecrated in the Cathedral of Saint-Denis, and especially because she was fascinated with a handsome prelate, this bovine Juno, like Homer's own, was the only one who could give the eagle his wings and send him on his way to change the course of History.

Indeed, History often allows some very strange impulses to guide her steps.

*

As soon as they reached Saumur, where the King took over the government from old Duplessis-Mornay, the "Huguenots' Pope," and raised the famous cry "Long live my people!", Marie de Medici displayed her nasty temper on finding that the Constable had taken the apartments that were to have been hers. Nevertheless, she accompanied her son to the siege of Saint-Jean-d'Angely where M. de Soubise, Rohan's brother, faced the royal army.

This siege lasted from May 31 until June 24. The Queen Mother soon became bored with it, for springtime had inspired her with fancies far removed from warfare. Paying no heed to gossip, she went off to spend several days in near privacy with her adored bishop at the little priory of Coussay. The incident was so extraordinary that no official document mentions it; fortunately for us, letters exchanged by the two of them and by observers were less discreet.

Richelieu's pride must have taken a bound when his ordinary house was host to Henry IV's widow, for it proved to the astonished world how attached and subservient she was to him.

Saint-Simon was the first to describe their walks, when the bishop's purple chimer would brush against the love-struck lady's immense span of farthingale. Their intimacy is not widely recorded, but that side of the relationship is scarcely enigmatic.

On the other hand, we do know the battle plans they drew up at the close of less serious interludes. On June 12 the Queen Mother returned to the army, in good spirits and ready for a quarrel. Luynes was furious about her little adventure and beat her to the draw, accusing her of try-ing to form a "Third Party" and of reinforcing Angers's defenses. This led to a good deal of coolness between them, despite soothing letters from M. de Luçon.

After the fall of Saint-Jean-d'Angely, Marie defied the Court again—unless she was acting out of purely personal interests. Once more she visited her friend, not at Coussay this time but at Richelieu, and re-turned with her head held high.

For the moment, Luynes was reveling in his easy victories—the glory for which actually belonged to Louis XIII, the man with the white plume, whose heroism and tenacity were already legendary. The Constable wrote to the Duke of Montbazon: "We will have cleaned up the whole busi-ness very shortly, and you can say that you have a son-in-law who made you proud, having risked his life for his God, his King, and duty to his office." So he felt quite justified in letting the Queen Mother know what he thought of her.

The Eagle and Juno

Richelieu learned from his friend Bouthillier, who had been living in Rome for several months and observing the Papal Court, that there was little hope of obtaining the scarlet hat. So he, too, prepared himself for the worst. Mother and son were at sword's point once again, and, at Blaye, Marie de Medici left the army.

With the whole region subdued from the Tarn River to the Aveyron, voices of reason urged the King to "rest on his laurels." Louis XIII resented this advice, saying that he was "on the way to becoming a true king of France." Luynes humored his master instead of helping him. The young monarch wanted to win a spectacular victory and take Montauban, military center of Languedoc, which he thought would fall without a single blow thanks to the defection of a Huguenot officer named Sauvage. So the army foolishly plunged straight into the heart of a region whose people lived by the fiery preaching of their ministers and were prepared to defend both their beliefs and the Church property they had expropriated more than fifty years before.

During the campaign, emissaries such as Marillac and the Archbishop of Sens ran back and forth between headquarters and the Queen Mother. From her end, they heard only complaints, recriminations, hypocrisy, and threats. When the Archbishop told Marie how much her departure had displeased the Constable, she flew into a rage: "If it is wrong not to swelter for no good purpose in the heat of Languedoc, then I am wrong, but not otherwise. If I were of any use in the present situation, I would forget about my health. . . . But scorn is something I cannot stand. It makes me furious."

Luynes was frightened and hastily reminded her of the illusory scarlet hat. On this subject Richelieu gave Marillac instructions verging on an ultimatum. "They [Luynes and Marillac] are aware that now is the time to do it, and there is definite assurance from Rome that if pressure is brought to bear, it will be done, but that Amadeau [Richelieu] will not lift a finger, since he knows that it will come about if they desire it; if they do not, neither does he. . . . He intends his conduct to be above reproof. *The Queen is so jealous of her independence there is no telling what she may do.*"

Undoubtedly Fancan and his hired pamphleteers were familiar with the "Laments upon the Constable's Sword" which the nobles recited among themselves to compensate for the humiliation of having to serve under such an inglorious commander as Luynes:

A coward, without faith, I hide in my scabbard
Who once for my King made many a wound,
And instead of that glory I must now be a laggard
While my blade's in a web that a spider weaves round.
The great Montmorencys in wars like these
Gave me a taste for torrents of blood.

Such was the morale of the King's officers in the face of Protestant fanaticism.

Of course Louis slept on the cold ground, drove himself to exhaustion along with his men, and did not flinch when a musket ball sailed right by him and lodged barely ten paces away. But none of this could counter-act the deplorable state of his army, now relapsed into feudal anarchy, or its disorganized supply services and ineffectual generals.

The usual intrigues were brewing in the royal circle. When he was criticized by the Catholic zealots for want of firmness, Luynes dismissed the King's Chaplain, Father Arnoux, who was so stunned by the move that he promtply turned to Richelieu as the Constable's undisputed successor.

News of the campaign soon spread anxiety throughout France and brought secret rejoicing to Richelieu. La Force was determined to defend Montauban to the end; Rohan would hold the countryside and provide support. Sauvage's treachery was exposed, and he was hanged. There was no choice but to besiege the city.

Luynes still hoped to arrange the customary type of settlement with the lords of the realm, but this time angry popular opposition made it impossible. On September 1, they opened fire on the city. On the 16th, the Duke of Mayenne was killed, a sad blow for the King's party and the provocation for a massacre of Huguenots in Charenton. By October 8 things were going so badly that Luynes, after another of his offers of negotiation had been turned down by Rohan, swallowed the ignominy of having England's ambassador offer to act as mediator.

The response was a single howl of dismay. Bérulle proclaimed that God surely could not wish such a wretched instrument of his will upon them. The soldiers gibed at their leader, calling the hillock protecting his command post "the Constable's breastplate." No one wanted to risk associating with him any longer, not even to step into the post of Keeper of the Seals, left vacant by Guillaume du Vair's death during the summer.

Luynes seemed to stumble right into the enemy's camp. He was careless enough to lecture the King publicly—"Easy there, Sire!"—and made it appear that upon his shoulders, which were already drooping, rested the entire responsibility of the kingdom. When he himself took over the office of Keeper of the Seals, they said he made a fine Constable in the city and, on the battlefront, a great Chancellor. Louis was sorry he had given this supreme power to his friend. At the same time that Louis's self-esteem was rising as a result of his new found military skill, his former idol was losing one by one all the glories with which he once had shown.

November brought bad weather, torrents of rain and mud. The troops needed shelter, provisions, medical care, and ammunition. An epidemic broke out, plague or scarlet fever, cutting their strength to about one-third and placing the King in danger. The siege had to be lifted, a stinging humiliation such as the monarchy had not known since the worst days of Henry III. Louis's pride was bitterly wounded.

Luynes saw that he was lost. Admitting that "God was not on his side," he did not dare return to Paris, since Richelieu had gone there with the Queen Mother in order to regroup the opposition. Clutching at anything to save himself, he attacked the little town of Monheurt and ran into stubborn resistance. There, on December 3, he came down with scarlet fever and, on the 8th, called for his confessor.

The King came to his bedside every day, torn between resentment and memories of the past. On the 12th, Monheurt surrendered and was put to the fire like a sacrificial offering. On the 13th, a false alert set royal quarters on edge, and His Majesty was advised to withdraw. "Withdraw?" exclaimed the furious young monarch. "I will die first!"

At dawn on the 15th, Louis was told that the Constable was near death. It saddened him, but he left without seeing the dying man again, and Luynes came to his end in utter isolation, attended only by a single servant. While transporting the body back to the duchy of Luynes, the servants used the coffin for a gaming table.

*

Now twenty, Louis XIII was already fully aware of his mission and his responsibility. The passing of the man whom he had loved too well marked a significant break in his life and ended the first period of his kingship.

The previous four years had not been a loss, for they had uncovered some of his own abilities and strength. They were terrible years for France, earning her the disdain of her threatening neighbors, leaving her conquered from within by a faction resembling a foreign power that gnawed at the very heart of her.

With a determination worthy of his Huguenot grandmother, Jeanne d'Albret, Louis set forth the balance sheet of his accomplishments and failures. One of his major assets was the ability to discern his own errors and not repeat them. Never again would he allow personal feelings to influence his political actions, or one of the handsome youths who struck his fancy to share in the business of government.

Everyone watched his next move. "The King's prudent conduct in Council was the beginning of a promising reputation." A lampoonist offered the following advice: "Open your ears, great King, and break out of your trance. It is time to take the helm." Yet Louis was in no trance; he knew where he wanted to go but lacked the guidance of a strong hand.

Defeat, disappointment, and perhaps, too, the premature end of his conjugal relations had revived his shyness and distrust. Gone was the bold assurance of his first military successes. Stammering and unsure of himself, he could not sustain long discussions or confront large groups of people over whom he was expected to exert his will. He needed someone to serve as confidant, moral support, inspiration, and spokesman, someone to intercede between himself and the rest of the world, who would listen willingly to his endlessly warmed-over hunting tales, who would rescue him from his solitude, and in whom he could confide. Where was such a person to be found?

Betrayed by fortune, by friendship, and by love, Louis's yearnings for the maternal bosom returned; perhaps he could at last gain this coveted refuge. He wrote to his mother: "My affection for you is stronger than any other feeling and will not let me dwell on these sad thoughts." He added that he was anxious to see her again.

Richelieu had reason to wonder whether he had reached port unexpectedly.

XXIII

A She-bear on the Rampage

IT is not true, as Richelieu stated in his *Mémoires* (which are particularly unreliable for this period), that Louis XIII complained bitterly of Luynes's "insolence" and the bondage he imposed on their relationship. On the contrary, the King showed great generosity to the dead man's family, except for his widow, but in her case he was working off a personal grudge, for the lovely Marie de Rohan had tried to seduce him and, having failed, she mocked him. Like most princes of his breed, he never forgot or forgave.

The memory that galled him most was his defeat before the gates of Montauban. It made him ill to think of it. Determined to avoid being dragged into such situations in the future, he took personal control of the government. "His Majesty," wrote the Nuncio, Corsini, on December 24, 1621, ". . . has gone to work at once and supervises all matters with great attention patiently attends every Council meeting, and brings such enlightened judgment to his task that he has won everyone's admiration and all his subjects are filled with joy."

Corsini's picture is much too highly colored. There was no admiration and no joy. In deciding to take charge himself, Louis XIII showed no less decisiveness or concern for the public welfare than did Louis XIV in 1661, but unfortunately, he lacked the lessons of a Mazarin, and his deplorable speech prevented this youth of twenty from imposing his authority. It was obvious that he was feeling his way, but instead of helping him, his ministers tried only to avoid displeasing him.

"These Councilors meet frequently with His Majesty," reported the Venetian ambassador, Giovanni Pesaro, "but they will take no initiative, since they are not certain of the King's intentions or what his attitude may be. Moreover, these gentlemen see the situation as such that, of necessity, either the Queen Mother or the Prince de Condé will gain the King's trust, and no Court favorite will be able to maintain his position without the support of one or the other."

Richelieu shared the same view: Condé had to be outwitted. Having been cautioned to control herself, the Queen Mother went to visit the Duchess of Luynes bearing assurances that in spite of the past, she was resolved to "love and protect her always." She instructed Marillac to express her tender devotion to her son—and also to find a way "to concoct something in her interests." Meanwhile, Condé scurried to the King "to ascertain the state of the market." [1]

Marillac did his best. He told the enigmatic sovereign that the Queen Mother did not want to govern; all she asked for was a seat in the Council and that attempts be made to come to terms with the Huguenots. The sphinx did not commit himself.

The Councilors, that is, Cardinal de Retz, Chancelor Brulart de Sillery, Puisieux, de Vic, and Schomberg, were extremely fearful of Richelieu because he had the Queen's protection. They allied themselves with Condé.

They would have done better to learn how to deal with the King's unpredictable moods. Knowing that he was touchy and distrustful, they brought the most insignificant matters to his attention, pestering him to the point where his doctors began to worry. One day Louis was so exasperated that he refused to see them, exclaiming: "I am not their servant!"

He decided to return to Paris. M. de Luçon came to greet him at Orléans and, according to his *Mémoires*, delivered a lofty speech recalling "that the most sagacious monarchs have always taken the helm of their Ship of State, but they were aided by good pilots to ensure safe steering." The journals of his contemporaries do not mention a word of this, and it is doubtful that he was actually so outspoken.

If he was, it did not serve his own interest. For the King still hesitated to throw himself into Marie de Medici's arms from fear of a man whose "intelligence," as the Nuncio put it, "was broad enough to tyrannize both

[1] Bassompierre, *Journal*.

198

mother and son." There was an additional motive for his hostility which Corsini dared not mention: the scandalous intimacy between Henry IV's widow and a very unsaintly priest.

Once again the victim of his own kind of scarlet fever, the would-be Cardinal seemed unaware of the King's hostility. He handed Puisieux a letter from the Queen Mother in which she defended herself against the accusation of having tried to form a third party and asked for the promotion "which he [the King] has promised me publicly." Puisieux, like Luynes, was extremely liberal with his promises.

On January 27, 1622, Louis XIII re-entered Paris to the accompaniment of joyously pealing bells, cannonades, and "universal" acclamation. He went straight to Notre Dame Cathedral to hear a *Te Deum* as if he had just won an important victory, then headed for the Louvre, where the two Queens awaited him. He "greeted and embraced each one tenderly." Like hawks, the Court watched and listened.

"Sire," said Marie de Medici, "I cannot conceal my joy at finding you returned to us in glory and good health after risking the perils of war and pestilence, and at seeing you are indeed master here."

"Madam, you have good reason to rejoice, and I shall explain it briefly since I am not a good speechmaker, and shall prove it as no other son has so loved or honored his mother. I speak from true and filial sincerity and affection."

He went immediately to the Queen Mother's chamber and remained there for a long time. Only then did he rejoin Anne of Austria, and he spent that night with her. The next morning, after his levee he returned to his mother, and went there again after Council. Marie believed she had won the match.[2]

On her return to Paris several months before, she had decided not to reside in the Louvre any longer and to build a palace worthy of her greatness, the Medici Palace. Interestingly enough, the site she chose was not far from Concini's old residence on the Rue de Tournon. The plan of the buildings (the future Luxembourg Palace) included an enormous gallery occupying most of the right wing.[3] Rubens, the painter and diplomat, subject of the Spanish King and protégé of the Infanta as well as Governor of the Low Countries, was commissioned to decorate it with a great series of paintings.

[2] According to reports from the Nuncio and the Florentine ambassador.
[3] The Medici Gallery disappeared in the nineteenth century.

RICHELIEU

The artist arrived in Paris on February 22, 1622; his purpose was not only to prepare his work but also to deter France from aiding the United Provinces against whom Spain was now at war again following the expiration of the Twelve Year Truce.

It is important to stress the fact that Richelieu, who instigated this project and who was determined to revert to a nationalist policy at the earliest opportunity, made this commitment to the Spanish party. Without this party's support or the good will of the Holy See, his ambitions had no chance of fulfillment. Nor could he succeed without finally convincing the King of his devotion and determination to restore harmony in the royal family. It was also good policy to recall and proclaim the power of Henry IV's widow.

In persuading Marie to commission the representation of events she normally would have preferred to forget, Richelieu intended to accomplish a number of purposes: to mislead Spain, to exalt the Queen Mother and present her as the extension of her husband, to depict the painful years following the regency in such a way that the Queen would emerge as heroine, and, finally, to propagandize discreetly her minister's work in the interest of peace.

Rubens and Richelieu conferred at length. The Ambassador was taken in by the Bishop and never doubted that he was serving the cause of Spain while building his own reputation; as an artist, however, he had a marvelous grasp of what was expected of him. He proposed to do a series of nineteen impressive paintings. In the abundant forms of unfolding allegories, truth would be subject to the same same delicate retouching as the ruined shape and features of the matronly object of this apotheosis.[4]

In the meantime, his promotion to the cardinalate was still the big question. Faced with added pressures, Puisieux hit upon a subtle expedient. They would solicit the hat for M. de Luçon and, immediately afterward, he would be appointed ambassador to Rome. The King would be pleased to see his mother freed from the Evil Spirit while Condé and the Council would have no further cause to fear him. As for

---

[4] Otto von Simson, Professor of Art History in Berlin, has published a very interesting study on this subject in the magazine *l'OEil,* but he makes several historical errors, particularly that of accusing Richelieu of having wished to prevent the reconciliation of 1619.

the Queen, her return to the Council would be her reward for an obliging attitude. Everyone would be satisfied—except the principal party.

Richelieu felt he must not refuse. Marie de Medici seemed to be pleased; he hinted to Puisieux that he would accept: "Believe me, I shall take every possible opportunity to repay the debt that I shall owe."

His *Mémoires* reflect his bitterness at having to concede to the Sillery faction: "They recognized a certain decisiveness in me; they feared my influence lest the King, in taking some notice of me, should decide to invest the principal share of his responsibilities in me. And to serve their design they employed various persons to spew up a thousand calumnies against my name."

The agreement was concluded, or so it seemed. The Queen Mother took her seat in the Council once more, "casting words of honor right and left," but very shortly she realized, or rather her mentor discerned "that she was only permitted to see the display window and was never to set foot in the store itself."

Progress in Rome was equally ambiguous. The Archbishop of Lyon was proposed for promotion along with M. de Luçon. Puisieux officially supported the latter while spreading rumors that Gregory XV unquestionably preferred the Archbishop, a former colleague of his. This led to a lively accounting between the Nuncio and the incensed Juno.

By March Marie de Medici was even angrier, for her protégé's affairs were getting nowhere. Her temper exploded during a reception at the Louvre given by Condé. On her way there, she stopped to see Anne of Austria and found herself face to face with Ruccellaï, the priest formerly in her service who had betrayed her, and ordered him never to show his face in her presence. Ruccellaï scurried to Condé for protection. Throughout the entire reception there was talk of nothing but that. Condé, always ready to stir up discord, asked the King to intervene.

Louis was extremely annoyed and sent the venerable Jeannin to calm his mother down, but before the old man could open his mouth, she unleashed a storm of abuse. The King came by, thinking that matters had been smoothed, and he, too, must have come under fire. The Queen Mother was determined not to tolerate any further insults to her dignity and intended to match Condé blow for blow. And if His Majesty would not give her satisfaction as regarded Ruccellaï, she would have the hide of that miserable wretch!

Louis asked her to control herself. It was a serious breach of etiquette to issue commands under the roof of the reigning Queen. Marie howled and wept. It took Richelieu, who now saw his plans in jeopardy, a solid week to soothe her.

Too late! The harm was done, and once again the Court was divided into two camps. The Princes, hostile to Condé, sided with the Queen Mother, but the King's deepest resentments toward her flared up once more, and he added a number of new ones to M. de Luçon's account.

Louis would brook no restraints and was all the more jealous of his authority since he derived no pleasure from exercising it. He made up his mind never to reunite with that mother of his who preferred a Richelieu or a Concini to himself. Here he was running to her with open arms, and even then he had to duck her angry barbs!

The first Prince of the blood seemed to him the only one capable of standing up to her rage. Condé was made Lieutenant-General of the Army and returned to the Council. It was easy for him to dominate Sillery, an octagenarian about whom one observer wrote: "He listens quietly, answers softly, digests heartily, and produces endlessly the most high-sounding nonsense." Puisieux, whose vacillation, fickleness and sudden reversals earned him the nickname "the hermaphrodite of State," had an equally narrow outlook. The aged President Jeannin was sinking fast. Richelieu was furious at having such pygmies in his way.

At the end of the winter there was again the frightening prospect of war, either civil or foreign. Holland appealed to France for aid while preparing to march in support of the Elector Palatine. The Spaniards were blockading Juliers. Worse than that, they imposed the Milan Pact on the Grisons, thereby violating the Treaty of Madrid and making themselves masters of Valtellina.

Meanwhile, encouraged by success and, at the same time, terrified by the anti-Calvinist repression which was rife throughout Germany, the Protestants were pursing their separatist goals. Which of the dangers should be dealt with first?

Marie de Medici told the Grisons's envoy: "I trust the King will not encourage the Spaniards to continue forging ahead as they are doing; for my part, I shall work for the general welfare and for peace, which is where I believe my children's interests lie." It was quite a statement to have elicited from the ultramontanist Queen who was so proud of her ties with the House of Austria; it seems highly unlikely that Richelieu could have gotten any more out of her or would have dictated to the Queen Mother the bold speech which is cited in his memoirs.

Louis XIII told the old Huguenot chieftain, Lesdiguières, who stayed on the sidelines during the rebellion: "In my kingdom I will not permit a single adherent of the so-called reformed religion to be oppressed or coerced in the observance of his faith. . . . But if, under the cloak or religion, some of my subjects undertake lawless acts in opposition to my edicts, I shall not hesitate to weed out truth from falsehood and punish them as well as protect those who remain dutiful."

He still brooded over his defeat at Montauban and had no conception of the international significance attached to this affair. Condé, the Catholic zealots, and the Holy See's agents were wasting their time trying to lure him back to Southern France to the detriment of French interests in Europe.

However, when the Articles of Milan were made public, Louis's ministers demanded that they be annulled and called up an army in Lyon. The Huguenots were foolish enough to take the offensive. Under the leadership of Soubise, they seized Royan, the tower at Mornac, and La Chaume and defeated the royal army commanded by Saint-Luc. With part of the coastline now in their possession, they seemed to be begging England's intervention.

Louis XIII no longer hesitated. He adored little theatrical stunts. On March 20, without revealing his plans to anyone, he left the Louvre, in hunting dress and without escort, and set out to take command of his army. He did not want his mother along—on that point his ministers were entirely in agreement. In order to keep her in Paris, they offered her outright "absolute authority in all matters, financial control and governorship of all provinces bordering on the Ile-de-France region; they gave her to understand that she thus would wield sovereign power." [5]

Undoubtedly the proud and indolent Juno would have accepted the proposal readily had she been free to do so. But Richelieu held her captive, and his fear was that if anything happened to the King, Condé, with the army at his call, would seize power.

Overnight, Marie became a paragon of motherhood, disclaiming any ambitions for herself. All that interested her was to be near her son; away from him, she would live in constant anxiety.

Louis XIII gave in and the Queen Mother left Paris the day after

[5] From the records of the Venetian ambassador.

his departure. Anne of Austria was ill and remained in the capital. She had had a second miscarriage several days before. The King was already on his way when he learned the details of the accident. Returning from an amusing party at the Princess of Condé's house, his wife was going up to her apartment accompanied by Mme de Luynes and Mme de Verneuil. Irrepressible Marie, the Constable's widow, had the childish idea—or perhaps it was criminal, since she carried a grudge against the King—to take the young Queen under the arms and, at a run, drag her the length of the Louvre's great gallery. Anne fainted; the next day she lost her child.

Louis seethed with rage. He sent his wife a harsh letter and ordered the two ladies to leave the palace. Mme de Luynes retaliated by marrying her lover, Claude de Lorraine, who was also the Prince of Joinville and later Duke of Chevreuse, fifth son of Henry of Guise who was murdered at Blois; the siren's beauty and her dowry of 200,000 écus had proved irresistible. Thus Marie de Rohan married into one of the foremost families of the realm, and it would have been a risk to close the palace gates to her. When all this reached Richelieu's ears, he had no idea how much it would affect his own career.

Louis XIII never forgave his wife for the irresponsible act which perhaps had cost France a Dauphin. For three years he had lived with an illusion of love that now faded, giving place to his antipathy toward those elements of his wife's character which he considered "peculiarly Spanish": her love of intrigues and of splendid wardrobes, her arrogance, and her use of Spanish jargon. Soon he became completely disdainful of this sensual, scatterbrained coquette, this lazy, gluttonous, pleasure-loving creature who had the bearing of an infanta but not a queen. She was exactly the reverse of his ideal.

As for the new Duchess of Chevreuse, there was war from the start between Louis and this formidable enchantress. Richelieu would have to take her on one day and would find the ordeal as strenuous as his struggle with the Hapsburgs.

XXIV

"Your Eminence Is Cardinal"

THE royal army was poorly equipped, and the Huguenot ranks were thinned, but their clashes were bloody nonetheless. Once again fanaticism pitted Frenchmen against each other with incredible ferocity. The Protestants of Nègrepelisse had massacred four hundred Catholic soldiers and were about to suffer the same fate when the city was sacked and burned. In Saint-Antonin, women were defending the ramparts.

The campaign opened with a personal triumph for the King. Under Soubise, a Huguenot offensive had overrun Royan, Sables-d'Olonne, and Oléron. The troops then dug in on the Isle of Riez, an impregnable position as long as the tide was high, but otherwise accessible to infantry attack. Louis gathered a cavalry force of five hundred on the opposite shore and, refusing to listen to his strategists or wait for infantry support, ordered an assault. At dawn on April 16 his horsemen, knee-deep in water, forded the inlet and took the Protestants by surprise, slaughtering three thousand of them and putting the rest to flight. Soubise escaped to England. The King had fought in the front lines and stayed in the saddle for eighteen hours with only a ration of bread and cheese to sustain him.

Three weeks later, the siege of Royan taught him about trench warfare. He told Bassompierre that he had no experience at this type of fighting and needed guidance. But his courage never left him, and on May 7 he narrowly missed having his head blown off by a musketball.

Victory was his reward. Except for Montauban, which they carefully avoided this time, all of southern France from Saintonge to Languedoc was brought to heel—but at what a price in human lives and misery. It was a great mistake for the King to have left Condé in command, for his savagery was in the tradition of Montluc and Baron des Adrets. He left behind him a trail of blood-bathed, pillaged towns, villages flaming like haystacks, and corpses strewn over the countryside.

Both factions were anxious to end the horrors that only Condé and his ruffian bands were enjoying. The King began to tire of his cousin's arrogant meddling; the break came when a horoscope predicted that the throne would pass to the royal familys' younger branch.

Puisieux exploited the Prince's fall and gradually became key minister. Condé was furious and as much as offered the role of favorite to Bassompierre, who laughed in his face.

Marie de Medici had left the troops in May and was looking after herself at Pougues—in the company, naturally, of the ever-present bishop. Louis XIII worried about her health and wrote to her often; despite everything, his love for his mother remained strong. He even wrote directly to Richelieu.

M. de Luçon was being extremely wary. He left his propaganda work to Fancan's pen and Rubens's brush, and any scheming in Rome was attended to by faithful Bouthillier. He himself assumed an unobtrusive, almost self-effacing, manner. Being companion and male nurse to the Queen Mother seemed to absorb him completely. In this way he managed to lull the suspicions of certain people, notably Jeannin.

The King had arrived in Toulouse on June 27, and it was there he felt the first symptoms of tuberculosis, affecting both his lungs and intestines, which was to take his life before the age of forty-two. Three months of haphazard eating and sleeping had sapped his strength. After a week's rest, he wanted to move on despite his fever, but the next day he suffered a relapse at Castelnaudary. Another week passed, and he started out again. Finally, in Béziers, he could go no farther. Héroard, his doctor, reported "acrid perspiration, throbbing at the temples and base of the neck, persistent thirst, and an enflamed uvula."

The young King nearly died; in his sleepless fevers, his thoughts kept wandering back to the irascible goddess whom Richelieu had tamed to angelic docility.

Puisieux wrote to his father, Sillery, using their private code: *"Lasalle* [Condé] is on pretty bad terms with the *Maître du Bâtiment* [the King] who is friendly with *La Porte* [Marie de Medici]." Without a twinge of conscience, he sent asurances of devotion to the Queen Mother.

Puisieux's brother, Ambassador de Sillery in Rome, was also advised of the situation, and he, too, got off a letter: "With no less devotion than impatience, I await whatever decision is made regarding the promotion."

Until that time, the Sillery family had been double-dealing with considerable help from Corsini, the Nuncio, who also aspired to a scarlet hat. Just as they were switching alliances, Cardinal de Retz, nominal head of the Council, died as a perfect courtier should: to make things easier for Their Majesties and the ministers. The Queen Mother, now certain of her power, immediately invited Puisieux to "make another overture for the Bishop of Luçon's promotion." At the end of her letter there was a post-scriptum in her own hand that was tantamount to a summons: "The special confidence I have in your avowed friendship, *which I should like to have occasion to reciprocate,* leads me to ask that you complete the task described in your recent letters as well in hand." Richelieu's style is discernible here. But neither he nor his protectress needed to worry any longer. Louis XIII, now convalescing, was determined to prove that "never did a son so love and honor his mother." Advised of a last-ditch maneuver on Corsini's part, Louis angrily commanded his ambassador to finish the matter.

Corsini had purposely neglected to inform the Pope of the King's latest instructions, and His Holiness was surprised by Ambassador de Sillery's sudden burst of effort to wind up the affair. Owing to decidedly false reports, the latter was under a happy misimpression that Marie de Medici's protégé was a defender of the Spanish cause and an implacable foe of heresy. On September 5, 1622, the Bishop of Luçon became Cardinal de Richelieu.

The news reached Louis on September 14 at the siege of Montpellier, which he had opened on August 31 to revenge his defeat at Montauban. Marillac was there and hastily wrote his congratulations to the new Cardinal, sending the letter to Marie de Medici who had left Pougues to join Richelieu in Lyon. "Your Eminence," he began, "the Queen herself will announce to you, if she so pleases, that you are Cardinal. For I would not dream of pre-empting Her Majesty in informing you of this good news." The letter reached Marie between La Palisse and Roanne, but hers was not the privilege of being the first to tell her friend.

A gentleman who had offended M. de Luçon and looked to regain his favor leaped into the saddle and galloped straight for Lyon, burst in upon Richelieu and fell at his feet: "Your Eminence is Cardinal!"

"The shock overwhelmed his natural restraint, releasing a flood of mad, delirious joy such as moody persons commonly experience at such times. He began dancing around the room in front of the astonished messenger. Once he had this out of his system, the new Cardinal regained his normally cool composure, sat down again, and made the man swear on his life never to mention what he had seen." [1]

By the time his patroness arrived, he was in perfect control of himself and undoubtedly put on an act of complete surprise. The austere Gabriel Hanotaux gives us this chaste description: "We know nothing about what transpired between Henry IV's widow and the new Cardinal. But we may well imagine the intimate effusions of a fading woman as she shared the triumph of the remarkable young man she had chosen to honor" (who had seduced her, would be more precise).

Gregory XV was totally void of intuition, and his messages to the King and to the newly elect, despite their stylistic beauty, are amusing in terms of the events that followed. To Louis XIII he wrote: "Your Majesty's prayers and suffrage have singled out this prelate whose great wisdom is recognized throughout Gaul as *the rampart of the Catholic religion, the scourge of brazen heresy,* and who has always preferred to merit high honors rather than to obtain them." To Richelieu: "In our struggle against the Prince of Darkness, your knowledge and piety, like a sword of salvation in your land, have *cut down the heretics' pride and chastened the nonbelievers.* . . . It will gratify us most highly if, in fulfillment of your purpose, you will continue to raise aloft in Gaul the grandeur of the Church and if, fearlessly and without trepidation, you crush the forces of heresy, trampling the venomous asps and serpents. These are the great duties which the Church of Rome requires and expects of you."

The Pope evidently anticipated that the new Cardinal would preach the civil war. He was singularly mistaken.

[1] Michelet, *Histoire de France.*

208

"Your Eminence Is Cardinal!"

Having come this far on the road to power, Richelieu had no further use for the hypocrisy or duplicity he had been forced to employ for so long. He issued no edifying statement and made no attempt to give the Holy Father an impression that he was still passionately fond of theology or controversy. He did not even consider a "pilgrimage" to Rome.

With the King he was no less honest: "I pray that through God's grace *my actions shall speak more significantly in my behalf than the robe with which you have seen fit to honor me.*" His appeal had no response. Cardinal de La Rochefoucauld replaced Cardinal de Retz on the Council. Louis had made a new effort to win his mother's heart, but he still had not forgotten the days of Concini or his jealousy of the Queen's cassocked protégé.

The Court, however, no longer doubted that Richelieu was on his way to the heights. Many people recognized the genius that Guez de Balzac appraised so generously: "There is a dearth of men who are wise and capable enough to govern; for, indeed, to produce another than is your equal, nature and Providence must combine all their resources and plan for the event long in advance."

Bouthillier was overjoyed. "What else is there to wish for now that M. de Luçon is Cardinal? God must be destining him for even greater things."

Only the ingenuous Gregory XV missed the point. M. de Luçon had not sought the scarlet robe in order to "raise aloft in Gaul the grandeur of the Church" but to facilitate his rise to power.

At the age of thirty-seven, Richelieu, needy youngest son of the gentry, pastor of an impoverished diocese, politician frequently obliged to act in a degrading manner, had now reached his rightful station among the princes of the State and far removed from the common lot of men. Little by little, he acquired the material comforts as well as the pride and cynicism that were trademarks of his rank. He also developed a taste for luxury and sought feverishly for means of increasing his income. For a pension of 5,000 livres he gave up his bishopric and was constantly harrying his business agents: "I wish to expand my profits as much as possible in a way that benefits the Church. . . ."

He loved fine buildings and objects of art. After selling his office of Queen's Chaplain, he was in a position to buy the house in Rueil belonging to Moysset, the financier, and began to furnish it while supervising the construction of the Medici Palace.

Politics, of course, remained his chief concern. He lost no time in speaking out in favor of reconciliation with the Protestants, thus disappointing the Holy See. Most of the Huguenot nobles shared his hope, providing it was worth their while. In exchange for a Marshal's baton, La Force and Chatillon had made peace each in his own province. Sully, whose dream it had been to establish an independent principality, opened up Quercy. At the age of eighty, Lesdiguières became a convert and was appointed Constable of France. He was a born mediator. He reminded the King: "Sire, Valtellina calls!"

Even Jeannin seconded him. For the situation in the valley was taking a violent turn. Invoking the Treaty of Madrid, the Grisons rebelled against Spain. But the Empire was not committed to the treaty and Archduke Leopold invaded the mountain passes, defeated the Grisons, and imposed a Draconian settlement. Henceforth Valtellina's forts were controlled by Spain and the Grisons's territory by Austria, thus linking once again the two arms of Hapsburg power and opening the way to gradual domination of Venice and Savoy and to "squeezing the iron collar" around the neck of France.

During this period the slaughter continued in Germany; Maximilian of Bavaria completed his conquest of the Palatine Electorate; and, worst of all, the King of England, hoping to save his son-in-law, Frederick, made an alliance with Spain, whom he was in no position to fight. There was talk of a marriage between the Prince of Wales and one of the infantas. France was totally isolated and as weak as she had been during the worst of the religious wars.

Louis XIII was painfully aware of this but did not want to suffer another humiliation at Montpellier. Condé bungled the siege and lost favor, this time for good, but it led to negotiations. The King of England intervened in the hope of involving France in the European struggle. On October 9 Montpellier agreed to open her gates and surrender. Peace was signed immediately.

It was a patched-up peace, like so many others. The King's authority was minimized, forcing him to bargain with his subjects despite all the effort, lives, and money he had poured out. Although it confirmed the principles of the Edict of Nantes, it did not remove the barriers dividing the Huguenots from the rest of the nation. The seeds of rebellion were still there: a crusading spirit among the Catholic zealots which, inevitably, inspired Protestant mistrust; the fanaticism of one party, the separatism of the other; the military strength of the Protestants, who still controlled La Rochelle and Montauban; the sovereign status of their leaders; and the Court's wavering attitude.

Condé was the proof. He quit the army in a temper and emigrated to Italy. The Council's efforts to stop him were useless. Suddenly the prospect of facing the Queen Mother alone, or rather the new Cardinal, terrified the ministers.

On his way to meet the King, Richelieu traveled down the Rhône, the river which is associated with the great events of his life. He thanked the monarch at Tarascon and followed him as far as Avignon.

The ministers were considering a league between France, Venice, Savoy, and the Protestant cantons of Switzerland. The Duke of Savoy, Louis XIII's brother-in-law, came to Avignon for this purpose. Following their meeting, a demand was put forth for application of the Treaty of Madrid. Spain balked at this and countered with a proposal to place Valtellina's fortresses under the Duke of Lorraine's command, provided his soldiers were Catholic. Nothing was settled.

The King's wanderings took him next to Dauphiné; he stopped in Grenoble, then set out for Lyon, where the two Queens were preparing to receive him. The Court, ambassadors, and foreign leaders were all watching for the outcome of this meeting which would tell them something about His Majesty's still puzzling political plans.

*

Louis XIII bore everlasting grudges. Nine months after the accident in the Louvre's great gallery, he had not forgiven either his wife or Mme de Chevreuse, who continued to see each other despite his interdiction. On the other hand, he was most eager to see his mother. Since the death of Luynes he no longer had an intimate friend in the sense his "ambidextrous" nature understood the relationship. It is well known that men of this sort seek safety at the maternal bosom when there is no male to protect them.

Despite Jeannin's plea on behalf of Anne of Austria, such were Louis's feelings when he encountered the two Queens. The Venetian ambassador hastened to inform The Most Serene Republic: "The reigning Queen greeted the King with great affection, but despite his long absence, His Majesty scarcely reacted and remained quite cold. The King had already called on his mother, a mark of honor which pleased and delighted her greatly and which showed him to be on closer terms with her than before."

Louis spent the night with his wife, "between eleven and dawn," as the Nuncio spelled it out, but it did not stave off the ill fortune of Anne of Austria.

Mme de Motteville saw it this way: "Now that Queen Marie de Medici had patched things up with the King, peace between mother and son sowed discord between husband and wife; and since the Queen Mother felt that for her to be absolute mistress of this prince, the princess had to be on the outs with him, she did her best to nurture their disagreements, with the result that her daughter-in-law had no credit and no peace from that day onward."

Did Richelieu have any part in these schemes? All we know for certain is that Anne of Austria associated him, as did everyone else, with the woman who became her persecutor and took a loathing to him then and there; for more than twenty years her hatred had far-reaching consequences.

According to the Cardinal's *Mémoires*, Marie de Medici immediately broached the subject of foreign affairs to her son, urging him to take a firm stand against Spain's maneuvers. But there is nothing to support this assertion. The obtuse Queen was infatuated by the Cardinal to the point where she took positions that were exactly contrary to her own ideas, apparently without understanding what was happening to her, yet Richelieu could never have persuaded her to deny the acts of her regency or to set herself up as an avowed enemy of the House of Austria and the aims of Rome. The future would soon prove this. If the seductive demon could still play Catholic zealots such as Bérulle and Father Joseph to his own advantage, how much more easily could he sidetrack the "she-bear." But he would have to act with extreme caution, concealing his real aims in the guise of petty Court intrigues, and avoid compromising statements.

All the same, as the Nuncio feared, there was a general desire to return to the "maxims of Henry IV," or at least to stem the current. Another conference took place in Lyon which the Duke of Savoy's son attended. Spain was not too worried, especially since the Queen Mother appeared to have triumphed—to the point of having the Concini's son released from prison.

"Your Eminence Is Cardinal!"

December 10, 1622, was a day of glory for Marie as well as for the being she had created. In the chapel of the archbishopric, amid great ceremony, the King placed the biretta on the head of Armand du Plessis. Cardinal Richelieu gave a speech which sent sophisticated minds into raptures, though to us it seems labored. But the finale was pure theatrical inspiration: turning suddenly, he approached the Queen Mother and laid his scarlet cap at her feet. In a voice trembling with emotion, he addressed her: "Madam, this scarlet token of office, for which I am endebted to Your Majesty's benevolence, will be a perpetual reminder of my solemn vow to shed my blood in your service."

Marie de Medici could not exist without her wise men and astrologers. If one of them had predicted how this oath would be fulfilled, the shock probably would have killed her.

XXV

Louis XIII Goes Hunting

A GOOD deal of progress had been made, but the major obstacle was still the King's hostility. Mustering his patience, Richelieu chose to ally himself temporarily with sheepish ministers who were doomed to defeat and to use his protectress as a shield.

The Venetian ambassador, Giovanni Pesaro, reported that "the King treats the Queen Mother with utmost honor, respect, and affection. She has been admitted to Council with a greater degree of authority than heretofore. Her Majesty is now on excellent terms with Puisieux. . . . *The Queen and Puisieux have taken an oath and are formally committed to keep all matters out of the hands of Cardinal de Richelieu of whom M. de Puisieux is extremely apprehensive.*"

Once again the Prince of the Church had to resort to this byplay. It was a great strain on him, and during this period his fevers and headaches returned, his nerves were on edge, and a host of other ailments assailed him. "The only course was to let time do its work and hope be a consolation." It gave him a chance to prepare for the future.

When Louis XIII returned to Paris, the Queen Mother, responding like an automaton to her friend's bidding, lost no time in broaching the question of priority in Council. Cardinal de Retz had left his ranking position to Condé, but the Prince was now far away, and old Chancellor de Sillery wanted to take it over. Marie urged that precedence be assigned to Cardinal de La Rochefoucauld; the Nuncio and the Spanish-Catholic faction gave her loud support. It is evidence of how far Richelieu was from inspiring the distrust of these people, since it was he who promoted the debate.

Without even having to lift a finger, the incompetent La Rochefoucauld won out. Giovanni Pesaro thereby concluded that "Cardinal de Richelieu's aim is to keep a cardinal in this position and to begin off-setting the Chancellor's influence." The latter straightway solicited the scarlet hat for himself!

After this defeat, the Sillerys had Schomberg, Superintendent of Finance, dismissed on grounds that he was too closely tied to Condé, whose return they feared. The King spoke of making a bold move by recalling Sully. His ministers promptly panicked and rushed to tell him that the treasury was bare, and unless immediate credits were obtained, the State would be faced with bankruptcy. Beaumarchais, financial minister in charge of revenues and one of the tax-farmers who made enormous fortunes out of the wretched conditions in the kingdom, offered to meet the deficit, but this type of generosity came with strings attached. Louis sighed and accepted. The Marquis de la Vieuville, Beaumarchais's son-in-law, was given Schomberg's post. Thus the Sillery faction was reinforced.

In his *Mémoires*, Richelieu went out of his way to blacken this family. Under Henry IV, Sillery had served the State well when it was purely a matter of executing the King's orders; but at the age of eighty (equivalent to 100 nowadays), he was not fit to govern. Like all the favorites and ministers of that era, he was out to make his fortune all along. "His pattern," wrote the Nuncio, "has always been to manipulate affairs to suit his private interests, either in terms of money or by taking the nearest exit from difficulties; his mode of operation is to get along by sticking a plaster patch over whatever appears imminently dangerous; but when wounds are not healed, they often become incurable. . . ."

His son was openly corruptible. Corsini reported: "I am on excellent terms with M. de Puisieux, the result of both the talks we have had and a few little presents. . . . He abhors the idea of an outright rupture with the King of Spain and prefers to oppose him indirectly." Spanish gold undoubtedly had something to do with Puisieux's restraint.

However, the do-nothing attitude in foreign policy could not continue much longer in the pace of public pressure. On the suggestion of

France's ambassador to Madrid, Fargis, Louis XIII accepted the Pope's mediation in the Valtellina affair, but he instructed Anne of Austria to present Spain with an ultimatum. She was to write to the King, her brother, and to advise the Spanish ambassador that Louis insisted on having the Treaty of Madrid applied. Otherwise, he would take strong measures.

Troops were dispatched to the frontier of Flanders. On February 7, 1623, France, Venice, and Savoy formed the League of Paris. The alliance was both offensive and defensive. Mildly intimidated, Spain pledged to turn Valtellina's forts over to papal troops but reserved the right to repossess them in case of need.

It was a mediocre victory compared to Hapsburg successes in Germany where Maximilian of Bavaria had won himself the Palatine Electorate and Bethlen Gabor, after threatening Vienna, had been forced to retreat. The double-headed eagle was triumphant everywhere, while France, unable to make a recovery, seemed as feeble as her tottering old Chancellor.

The French people's deep-rooted nationalism was beginning to ferment and made the King's ministers highly unpopular. From the shadows, Richelieu cleverly channeled this potent force, he who owed everything to the defenders of the Catholic "International"!

No candidate for power was more hated and idolized, more feared and trusted, more disparaged and esteemed than he—to the point where he became the fascination of large numbers of people whose backgrounds and principles were completely opposed to his. France would not encounter such a phenomenon again until the twentieth century in the persons of Clemenceau and De Gaulle.

Like these two men, Richelieu, on the eve of his cardinalate, was haunted by the nightmare of the "establishment." As he put it: "My misfortune was that those who were assets to the State bore me a perpetual grudge, not for anything I ever did to them but for the potential good they saw in me. . . . It is common knowledge that under weak ministers it is equally dangerous to have either too good or too bad a reputation, and that illustrious men have fared worse than the guilty ones."

Corsini put this into his own idiom in a letter dated January, 1623: "The Cardinal of Luçon will never see eye to eye with the Sillerys, for they are too distrustful of his intelligence and ability." Nor was this apprehension limited to the top circles. The lowliest agents of Florence's resident minister echoed it: "I have been kept informed," wrote this diplomat, "by cleaning women and the apothecary [of the Queen Mother], people with whom I am in close touch since they are my compatriots. They often come to me to pour out their feelings, and especially their reactions to the proud and selfish domination of the Cardinal, who, out of either ambition or greed, seeks to minimize all of the Queen's other servants [this accusation was well-founded]. . . . They told me that this Cardinal would bring disaster again to the Queen because the King cannot stand him. . . . They also said that, on this same subject, the King had taken a good gibe at the Queen, but she pretends not to understand what he means."

On the other hand, Richelieu inspired the deep attachment of his intimates to whom he was attentive, helpful, and even affectionate. "I am yours," he wrote, probably to Father Joseph, "in Latin, French, or Greek, which ever you like. I am devoted to you out of respect for your ability and because your candor and affection compel me to it."

The Capuchin mystic campaigned tirelessly in behalf of his friend. By serving him, he was certain that he would accomplish indirectly a task as important as the illusory crusade, for "he was a man with no ambition for himself but limitless ambition for France, whom he regarded as the great instrument of Providence."[1] He seems not to have realized that he was denying his past, and that from championing a sort of Church-dominated European federation, he had developed into an advocate of pure nationalism.

Fervent Bérulle, too, was even more blind, or rather he saw out of only one eye. A celestial message had revealed to him that La Rochelle was destined for destruction. In his imagination, only the Bishop of Luçon was capable of so marvelous a feat, which, in fact, was accomplished, but in such a way as to crush all the priest's hopes.

Father Arnoux, a spokesman for the Jesuits, could not see very far ahead. "When are you finally going to take the helm?" he would ask Richelieu.

A large section of the intelligentsia had become infatuated with the Cardinal and practically worshiped him. Malherbe wrote to Racan: "You know that I am not given to flattery or deceit, but I swear there is

[1] Victor Cousin, *Fragment Philosophiques.*

217

something superhuman about this man, and if our ship is ever to survive the storm, it will be because his glorious hand is on the rudder."

Praise of this order became grist for the propaganda mills of Fancan and his pamphleteers, who openly appealed to the nationalist sympathies of "good Frenchmen." *La France Mourante* denounced government abuses and prevarications and painted a grim picture of the country's position, demanding a change of policy. "You should willingly support your allies, Madam [he is addressing France], get behind them both in Germany and Italy, send them all the nobles and soldiers who are bent on making war and thus prevent them from enlisting in the Spanish cause . . . restore the reputation of this Crown whose luster grows more tarnished each day in the eyes of foreign nations, and weed out of your Councils all those who have the odor of Spain."

This was Richelieu's future program. But Richelieu remained under cover, while Fancan, up in the front line, was under the impression that he was leading the march. We already know the reward that awaited this valuable and fearless agent.

Many conflicting rumors assailed the young King, now twenty-two, on whom everything depended and whom nobody seemed able to fathom. The Sillerys had made the mistake of trying to flatter his seeming frivolity, and all the while he never forgave their inability to bring him fame and "glory."

Despairing at his own inadequacies and nagged by uncertainty, distress, even remorse, Louis XIII took to hunting with a passion.

"What an idiot!" was the exasperated comment of Mme de Chevreuse. The Court and Paris itself were almost in agreement with this unrequited flirt.

Withdrawn and taciturn, fumbling for words and wooden in his movements, a lustreless appendage to resplendent gatherings, the King succeeded in imposing respect but not in making himself understood. Observers noticed his awkward attempts to imitate his father: he tried to play the "gay blade," told vulgar jokes in a quavering voice, took dancing lessons. These touching efforts brought smiles of pity, and pity had no relation to the indulgence which politicians and courtiers habitually displayed, providing they could base their calculations on a well-defined personality: he had to be either a sluggard or a father of his people or a tyrant. But which was he, this timid youth with his violent tempers, this distrustful and jealous despot who delivered his authority into the hands of a favorite, this wavering shadow one could never pin down, this puritan with a passion for boyish amusements, this injured spirit that was at once an implacable judge,[2] this mixture of anguish and uncertainty, pride and self-effacement, boldness and docility?

The King did not like "to act on his own," yet would not tolerate having decisions made without his consent. "Long-winded affairs" disgusted him, yet he threw himself into mammoth undertakings. He had a taste for amusing and entertaining things, yet nobody was as meticulous as he. Steeped in the sense of his grandeur, he was still miserly enough to deprive one of the Court ladies of a bowl of soup. He raised Luynes to fortune far above the Concinis, yet would not grant the most absurdly small favors. "I am sinking, sinking," he moaned to the fortune hunters, "we are out of funds."

Most contemporary writers attribute such ambivalent behavior to feeble-mindedness. They seem to discount the fact that when moral judgments are constantly repressing the impulses, Nature can produce some alarming results by way of revenge.

The friends of Mme de Chevreuse were contemptuous of the King for not obeying his impulses when his very credit rested upon his restraint. It has been said that "great events and great responsibilities are the props of mediocre minds." Mediocre minds perhaps, but certainly not fainthearted ones. Louis would have been a nonentity without the courageous determination he put forth—and managed to turn against himself with unparalleled effects.

This monarch, who had the makings of a cenobite, derived a sense of satisfaction from bitter self-mortification. Instead of enjoying pleasures, he denied himself; he savored, almost reveled in, his own suffering; indeed, he went beyond that and became his own worst tormenter.

But here was no royal friar fingering his beads or meditating on the tombs of his ancestors. His worst moods of despondency were not permitted to interfere with the rigid rhythm of his existence or his need for activity. For a requiem to be performed in celebration of his own death he composed a series of lighthearted musical pieces, the love song "Amaryllis," and any number of ballets. "Their August Majesties are equally at home when the ocacsion does not call for grave demeanor,"

---

[2] In 1617 he had denied pardon to Baron Guémadeuc, condemned to die for having fought a duel, saying: "I must choose justice over mercy." Seven years later the Cardinal used the same phrase.

was the comment of the *Gazette de France* at the close of one of those entertainments during which the "hypochondriac" revealed himself in an entirely unexpected light.

Though he had no gift for dancing, Louis's vanity made up for it in other ways. One would never had known that the Louvre housed the most economy-minded of monarchs. In the magnificently decorated great hall above the entrance floor, sumptuous audiences attended "extravaganzas" which no one in our day could afford to put on. The flower of royalty and the nobility mingled with the performers, who sometimes numbered as many as 250. Extraordinary stage contrivances were used and costumes in which gold and precious stones replaced everyday materials. There were giants and dwarfs, rope-walkers, fantastic beasts, mythological divinities, knights and enchantresses, solemn tableaux, and, most often, light comedies.

Often it was Louis who wrote the plot, the verses, and the music. He even did choreography and designed costumes. What clownish hand was behind a burlesque Mohammed with his turban and false beard, or a masked devil with horns, or the tawdry glitter of an old woman who danced for three-quarters of an hour without a breath? It was the King's, the stern-faced, solemn King who was known to discredit a courtier for telling an off-color joke and, in a playful mood, was capable of snipping off the beard of one of his officers. Yet on the battlefield he was seen mimicking the contorted faces of the dying. Which is the true picture of Louis XIII?

We may look for an image of him at Versailles as it used to be, in its soft gray landscape, its vineyards dotted here and there with an isolated thatched cottage, in the mist rising from its ponds in the haze of autumn, in its infinite forests abundant with game. "This landscape held a secret charm for Louis XIII. There the air was cool and refreshing. For him, this scorned piece of earth symbolized freedom." [3]

In 1623, under the category of "Trifling Expenses," a credit was allocated for the construction of a "petite maison," a hunting-lodge, at Versailles. The main building was to be approximately eighty feet long by twenty feet deep, with two rectangular wings forming a court. It would have walls of brick and stone. Such was the projected "house of cards . . . the design of which could scarcely swell the head of an ordinary

[3] Louis Vaunois, *Louis XIII.*

gentleman." [4] It became the King's refuge during the crises of his reign and of his life.

Meanwhile, he brought the hunter's curse to the forest kingdom. "The King is so addicted to hunting," reported Corsini, "that he is oblivious to sun or rain, night or day, heat or cold, hunger or fatigue. May the good Lord take care of him, for I do not see how a human body can withstand such strain."

The Nuncio was aware that these excursions far from the royal residences were open invitations to a hopeful favorite. And sure enough, along came someone who seemed ready to step into Luynes's place, at least in Louis's affections. It was Toiras, Captain of the Guard. Puisieux immediately tried to get rid of him, but the handsome Captain raised a terible row, and Louis took his side against the Secretary of State. Once more there was panic in the beehive, but it was uncalled for: the King no longer allowed his emotions to influence public affairs.

Neither the charms of Toiras nor his own exhaustion could still the dictates of a conscience that commanded him to be a great king, or remove the image of the man in scarlet whose brilliant presence began to disturb him without overcoming his hostility and fear. At Court, he looked in vain for someone to lean on. The sticky web of intrigues threatened to draw him in and sometimes forced him to cut it away mercilessly. Thus he abolished the office of Superintendent of the Queen's Household, which was disputed by the widows of two Constables, Montmorency and Luynes. Mme de Chevreuse swore vengeance and took it by exacerbating the discord between the two sovereigns.

So Louis was left with only his mother. And she never ceased talking about the detested Cardinal, sending him to the King whenever she could, hoping to create a relationship between the two. During these audiences Richelieu wore velvet gloves, mustered all his charm, bewailed his poor health, and let it be known that he was not after power but would accept it only if the welfare of the State warranted it.

Those were the key words: the welfare of the State. This idea seemed to have been dead for the last thirteen years. But, unknown to the Court in general, it lived on in the mind of Louis XIII, and the Cardinal was destined to revive it. Other magic phrases, too, awoke sympathetic echoes in the King: the grandeur of France, the glory of the Crown. Yet Louis, to all appearances, remained unyielding.

[4] Bassompierre, *op. cit.*

There was one diverting incident. James I of England had a decided preference for a marriage with Spain rather than the French match proposed by Luynes. The Prince of Wales, under the influence of Buckingham, his favorite as well as his father's, set out on a romantic adventure. He and Buckingham went secretly to Madrid to take a look at his fiancée, the Infanta Maria.

On the way, the two young men stopped in Paris. In disguise, they attended a ballet in which Anne of Austria, reciting verses by Boisrobert, abdicated the queenship to her mother-in-law, who, of course, took the role of the Queen of Olympus:

> You strip me of my fame and honors. . . .
> Yet my husband is your gift to me,
> Such happiness is glorious proof
> No other Juno could there be.

XXVI

The Narrow Doorway

CONDÉ was back in France but did not appear at Court. He sent his wife to Paris with instructions to try to patch things up with the Queen Mother, who made a brief stay in the capital at this time. She said she was coming there to see the first pictures Rubens had completed. Soon this pretext became the major motive behind her trip.

Rubens's rendering of the early part of her saga was completely satisfactory to both the Queen and to Richelieu. Looking at the series depicting her life with Henry IV and her government, the least knowledgeable person would not have guessed the fundamental revolutions brought about by the murders of Henry IV and Concini. The marvelous canvas representing Marie de Medici's coronation bespoke the confidence of her husband and the legitimacy of her regency, and, instead of calling attention to the tragic rupture, it gave the impression of continuity.

As for the events of 1617, nothing could surpass their noble and serene presentation. Again, no suggestion of disruption and, of course no trace of Marshal d'Ancre. Aboard the vessel of state rowed by cheerful allegories, a tenderly smiling Queen Mother turned over the helm to a grateful Louis XIII.

The question was whether the painter could tell subsequent events with equal skill. Richelieu was concerned about this, although he had already advised treating the delicate subject matter "through mystical symbols and with all possible respect to the son." It is probable that he would have preferred to do without the last five paintings but that the Queen, with her usual stubbornness, insisted on pictorializing her departure from Paris following her disgrace, her escape from Blois, the Treaty of Angoulême, the renewal of hostilities and, with its significant title, the *Final Reconciliation after the Constable's Death*.

The Departure from Paris (the study for which is in the Munich Museum) was destined to disappear permanently from the series. The episode was too delicate for comfort. In the remainder of the series, Rubens maintained his marvelous grasp of Richelieu's intentions. The *Reconciliation*, with its "mystical" presentation, offers the best example. Mother and son appear as saints united in an apotheosis, while Virtue crushes the Beast of the Apocalypse, the sole cause of discord, namely, the unfortunate Luynes.

Never was a program of propaganda more cleverly conceived. Two years later when Louis XIII visited the gallery and admired the paintings, he was not offended to see the man he had cared for so deeply depicted as a monster.

*

The politics of the Holy See were in the hands of a dying man with grandiose ambitions, Gregory XV, and his nephew, Cardinal Ludovisi, a petulant youth of twenty-five. As soon as Spain offered him control of Valtellina's forts, the Pope sent his own brother to take them over and, at the same time, made an agreement with the Spanish governor of Milan and Archduke Leopold whereby the House of Austria remained virtually in command of the valley. The Prince of Wales's engagement to the Infanta was a token of victory in his eyes, and Gregory XV would not have hesitated to exploit it by embroiling France and Spain in a war, but death stepped in and ended this project.

Richelieu did not attend the Conclave. The entire framework of European politics would depend in great measure on the choice of a new pontiff. Instead of trying to protect the interests of his own country in Rome, the Cardinal preferred to pursue his maneuvers at Court.

The French party won out nevertheless. Cardinal Barberini, twice-appointed Nuncio to Paris, had received his beretta from Henry IV during the festivities celebrating the Dauphin's birth. He was elected

Pope amid shouts of "Vivo Barberino! Via Francia!" Unfortunately, the King's ministers had already capitulated and accepted the intolerable situation in Valtellina. Although the new pontiff, Urban VIII, did not have his predecessor's crusading spirit, he maintained Rome's link with Spain, and it was useless to try to sway him.

Louis XIII developed a strong dislike for the Brulart de Sillery clan. His mother gave a magnificent reception for him at Monceaux. "The trip," reported the Nuncio, "even though Puisieux had received formal assurances of favor from the King, brought rumors of change. . . . When the King displays more than his usual courtesy to you, it is generally a sign that his feelings have shifted."

The ministers lost their heads and began quarreling among themselves. Puisieux wanted the office of Keeper of the Seals but his father refused to give it up. La Vieuville, whom he had counted on as a sure ally, turned against him, and Toiras was now his avowed enemy, seeking every possible opportunity to reconcile Marie and her son.

Nor was there peace in the Queen Mother's quarter. Some unexplained dispute must have arisen between her and the Cardinal, for he left her suddenly during the month of September, claiming that he had to supervise some decorating work at the Château de Richelieu. But before he had reached Orléans a messenger from the repentant Juno brought him back to her.

Once more, despite his position of guarded neutrality—which he made sure to publicize—Armand du Plessis represented a leader of the opposition that would soon come to power. As Corsini put it, he counterbalanced everything the ministers did. When negotiations over Valtellina resumed, the Nuncio sought his support, and Richelieu wisely remained noncommittal. "He told me," wrote Corsini, "that the ideas currently in force were mistaken and most harmful, but that we must have patience for the day certainly was approaching when France would show her strength. . . . He also commented that it was advisable to make the best of a bad situation."

The plague ravaged Paris. At Saint-Germain the Court was torn in all directions with its incessant scheming. The King was off hunting. Ambassadors gravely reported that he now preferred fox-hunting to fowling; they undoubtedly felt it was all he had on his mind. In fact, the problem of France's future was racking the young monarch's conscience.

225

Though the Sillerys were now discredited with him, he did not want to dismiss them before choosing their successors, and he knew how important the choice was. One more mistake could prove fatal. Louis was aware of his need for a strong man but was repelled by the idea of having to submit to him.

Sully? Condé? Richelieu? He feared the first and loathed the second. As for his mother's protégé, he did not dispute the Cardinal's brilliance but could not overcome his deep-seated aversion to this "dominating" person, a man he felt would stoop to anything. Richelieu, for his part, felt the decisive moment approaching and dared not budge for fear of making a slip. There was something pathetic about the expectations of the two.

With the help of Toiras, La Vieuville sharpened his weapons. He was a shrewd opportunist, and his tight-fisted control of public funds was calculated to please the monarch. Louis thought he had found a way to avoid an unbearable yoke and decided to dismiss the dishonored ministers.

On the morning of December 31 he was unusually gracious to Chancellor de Sillery; that evening he demanded the State Seal. It took the old man's breath away; he balked, reminding the King of his long years of service. Louis had to pull his robe over his mouth to stifle his laughter.

He held off dismissing the Sillerys for another month. Bassompierre, his confessor, pleaded for them. But La Vieuville was impatient to take over and made an agreement with the Queen Mother and Richelieu. The three of them mapped their strategy. It was scarcely necessary, for the King had made up his own mind.

First, he exiled Sillery, offering him a chance to defend himself before Parliament against charges of malpractice. The old man did not accept the offer. On February 5, Puisieux followed him into exile.

Was this to be the Cardinal's long awaited moment? He was greatly mistaken if he thought so. One of the reasons the King showed favor to La Vieuville was that the financier claimed he had persuaded his new associate to accept the post of ambassador to either Rome or Madrid. According to the Florentine minister, "this undoubtedly puts another obstacle in the path of complete reconciliation between the King and his mother."

And what an obstacle! Marie de Medici raised a furor while Louis, still unresigned to the prospect of submitting to the Cardinal's "tyranny," formed a ministry of mediocrities around La Vieuville: La Rochefou-cauld, d'Aligre, La Ville-aux-Clercs, Phélippeaux, d'Herbault, and d'Ocquerre.

La Vieuville's day of glory was brief. A "storm of abuse" was gather-ing against him which Richelieu ordered from Fancan and his pamph-leteers. Three virulent tirades appeared, *Le Mot à l'Oreille* ("A Little Piece of Advice"), *La Voix Publique au Roi* ("The People Address the King") and *La Chasse aux Larrons* ("Hunting the Robbers"), all of which leveled bitter attacks at him as well as at Beaumarchais, his father-in-law, in terms which no modern polemicist could surpass for invective. Louis XIII read *La Voix au Roi* and was profoundly disturbed.

At that point the Pope dealt with, or thought he was dealing with, the question of Valtellina. The valley fortresses were to be demolished and their land restored to the Grisons who were denied the right to take arms, while Spain was to guarantee free transit between Italy and Germany.

Ambassador de Sillery, perhaps out of vengeance for the exile of his father and brother took it upon himself to accept the plan, which was entirely favorable to Catholic Spain. It is not true, as Richelieu's *Mémoires* state, that word of this reached Paris after he entered the Council. Louis XIII learned of it long before then, and his violent re-action was to be translated by the Cardinal several months later. The King's ministers did little other than make protests to the Nuncio.

On the other hand, an unexpected opportunity arose to put the House of Austria in check. Handsome Buckingham had behaved deplorably in Madrid and had taken an ardent dislike to the Conde de Olivares, Philip IV's chief minister. As a result, England and Spain had a falling out. Eager for revenge, hotheaded Buckingham got the idea of forming a league between England, France, the United Provinces, and the Protest-ant princes of Germany. He revived the long-discussed match between the Prince of Wales and Henrietta, Louis's sister, and sent his friend Lord Holland, who was almost as attractive as he, to Paris. Holland paid court to and won favor with the Queen Mother, then became Mme de Chevreuse's lover. It was a good way to get firsthand information on the intrigues at the French Court.

The King announced that his mother would be free to arrange what-ever marriage she chose for Henrietta. One would expect that Marie, who was so hopelessly pro-Catholic, would have been shocked at the prospect of a heretic son-in-law. But Richelieu, whose anti-Spanish activities were still concealed, overcame her scruples by flattering her vanity, assuring her how proud she would be, as mother of France's king and mother-in-law of the Spanish monarch, to become also the mother-in-law of Charles I of England.

The Pope, Henrietta's godfather, was not touched in the least by this argument. He spouted his indignation and predicted the probable catastrophes that would follow. Such a marriage was impossible as long as England enforced her strict repression of Catholicism. And even if she lifted it, would not Henrietta of necessity be hated by her future subjects?

There was another alternative, but it was risky. One of the fiercest *condottieri* of the German war, Count von Mansfeld, the unfortunate commander of the Protestant armies, came to offer his services to France. He was already in Compiègne, to the great displeasure of Louis XIII.

La Vieuville was not up to the situation. He thought of an expedient to involve Richelieu in responsibility for his own decisions without opening his way to the Council, he offered him precedence in a Council of Dispatches which would have charge of foreign policy.

The reply was a masterpiece. Smothering the minister with his irony, the Cardinal also tried to reassure the King—and to get a decision from him one way or the other: "The Cardinal is overwhelmingly grateful to M. de La Vieuville for the marks of his esteem and good will. . . . But he himself will admit that the proposal in question would be neither in the King's interest nor an aid to close and desirable understanding between His Majesty and the Queen Mother and that it would be dangerous to the Cardinal himself: a disservice to the King because of the said Cardinal's lack of knowledge in regard to foreign affairs during the last few years, and to himself *because of his frail health which leads him to seek occupation in private life rather than in such a demanding post.* Moreover, this office calls for decisions that are so far-reaching and so dependent on wise judgment that *they can only be expected of the King and His Majesty's Council."*

Marie de Medici took the offer as an insult. Her incomparably brilliant protégé deserved a place in the King's highest council, the Council of State, and nothing less. With her shrill voice raised to the pitch that had so irritated Henry IV, she drummed away at her son, trailing him stubbornly from Saint-Germain to Monceaux to Compiègne.

The Narrow Doorway

Satisfied that she had shaken his resistance, she then reversed her tactics and settled down to sulk conspicuously in Paris. La Vieuville was frightened and went to see the terrible matron, who gave him strict orders to assure the Cardinal's nomination personally. "Ah, Madam" he moaned, "you ask for something that will unquestionably ruin me. And I wonder whether one day Your Majesty will not regret having advanced someone she really does not know yet."

However, he did what he was told. Louis did not say a word. The next morning, watching as the Cardinal passed in front of his window, he said to Marshal Praslin: "There goes a man who wants to sit in my Council, but I cannot bring myself to accept him after all he has done to me."

The entire Court trembled at the thought of another Marshal d'Ancre in scarlet robes.

But Marie de Medici was in a froth, just as she had been over the issue of her coronation. Henry IV had given in, hoping to achieve peace in his household. Louis XIII wanted to hold on to this semblance of maternal love without which he would feel alone in the world.

On April 29, 1624, during his morning visit with his mother while she was still in bed, he announced the Cardinal's admission to Council "in order that the world might know his real and not illusory desire to share her complete trust."

*

He had no intention, however, of delegating power to the man he still feared. The Nuncio explained it very well: "It was decided to admit the Cardinal to the Council, but the jealousy of the other ministers must account for the limited authority he is to enjoy; namely, the Cardinal will sit in the Council to give his opinion on current matters, but, as the King's minister, he will have no right to carry on any negotiations under the King's roof or have any dealings with anyone as regards His Majesty's affairs; and the reason is that they do not wish him to reach for this power which, with his rang of Cardinal and his naturally superior intelligence, he could quickly attain."

Richelieu was extremely resentful. The Nuncio went on to report that "his tone of voice, his gestures bespoke his bitterness." But he did not make the error of refusing to cross the threshold of the ministry because the doorway was too narrow. No, he tried to invest his near-furtive entrance with imperial dignity.

His reply to Louis's offer was haughty and guarded; it even stipulated certain conditions. He would not accept without reminding the King that he, Louis, "had been offended by him somehow in the past" and that the Cardinal "would have enemies right and left."

"If, despite these considerations, His Majesty is firmly resolved, the Cardinal can only obey. But he beseeches His Majesty to graciously . . . free him of the visits and solicitations of individuals who, in wasting time that should be spent in His Majesty's service, would end up ruining his health; and furthermore, since he is assuming this office without either seeking or desiring it, but out of pure obedience, it will be evident to His Majesty that he neither will have nor can have other aims than the prosperity and the greatness of his kingdom, so that in the very strength of this conviction the Cardinal may find assurance that all the artifice of evil-wishers will carry no influence with His Majesty to the detriment of the Cardinal's integrity."

How skillfully he managed to blend deceit with truth! Posterity, to a great extent, was to be the dupe; the Nuncio certainly was not. He noted: "Anyone who knows the Cardinal is not that ill and is extremely ambitious will perceive that in the matter at hand, this supposed preference for a tranquil life was a necessity arising from other causes."

In any event, Marie de Medici made a pilgrimage of thanks to the Madonna of Liesse.

XXVII

The "Long-remembered" Day

ONCE inside the Council chamber, the panther bared his claws. His prodigious memory produced an endless flow of examples and quotations to prove that cardinals had precedence over princes of the blood, the Constable, the Chancellor, and, most important of all, the Superintendent of Finance. His mother's shrieks and tears made the King yield. A royal edict dated May 9 sanctioned the aspirations of members of the cardinalate but for the sole benefit of one among them.

Whereupon a merciless struggle opened in the heart of the ministry such as many a Cabinet would experience under the Third and Fourth Republics. The similarity was pointed up by Richelieu's recourse once again to the lampoonists; in our day it would be a press campaign. *L'Action Française* was in some ways less vicious in attacking the targets of its hate.

La Vieuville could not lift a finger without unleashing a torrent of abuse. He was accused of every known crime and made to look ridiculous. "His head resembles those mares of the South that can breed nothing but air." A groom blamed the stable boy for saddling a horse back to front "like the head of La Vieuville." He was made out to be a robber, an eccentric, a trouble-maker, a traitor. He was "Judas's Veronica!"

Richelieu gave his personal opinion on foreign policy in an anonymous pamphlet: "Your Majesty must find a bold solution for matters that affect his very survival; he should not hesitate to see Mansfeld and to support his former allies without heeding the theories of monks and the Nuncio who are only concerned with the Pope's interests and not your own. If everyone tended to his own business, affairs would be in much better shape."

The surprising thing is that concurrently the "monks" under Father Joseph's influence were campaigning vigorously in behalf of the man who was attacking them. Unfortunately, we have no records showing how this extraordinary Janus managed to convince both parties that he belonged to each.

Needled unmercifully, La Vieuville felt compelled to produce results at any cost. His enemies accused him of cowardly concessions to the Pope and to Spain, while the Queen Mother pressed for the English marriage. This finally drove him to initiate the policy which was to be his successor's.

Subsidies were promised to the Low Countries, and Mansfeld received some while negotiations for the marriage were suddenly speeded up, all of which gave fresh hope to the English Court. But the religious issue was still a burning one, for King James and the Prince of Wales had taken a solemn oath in Parliament never to yield on this point.

La Vieuville, "like a drunken man, could no longer take a step without reeling" and consulted none other than his rival. Richelieu, displaying a sudden surge of concern for the Church, advised that it was absolutely necessary to obtain solid guarantees in behalf of Great Britain's Catholics. The Council approved. La Vieuville thought it over and saw the trap—then plunged head first into another one. Without consulting the King, he intimated to Lord Holland and to the new ambassador, Lord Carlisle, that he would be satisfied with a confidential letter from James I pledging his word on the religious question.

The French ambassador in London got wind of the affair and warned his sovereign. Louis XIII was furious and took an immediate dislike to the unfortunate La Vieuville. Nothing wounded his kingly pride so much as a challenge to his authority and, according to Richelieu's expression, "One did not fall from his grace gradually; one plummeted."

As of that moment La Vieuville was a condemned man. But the King still looked for some way to circumvent the Cardinal, that strange breed of man who seemed to work his effects on him from all directions.

He recalled Condé to the Court, then changed his mind about handing him the reins of government. As a last resort, he summoned Sully, "that great statesman and great minister of the King, his father."

At the beginning of August, Henry IV's chief adviser arrived in Paris, hailed by cannonades from the Arsenal, for he was Grand Master of the Artillery. We do not know exactly why Louis XIII decided not to rely on him. Sully was sixty-four years old (about eighty in our day) and his blunt, rough-and-ready manner was legendary. He was a Huguenot. His return would have been regarded as an insult to the Queen Mother, whose coronation he had once tried to prevent, and whom she in turn had disgraced. In all likelihood, this last factor was the deciding one; the old war lord went back to his estates and to life on a royal scale.

The dreaded deadline was at hand: alone, Louis XIII faced his mother and Richelieu. He consulted the Cardinal about certain changes in the Council. The good apostle was presumptuous enough to advise against them, then appointed a few of his own friends, Schomberg, Marillac, Molé, and Champigny. Louis gave his consent.

Seeing that he was really in charge, Richelieu went further and swamped the King with "an exhaustive analysis of the mismanaged affairs of his government in past years," reminding him that one more error could be fatal. Louis knew it all too well.

He went to Saint-Germain, then on to Versailles where, down to the kitchen equipment, he inspected in great detail "all the furnishings purchased by M. de Blainville, first gentleman in waiting." After several trips between the two estates, he proceeded to Compiègne and supervised military drill in the square at Rethondes, then returned to Versailles. This was his way of meditating.

In the meantime, La Vieuville made a last-ditch effort to survive by clutching at Richelieu, who, "knowing how to conceal the truth but not how to violate it," coldly presented him with a raw forecast of his downfall. The King was now with his mother at Rueil, and La Vieuville rushed there to offer his resignation: "I am aware, Sire, that you no longer wish me to serve you." Not a word from the King. Like a drowning man gasping for air, the minister asked permission to accompany His Majesty to Saint-Germain. His Majesty nodded.

That was August 12. The 13th arrived, the "long-remembered" day. La Vieuville attempted to justify himself to his sovereign and was dismissed. As he crossed the palace courtyard, Tresmes, Captain of the Guard, placed him under arrest and conducted him to the fortress of Amboise.

A meeting of ministers was called in which the King reported what had been done with La Vieuville; turning to the Cardinal, he announced that he intended to make changes in the Council. Richelieu gave a long address which contained the framework of his program, and concluded: "Sire, the government must be run in such a manner as to leave no doubt that Your Majesty is personally conducting all matters, which is as it should be."

Initiating a practice that became a habit, Louis replied laconically; he approved what the Cardinal had said and confirmed the censure of La Vieuville, the Sillerys, and even Luynes. "Henceforth it will be a pleasure to supervise all my affairs, since they will be conducted in an orderly fashion."

This was at once a tribute and a warning. Richelieu could expect no mercy if the power vested in him did not ensure the security and welfare of France.

On the same day a royal letter countersigned by Loménie, one of the Secretaries of State, informed Parliament of the changes made and confirmed the Cardinal's designation as chief councilor.[1]

Foreign observers were impressed most notably by the power of Marie de Medici. Florence's minister commented: "With Cardinal Richelieu in the seat of power, the Queen Mother's authority is now firmly established. . . . It would seem that Her Majesty is bent on building her prestige upon her son's love."

To the Venetian ambassador, Richelieu confidently asserted: "These frequent changes are evidence of disorder, but in the future the rule of order will prevail and the benefits that stem from it."

He lost no time in asking the Capuchin Provincial of Tours to allow Father Joseph to work with him. As he expressed it, "After God, Father Joseph has been the major architect of my present good fortune." *He was already ungrateful to his old flame!*

François du Tremblay was ecstatic: "I watched that young eagle develop talons and fly straight up into the sun!"

Sully bore no rancor and shared his enthusiasm, proclaiming: "The King has just been divinely inspired!"

[1] He did not become chief minister until 1629.

XXVIII

The Greatest Servant and the Best Master

ACCORDING to Jules Lemaître, the dramas of Corneille illustrate "the triumph of will alone, or, at the utmost, of will dedicated to some extraordinary task." The rise of Richelieu offers such an example if one concedes that Armand du Plessis made a devotion of his calling for statesmanship. From Bonaparte to the modern dictators, men have glided from obscurity to omnipotence before the eyes of stunned and admiring worlds, their passage the result of great upheavals and spectacular windfalls.

Richelieu was no less able or ambitious than they, but he lacked the advantage of circumstances commensurate with his stature. Undoubtedly he would have liked to emerge full-blown, like a demigod, from a battlefield or revolution. But the choice was not his. He was forced to make his way painfully and deviously, relying on the tools of adventurers and favorites, flattery, deceit, and self-abasement.

Henry IV used to say that his fierce love for the French people made *all tasks easy and honorable*.[1] Richelieu shared the same feeling because he knew his own value, because he was ambitious for material rewards, and because his scorn for others was so great that he had no scruples on their account and no concern for their opinions.

Like Father Joseph, he was a priest who regarded France as an in-

[1] Inscription on the statue of Henry IV in the Palais-Bourbon.

strument of Providence and the King as the personification of France. He never doubted that he was serving God by serving His representative on earth. This compelled him to make the supreme sacrifice of imperiling his own salvation; he accepted the risk just as he accepted the crushing burden of power. "A righteous man in the eyes of men," since he subordinated everything to the interests of his country, he abandoned the hope of being "a righteous man in the eyes of God." It was he who wrote: "Many men would save their souls in private life who damn themselves as public figures."

Well, damn himself or not, he would "watch the whole night through so that others might rest in the security of his vigil." He was prepared to risk his soul and to show the French people no mercy in order to raise France to grandeur.

Father Joseph pursued a similar ideal, but in a totally disinterested manner. He asked no reward except the success of his cause. But Richelieu had worldly ambitions on top of his desire for self-fulfillment. His lust for power in no sense damped his drive for wealth and honors, for gratification of his pride, for vengeance: "The greatest responsibility of kings is the tranquility of their subjects, the preservation of their realm, and the good repute of its government; to these ends its is necessary to punish all offenses against the State so effectively that the severity of retribution roots out the very notion of repeating them."

Identifying oneself with the State entails the danger of occasionally confusing political vengeance with personal malice.

On his way to power, the Cardinal responded to the basest human motives, but once at the top, the only faults he retained were those of heroes. The rest fell away like borrowed garments. Before the eyes of the French people, in all the splendor of his scarlet robe, there rose the majestic, implacable model of Philippe de Champaigne's portrait, with his piercing gaze, long, determined nose and tight-set mouth, his wiry slenderness, his expression that is at once distant, bitter, impassive, commanding, and almost sickly.

Though only thirty-nine Richelieu was no longer in the prime of life. His body endured a daily round of punishment, sometimes of the most humiliating sort: fever, headaches, intestinal pains, boils, ulcers, hemorrhoids, tumors, and probably fistulas which could prevent him from sitting down for several days. Matthieu de Morgues, who became his mortal enemy, told him: "Headaches, burning sensations in the blood, raging fevers that never leave you, syringes, lancets, hot baths—all these are reminders not only of your mortality but that life is yours solely at the price of its tyranny."

Sheer determination kept the Cardinal in control of his physical ills; it was of no avail against his nervous disorders. He was chronically subject to uncontrollable emotional seizures and especially to severe depressions that brought him close to collapse. It was fortunate indeed that he could rely on Father Joseph's rough, friendly concern and vigilance. But what was worse, the madness of the du Plessis lurked in the recesses of his brilliant mind, always threatening, sometimes attacking.

In his delirious moments, Alphonse, Armand's elder brother, believed he was God the Father. It became a traditional saying in the royal family that His Eminence was known to take himself for a horse! Richelieu's life became an endless struggle against the enemies within and without, against illness, against the forces that preyed on his mind.

And, even more than this sinister coalition, he would have reason to fear the strange creature at whose mercy he was: the King.

Having reached his long-sought goal, Richelieu did not attain the supreme reward of men of his stature: unlimited power. He would never know the solitary exaltation of the dictator who has imposed absolute submission. For over his shoulder constantly peered the monarch he had misjudged for so long and whose moods were now his major concern.

Louis XIII and Richelieu were both sick men, neurotics; yet, paradoxically, this common bond separated them as much as the yawning gulf between their minds. Apart from the question of his filial jealousy, the King's smoldering distrust and fear derived from this very similarity and contrast. He had no idea what effect his strange and compelling temperament had on the driving personality of his minister.

Unlike his father, Louis XIII lacked the ingredients of a popular idol: the swagger and dash, the poise, the vitality, the whole apparel of kingship. As an ordinary citizen he would have had small chance of rising above the crowd. His timidity and awkwardness, his stutter, his obvious fear of women, and the peculiar twists of a personality inclined toward misanthropy did not bring the world to his doorstep. His ignorance, together with the tremendous gaps in his education and a certain childishness, cast doubts on the soundness of his mind, which was just, determined, and honorable, but of quite ordinary caliber. As a soldier he showed great promise; his valor and devotion to his troops earned him more praise than any ability as a strategist. At Court, his outspoken bluntness was bound to cause smiles. In all probability, he would avoid palace life and spend whatever time he could either on his estates or with the army, hunting or caring for his health. Then again, his repressed desires might suddenly break through, leading to excesses inevitably followed by guilt and penitence. And, in the end, the sole vessel of his immortality might be some nasty little anecdote of Talle-mant de Reaux [2] holding him up to ridicule.

But this was no common variety of young man. The image of himself that he carried was a tremendous burden: the King of France, a composite symbol of his ideals, his principles, and his faith. He no more doubted the superhuman power of the Lord's Anointed than his miraculous power to heal the sick. He believed that his word was a holy commandment, opposition to which was an unpardonable crime. He was imbued with a doctrine that Richelieu had no need to explain to him: the absolute power of divine right. Sovereign, state, nation became a unity. He was a despot who required total sacrifice. It was natural for the lords of the land to worship the ground he walked on and for the common folk to say: "The earth is yours, Sire. It is enough for us if you are in good health."

Later, Corneille was to exalt this abdication of the individual, the cruel triumph of civic duty over personal commitment, the religion of the Roman Empire. He magnified the autocrat to whom the universal order of things was bound; he extolled the glories of ancient Rome, whose relentless, inspiring harmonies stirred him as they did the law-makers responsible for founding the absolute monarchy. Well ahead of Corneille's time, Louis adopted this conception of government; before he had ever heard of *Cinna*, he chose as model a ruler who was master of himself as well as of the universe.

His profound attachment to this idea aroused echoes of moral heroism in "the lean-limbed Jupiter with the pointed mustache." [3] If the Vice-Deity demanded complete obedience from his subjects he also required total abnegation of himself for the King's sake. Devotion to the people's service suppressed his own feelings, however compelling or simply warm and human they might be, even his religious scruples. The

---

[2] Gédéon Tallemant des Reaux (1619–1692) authored the *Historiettes,* savory commentaries on people and customs of his era. (Trans.)
[3] Michelet, *op. cit.*

iron rule to which he bound himself made him a slave to his mission. Those he governed were under his absolute control, but he remained their servant, for their safety and welfare was the price of his omnipotence.

Louis XIII adored the Chronicles of Joinville and longed to emulate Saint Louis; in fact, he did orientate his rule toward a type of rough-cut, stubborn saintliness. With him, the conception of monarchy reached its pinnacle. Henry V had not given it this mystical character. Louis XIV would endow it with more brilliance, yet he removed its essence, because too often he identified the sovereign with his own person instead of effacing himself for the sage of the sovereign's image. Louis XV, a casual and lucid spectator, watched the image fade. Louis XVI betrayed it because he loathed the idea of reigning. When he took the throne it was with the comment: "What a burden! I feel as if the whole universe were about to collapse on top of me!"

At the time of Concini's death, Louis XIII commented: "It is high time that I take on my duty."

Before taking on his duty as he conceived it, he forced himself to face the contradiction between the weak person he was and the monarch he ought to be and bravely resolved to lift himself to the higher level. The history of his life thereafter would reflect the evolution of this effort.

And the effort was all the more touching since he could not and would not tolerate help or guidance. Again, it was an illustration of "will dedicated to some extraordinary task," and one day Louis's triumphant purpose would be proclaimed in his famous statement,[4] which Corneille might well have put into verse: "I would not be king if I had the feelings of ordinary men."

The phrase must be understood as a summary of his ideal of kingship. It would be less moving, and therefore less akin to Corneille, if it honestly reflected the truth. In fact, Louis XIII was altogether exposed to the ordinary range of emotions; at the same time he felt compelled to renounce his share of the common human experience, for his conscience commanded him to rise above it. He did so, and in the end, the task of kingship swallowed up the man.

He reached for and would attain the majesty inherent in his vision

---

[4] Made when he was begged to spare the life of Montmorency. [Henri de Montmorency, Huguenot Governor of Languedoc, rebelled with confederate Gaston d'Orléans and was beheaded in 1632. (Trans.)]

of a born ruler of France. He allowed himself no frailties, no pity, no frivolous pleasures, no facile virtues. Not once would he refuse the cup of bitterness that was constantly handed him. His somber, stonily remote countenance was not typical of his countrymen, nor did it reflect the bizarre accidents of personality written on the faces of Spanish royalty. Louis's features were marked by the day-to-day struggle he waged; they were the price of severe self-discipline that raised an ordinary human being to solitary grandeur.

But sometimes the taut spring slackened: the King would lapse into despair, convinced that his own inadequacies made the ambitious dream unattainable. He lost heart over fugitive success, regretted the pleasures he had given up for labors that brought him only bitterness. Remorse plagued him. Such crises became a nightmare for Richelieu, for at those moments doubt and depression racked the monarch like a disease, and a puff of wind could change the destiny of France.

Louis XIV spoke of his "delightful" occupation. Louis XIII faced his duties with moral inhibitions and a gravity of purpose which made it impossible to conceive of such an expression. From the age of sixteen onward, he imposed on himself a rigid discipline, which perhaps would have been less stringent had he not sensed a hopeless imbalance between his task and his means. Few men could combine such modesty and pride; and few would delude themselves less. Absolute monarch that he was, he knew he could not govern alone. It was clear to him what he wanted to build, but others had to be the architects and joiners. His role was to see that they did the work properly, and he never forgot they were in his service.

He wanted to know everything, examine everything, follow the hourly progress of the work. He also demanded initiative and daring of his agents. His second-rate ministers completely failed to understand this. Richelieu, profiting from his experience, would not repeat his former errors and came to realize that the challenge of his patron's difficult temperament was one of the very reasons for his success.

The King deserved the surname he acquired by chance: he was just.[5] Though he controlled his representatives with a rough hand, they could rely on him at any instant. Were he needed for conference, or in any trouble spot in the kingdom, or to lead a military expedition, he was there. His health, pleasure, convenience, even the laws of etiquette meant

[5] He was born under the sign of Libra.

nothing to him. He was not yet twenty when his doctor, Héroard, became alarmed that the supposedly "lazy youth" was greatly overworking himself. In the years ahead, he nearly died of diseases a number of times in the course of his campaigns. Henry IV was the father of his people; Louis was more their guardian, always on the alert to punish offenders and put down trouble. Though their affection for him was instinctive, the French people had no idea of the debt they owed this pale knight errant. Louis "was untouched by praise to the point where he deliberately suppressed it"; he simply did not care about it. "He knew what humility was. He knew how to practice it at his own expense," wrote Saint-Simon.

Humility or modesty? Or perhaps the pride of one who has immured himself in the world of sacred obligations.

His former ministers had tried to cling to power by flattering the King's weaknesses. Richelieu chose to do it by gratifying the yearning for grandeur that this perplexing young monarch so cherished.

He succeeded. Even before repudiating the last of his fears, Louis became convinced of the Cardinal's genius. The conviction absorbed him so completely that everything else became secondary. Whatever happened, his conscience would not allow him to deprive himself "of the greatest servant France has ever had."

Richelieu went through stages which were quite similar. During his first period of government service, though he defended the authority of the monarchy, he shared the Queen Mother's contempt for the King. The dramatic events of April 24, 1617, opened his eyes to the thunderbolts this little known Jupiter could hurl. His journey among the rebel Princes afterward proved to him that no lasting order could be built except by the King and with his support. Now he was at the right hand of a man whose momentary whim or displeasure could alter the face of Europe. His discerning eye had spotted the pure, incorruptible metal that lay hidden beneath markedly odd gangue. In turn, Louis XIII had found the man he called "France's greatest servant." "The best master in the world," was Richelieu's reply.

So began an association which, in the critical times ahead, would change the map of Europe and bring France to the pinnacle of her greatness.

Bibliography

PRINCIPAL SOURCES

Archives Nationales, Paris (Manuscrits)
Archives du Ministère des Affaires Etrangères, Paris
Archives du Ministère de la Guerre
Archives de la Bibliothèque de l'Arsenal
Archives de l'Institut de France, Paris (Fonds Godefroy)
Bibliothèque Nationale (Départment des manuscrits)

Vatican Archives (Dispatches of the Papal Ambassadors)
Florentine Archives (Archivio Mediceo Francia)
Reports of the Foreign Ambassadors
Reports of the Venetian Ambassadors (published by Alberi)

LETTERS, MEMOIRS, EYEWITNESS ACCOUNTS

Andilly, Arnauld d', *Journal*
Bentivoglio, Cardinal, *Correspondance*
Bouffard de Madiane, Jean de, *Mémoires*
Brienne, Henri Auguste de Loménie, Comte de *Mémoires*
Déageant, Guichard, *Mémoires*
Fontenay Mareuil, François Du Val, Marquis de, *Mémoires*
Force, Maréchal de la, *Mémoires*
Héroard, Jean, *Journal*
Houssaye, Amelot de la, *Mémoire secret pour servir de supplément a l'histoire
de la vie du Cardinal de Richelieu*
Mercure François (1615-1624)

Bibliography

Montglat, François de Paule de Clermont, Marquis de, *Mémoires*

Mourgues, Mathieu de, *La Cordonnière de Loudun*

—— *Pièces pour la Défense de la Reine, mère du Roi*

Pontchartrain, Paul Phélypeaux de, *Mémoires*

Richelieu, Cardinal de, *Histoire de la Mère et du Fils* (attributed to Richelieu)

—— *Lettres, Instructions Diplomatiques et Papiers d'Etat* (published by Avenel)

—— *Maximes d'Etat et Fragments Politiques* (ed. 1880)

—— *Mémoires*

—— *Testament Politique*

Rohan, Henri, Duc de, *Mémoires*

Saint-Simon, Louis de Rouvroy, Duc de, *Mémoires*

—— *Parallèle entre les trois Rois Bourbons*

Tallemant des Réaux, Gédéon, *Historiette de Richelieu*

Villeroy, Nicolas de Neufville, Seigneur de, *Mémoires*

BOOKS

Arconville, Mme d', *Vie de Marie de Médicis*

Aubery, Antoine, *Histoire du Cardinal de Richelieu*

Bassompierre, François de, *Journal de ma vie*

Batiffol, Louis, *Le Roi Louis XIII à vingt ans*

—— *Richelieu et le Roi Louis XIII*

Bazin, A., *Histoire de la France sous Louis XIII et le Ministère de Mazarin*

Belloc, Hilaire, *Richelieu*

Burckhardt, Carl J., *Richelieu*

Charvériat, ——, *Histoire de la Guerre de Trente ans*

Duchesne, André, *Histoire généalogique de la Maison du Plessis de Richelieu*

Dupuy, Pierre, *Histoire des Favoris suivie de la Rélation de la mort du Maréchal d'Ancre*

Fagniez, Gustave Charles, *Le Père Joseph et Richelieu*

Girard, ——, *Vie du Duc d'Epernon*

Griffet, Le Père, *Histoire du Règne de Louis XIII*

Huxley, Aldous, *Grey Eminence*

Jouvin, A., *Le voyage de France*

Lacroix, Abbé, *Richelieu à Luçon*

Le Clerc, J., *La Vie du Cardinal Duc de Richelieu*

Levassor, Michael, *Histoire de Règne de Louis XIII*

Mouton, Leo, *Un Demi Roi, le Duc d'Epernon*

Pavie, Emile, *La Guerre entre Louis XIII et Marie de Médicis*

Pluvinel, Antoine de, *Manège Royal*

Préclin, E. et Tapié, Victor, *Le XVII° Siècle*

Pure, Abbé Michel de, *Vita Eminentissimi Cardinalis A. J. Richelii*

Rapine, Florimond, *Relation des Etats Généraux*

Richard, Abbé René, *Histoire de la Vie du Père Joseph*

Siri, Vittorio, *Memorie Recondite*

Topin, Marius, *Louis XIII et Richelieu*

RICHELIEU

Vaudoré, Fontenelle de, *Histoire des Evêques de Luçon*
Vaunois, Louis, *Vie de Louis XIII*
Zeller, Berthold, *Le Connétable de Luynes, Montauban et la Valteline*
——— *La Minorité de Louis XIII*
——— *Richelieu et les Ministres de Louis XIII*

Index

Index

Index

Adir... DATE ....y College Library